P9-DJL-456

DATE DUE

DEMCO, INC. 38-2931

This book may be kept
FOURTEEN DAYS
A fine of TWO CENTS will be charged
for each day the book is kept overtime.

ST. JOSEPH'S COLLEGE LIBRARY

PRODIGAL SHEPHERD

PRODIGAL
SHEPHERD

by

FATHER RALPH PFAU

and

AL HIRSHBERG

HV5293.P52   ST. JOSEPH'S UNIVERSITY   STX
Prodigal shepherd,

3 9353 00022 8286

HV
5293
P52

34800

J. B. LIPPINCOTT COMPANY

PHILADELPHIA • NEW YORK

Copyright © 1958 by Father Ralph Pfau and Al Hirshberg

Second Impression

Printed in the United States of America

Library of Congress Catalog Card Number 58-9535

A short version of this book has appeared in *Look* magazine under the title, "A Priest's Own Story."

Apart from the author, whenever a person is mentioned who is a member of Alcoholics Anonymous only the first name has been used in order to preserve the individual's anonymity. The sole exception is in the case of Doherty Sheerin who was the founder of Alcoholics Anonymous in Indianapolis. The name of Mr. Sheerin, now deceased, is used with the gracious permission of his widow, Mrs. Dorothy Sheerin.

The author has undertaken to write the story of his life in response to thousands of requests from all over the world. It is written for publication with the permission of Father Pfau's ecclesiastical superior, the Archbishop of Indianapolis.

FOREWORD

SOME AUTOBIOGRAPHIES, like those of Helen Keller, George Washington Carver, Earl Carlson, Harold Wilkie and Christy Brown, record the victory of the will to live over crushing initial handicaps. Others like those of Harold Maine, Terry McAdam and Lillian Roth describe a good start, a terrible disaster and a re-constitution. Still others record progressive disintegration.

In Father Pfau's biography there was a good start, and no terrible disaster. In fact, a unique feature of this honest, moving, record is the seeming lack of any external wound to account for the collapse. Here was a man who elected to become a priest, but who regretted that decision as soon as he made it and struggled with his indecision for years. He never touched alcohol in any form until adult life; he never joined in drinking parties, nor drank to drown his sorrows, for, relatively speaking, he had none. He wanted to teach—and was not permitted to do so. But is that a reason to drink?

This is a good book for those who have not discovered how impossible it is to say that X causes Y. It is a good book for those to read who do not realize the struggle through which an alcoholic goes all his life. It is the honest story of a friend of mine, a priest, whose Archbishop was wise enough to see the great usefulness a controlled alcoholic could be in strengthening the resistances of fellow priests and others who cannot make it alone. Here is another forceful document, pointing on the one hand to the insidiousness and power of self-destructive habit and on the

7

other hand to the victory that is possible, granted certain help and a certain basic strength of character. Every psychiatrist will back up Father Pfau when he says, "There is no such thing as moderate drinking for an alcoholic." Once one discovers his trend toward addiction, he must never take another drink. Never!

At the end of his book Father Pfau says, "I had nothing to do with it. God did it all." But all that goes before this shows how much Father Pfau did have to do with it, in a way he believes—and so do I—that other alcoholics can imitate.

Karl Menninger, M.D.

PART I

ALL MY LIFE, I will carry three indelible marks.

I am a Roman Catholic priest.

I am an alcoholic.

And I am a neurotic.

For many years, I was doubtful of the validity of the first and unaware of the existence of the other two. I was never sure I wanted to be a priest, and I know now that I did not choose the priesthood. It took me a long time fully to realize that I was chosen, and what I was chosen for.

My parish is the world—the world of alcoholics.

Admitting that I am an alcoholic did not come easy; it never does. I always thought that an alcoholic had to be a lost soul, a beaten, forgotten man, a rum-soaked derelict who drank himself into a perpetual stupor and who, because he drank liquor instead of eating food, finally died in a gutter of cirrhosis of the liver, or some such dreadful ailment. To me, he had to be at least unmoral, if not downright immoral, unable to control his lust for liquor because his will was weak.

And, since I was not that way, I couldn't believe that I was an alcoholic.

My will wasn't weak. I drank when I felt like it, but I thought I was pretty sensible about my drinking. I never drank in the morning. I never drank myself into a stupor, or got sick, or passed out from drinking. I seldom went a day without eating. I had long dry spells. How could I be an alcoholic?

But after fourteen years of intermittent drinking, which sometimes found me taking in a fifth of whiskey a day, I learned, with the help of Alcoholics Anonymous, that I am neither unmoral nor weak-willed. I am sick, as sick as I would be if I had diabetes. I am an alcoholic. And, just as the diabetic can't take sugar, I can't take alcohol.

I must live as an alcoholic until the day I die. I must never again take a drink.

I have had four nervous breakdowns and one near-miss. At one point, I thought they were the result of my drinking, but I know now that, basically, they came from other sources. My first breakdown occurred before I had touched a drop of liquor; my fifth began after I stopped drinking. I was too young, too bewildered, too upset to know what caused my first. By the time I began my fifth, I was an old hand at breakdowns—a sober old hand—and, after some groping around, I knew exactly what to do.

I had all these breakdowns because I am a neurotic. I must always live as a neurotic. I must never again allow myself to become so self-analytical that I am swamped with hidden, indefinable fears. I must never again allow myself to become over-tired, or try to do too much, or be put under heavy pressure, or do any of the things that feed my neuroticism. I must solve problems as they arise or I must accept them. I must never permit myself to become so emotionally attached to anything that I can't, if necessary, give it up.

If I am not neglectful in my living habits, I can make a happy and secure adjustment; indeed, I have already done so. I pray daily for the strength to continue.

I know I shall die an alcoholic, but I want to die a sober alcoholic. I know I shall die a neurotic, but I want to die a well-adjusted neurotic. I know I shall be a priest for all eternity, and, while I live, I want to be a good priest.

This is my story—the story of a priest, an alcoholic, a neurotic. It is not an easy story to tell, but I must tell it, for I know there are millions of people faced with problems similar to mine.

I hope some of them find the answers in these pages.

CHAPTER 1

In 1922, it was a long hundred and fifty miles between Indianapolis and St. Meinrad Seminary. First, you went to Huntingburg, Indiana, a hundred and thirty-five miles south. But, while it was most of the distance in mileage, Huntingburg wasn't halfway in time consumed. After you got there, you had to wait for a train to Ferdinand, twelve miles to the southeast. You went the rest of the way by buggy—or shank's pony.

I was two months short of my eighteenth birthday when I made the trip for the first time. Every detail is still etched in sharp relief in my memory, for it is not easy to forget the first step in the transformation from the lay world to the priesthood. Besides, this was my first long journey away from home.

In later years I often reflected that my mother must have hoped I would enter the priesthood from the day I was born. When I was a small child—perhaps five or six—I remember being in a room with her and a group of her friends. She patted my head and said, "This is Ralph. He's going to be a priest."

Under a warm September sun, five of us, all newly graduated from Cathedral High School in Indianapolis, met at the railroad station, and boarded the train to Huntingburg. I sat by the window, and watched the Indiana countryside flash by as the wheels of the train clicked in pleasant rhythm beneath me.

Most of us were lost in thought at first, but that didn't last long. We were all about the same age, and it is impossible to lose five seventeen-year-olds in thought for any great length of time. Long before we reached Huntingburg, we were chattering and laughing and acting, albeit a little nervously, as though we didn't have a care in the world. We were just a bunch of youngsters, about to embark on a new, and great adventure. The serious thoughts and aims that had led us this far were buried under a thin veneer of lightheartedness. We were all a little scared, but none of us wanted to admit it.

At Huntingburg, we hung around for two hours waiting for the train to Ferdinand. This turned out to be a one-coach Toonerville Trolley which, we found out later, was popularly known as the "Ferdinand Flyer." It had its own schedule. It ran when it felt like running, stopped when it felt like stopping and broke down when it felt like breaking down. The man who built its roadbed must have also been the inventor of the roller coaster; we bounced and heaved and stumbled along a set of railroad tracks which buckled like licorice sticks. This was my first ride over a bumpy route that I was to see much of in the ensuing years.

Somewhat to our astonishment, for we were certain that the rickety little train would never make it, we arrived in Ferdinand without incident. It was a hot, dusty day, and we were all sticky with sweat, and anxious to get where we were going.

We didn't know it, but the worst of the trip was still ahead of us.

One of the boys remarked as he climbed wearily off the Ferdinand Flyer, "It *can't* be much farther."

"Only a buggy ride," commented a seminarian who was standing on the platform.

"A buggy ride?" I asked.

"When the horse doesn't balk," he said, "or when the buggy doesn't break down."

"What happens then?"

"You walk."

"How far?"

He shrugged.

"Three and a half miles or so," he said.

We had to wait our turn before we could hire a buggy to take us from the station to the seminary. About an hour and a half after we got off the train, we climbed aboard a one-hoss shay with a fringe on top and we were off, literally in a cloud of dust. It was clear and sunny, but we didn't see a thing the whole trip. The horse's hooves kicked up a blinding curtain in front of us, and the wheels of the buggy did the same thing in the rear. All we could do was sit and wait for the driver to tell us we had arrived.

The first look at St. Meinrad was—as, indeed, it still is—a breath-takingly beautiful sight. The seminary is on top of a hill, and is completely surrounded by woods. The light tan buildings are made of St. Meinrad sandstone. The material was hewn from the seminary's own property at Monte Casino, about three miles away. The church, which has two towers, dominates the entire area, and can be seen for many miles on a clear day.

At the time I first went there, the principal buildings at St. Meinrad were the abbey, the minor seminary, the church and a brand-new major seminary. There was also a building housing the abbey press, and a smaller building that was the powerhouse. To the east was a valley leading to a lake and fringed by a large woods of fir trees, which we knew as "Paradise." The town of St. Meinrad was at the foot of the north side of the hill. To the south and west were the fields and barns and farm lands which supplied most of the food to the seminary.

We were assigned to a sixty-bed dormitory in the minor seminary. There was a chair between each bed and there was a row of hangers on the wall. We kept only the essentials in the space assigned to us. Everything else went into lockers in the basement. There was no inside plumbing. We used outside toilets at a building about sixty yards away. That area was called "Texas," much to the distress of students who happened to hail from that state.

The priests in charge at St. Meinrad were members of the Benedictine Order, founded by St. Benedict in the fifth century. It is one of the oldest orders in the church. One of its primary functions in the diocese of Indianapolis is the training of boys for the priesthood. St. Meinrad today is an archabbey of the Benedictine Order.

It was late when we arrived, and we had time only to get

settled, have supper and attend evening prayers before retiring.

We were awakened the next morning by a bell at five-thirty, and we had to be in chapel by six. There, led by the Rector of the minor seminary, Father Dominic, we had a half-hour of meditation. Father Dominic was a heavy-set, balding man, with a fringe of iron-gray hair. He spoke in a soft, but clear and eloquent voice which rolled like the notes of an organ. I noticed the first time I ever saw him that he had an odd habit of scratching his left side with his right hand and vise versa, and sometimes, in those early hours of the morning, I would steal a look at Father Dominic to see which side he was scratching with which hand.

Each one of us had a meditation book, read aloud by Father Dominic and rhythmically punctuated in Latin with "Punctum 1," "Punctum 2," "Punctum 3" (point 1, point 2, point 3). These were for purposes of guiding us, but, unfortunately, the hour was so early that it was a struggle to stay awake—and many times we didn't. In order to keep us from slumbering through that half-hour of meditation, two prefects—students from the fifth class—were assigned to prevent eyes from closing and heads from nodding.

Meditation was followed by Low Mass in the chapel, and all students received Holy Communion each day. High Mass was always in the abbey church in which was a transept with choir stalls, with two rows of seats and kneeling-benches on each side, facing each other. They were referred to as "choir" stalls because there the monks solemnly sung their Office each day in Gregorian chant. There was a sung Mass—a High Mass—every day at St. Meinrad.

The students used the pews which were set across the church back from the choir stalls in the rear. There were about twenty-five rows of pews, each seating about twenty students.

Mass was followed by breakfast at seven-thirty. Each student took his turn at waiting on table for a week at a time. The dishes of food came into the dining hall on a large turntable at one end, and the waiters picked them up and distributed them from there. After breakfast, there was a brief recreation period, followed by High Mass, then, in quick succession, classes, dinner, recreation until two P.M., classes until four, then study and supper at five-thirty. There was another recreation period, which ended at seven-thirty, then we studied until night prayers and retired at nine.

This was a pretty rigid routine, but I didn't mind it, for I had expected it to be harder. So many members of my family had entered religion that psychologically I was well prepared for seminary life. My brother Jerome entered St. Meinrad six years ahead of me and was in his last year when I started there. Out of a family of eleven, four of my mother's sisters were nuns and two of her brothers priests. My uncle George Smith was our parish priest at St. Philip's Church in Indianapolis. Another uncle, Father Alphonse Smith later became Bishop of Nashville, Tennessee.

I was the youngest of seven sons. There were no daughters. One of my brothers died before I was born. I hardly knew my father, who was of French extraction. He passed away when I was four. My mother's forebears were German.

When I was a child, daily Communion was a very common thing among Catholics in Indianapolis. Bishop Joseph Chartrand set the example, and we were trained to follow it. After my First Communion, I received Communion at six o'clock every morning for years. I did this because I wanted to, not because I had to. That was one of the reasons why it was so natural for me to accept as inevitable the fact that I was going to be a priest.

During these years I never thought much about girls. I had other interests, and, besides, I was almost painfully shy. Once, when I was in eighth grade, I saw a girl whom I liked at a party. We didn't speak, or even meet—I just admired her from a distance. I thought about her later, and wondered if I would ever develop enough nerve to try to see her again. Finally, I wrote her a post card, and mailed it. The weeks went by, and I never heard from her.

It was only later that I realized that I had been too shy to sign my name to the post card.

My studies in my first year at St. Meinrad were equivalent to an extended high school course, with such subjects as advanced Latin, trigonometry, science, English literature and history. We had a six-day week, instead of the five-day week I was used to in high school, and we wore cassocks, instead of street clothes. Otherwise, my first year at St. Meinrad was much as it would have been at any strict preparatory school.

Shortly after I entered the seminary, I met Father Anselm Schaaf, O.S.B., one of the gentlest, kindliest, most understanding men I have ever known. He was a man of medium height, with steel-gray hair and a serenely calm face. His chin was strong, his nose prominent and his lips were softened by the almost perpetual smile that played about them. But his most striking feature was a pair of deep blue, deep-set piercing eyes. When he looked at you, he seemed to be reading your thoughts, and I often felt that he actually did read mine.

I learned after I had been at St. Meinrad a few months that Father Anselm was a brother of my favorite nun at St. Philip Neri. It was Sister Mary Agreda who had made me go on into school when I had sulked on the steps on my first day there.

When I first knew Father Anselm, he was teaching Scripture at St. Meinrad. Later, he became Spiritual Director of the major seminary, then Rector and finally Prior.

Studying for the priesthood is a stern business, yet we always managed to enjoy our share of laughs at the seminary. One of the prime sources of humor was the food, which, according to the standards of most people, was terrible, but was only typical institution food—plain but plentiful.

As it happened, I got along fine at the table, no matter what was placed before me. This gave me a big advantage over some of my classmates, some of whom gagged at many a meal, mostly because they were over-fussy.

One breakfast was known throughout the seminary as "Nonsense." It was a corn mixture, similar to corn bread, and I loved it. It was chopped up and fried, and was eaten with butter and molasses. Most of the fellows liked it. It was a stomach-filling meal in itself.

On Sundays, we had homemade pork sausages, in long, luscious links. For lunch, we usually had cold meat, or cheese, potatoes, salad, bread and butter, and coffee. To me, this was a good, solid lunch, but there were always a few who disliked it.

There was one poor fellow named Dick, who almost starved to

death. He came from a wealthy family, and was used to rich, well-prepared food. Meals, for him, became an ordeal, and I'm afraid we didn't make life easier for him.

One day, for example, he had to get up and leave the table. All I had said to him was, "What's that floating in your soup?"

It was only a crouton. He thought it was a bug.

We had brick cheese, which the Brothers made right at the seminary, for lunch on Fridays, and dinner that night was always jack salmon, caught in the Ohio River. I loved the cheese, but never cared much for the fish.

The Brother cooks at the seminary had a genius for serving "identical beef." No matter what cut we had—in fact, no matter what kind of meat they gave us—it nearly always appeared on the table in big hunks, in gravy. Pork, lamb, veal, everything got the same treatment as beef.

While the cooks at St. Meinrad at that time could hardly compete with Oscar of the Waldorf, the bakers could hold their own in any company. They made delicious whole-wheat bread which we all gobbled up when a Brother brought thick slices of it around in a big basket at four o'clock every afternoon.

That was our snack-time. Each of us had his own lock-box in the basement where we kept provisions sent from home—stuff like cookies and candy and cake and jelly and peanut butter. During his first year at the seminary, I'm sure Dick lived off the food in his lock-box.

Because his eyes were perfect and one of mine was crossed, Dick envied me no end. One of the few excuses we had for getting home was to have our glasses checked. Those of us who wore glasses had more checkups in our first years at the seminary than we had previously had during our whole lifetimes.

Most of the boys developed a sudden concern over the state of their teeth, along with an unusual affinity for dentists. A tooth-ache wouldn't get you home, but it could get you as far as Ferdinand, where there was a dentist. But the big attraction there was Old Ma Leppert's dining room. She served a marvelous fried chicken dinner for a dollar.

The infirmary sometimes provided an escape from routine, but if you didn't have something obviously wrong, you had to have a temperature to stay there. I was there once when my bad knee kicked up. One afternoon, I was joined by a classmate called Bill, who had managed to develop a sniffle.

It was gone when he woke up the next morning, and he was quite disturbed at the prospect of having to resume routine quite so soon.

"I wish I could stay here another day," he said wistfully.

"Why don't you?" I asked.

"How can I? I don't have a temperature."

"Make one," I said. "Put the thermometer in your coffee when the Brother brings it around."

When the good Brother Infirmarian looked at the thermometer after pulling it out of Bill's mouth, I thought he was going to faint.

"Heavens above!" he cried. "One hundred and ten degrees!"

He reached for Bill's forehead, but Bill had turned his face to the wall. He was moaning softly.

"One hundred and ten degrees!" the Brother exclaimed again. "We'll have to call a doctor."

He walked out of the room for a few minutes, then reappeared. Bill saw him just in time to turn his face to the wall again and resume his moaning.

"How do you feel?" the Brother asked.

Bill moaned piteously.

"Let me feel your forehead," said the Brother gently.

He rested his hand on Bill's forehead for about thirty seconds before he realized that he had been had.

"Sit up!" he said sharply.

Bill, his face sheepish, sat up.

"Open your mouth!"

Docilely, Bill complied. The Brother angrily shoved a thermometer into his face, and stood by tapping his foot on the floor while waiting for it to register.

"Young man," he said, sternly, after looking at it, "you have no temperature."

"I know it," said Bill in a small voice.

"Get out of here—quickly!"

Bill got out.

That was more than thirty-five years ago. Today, Bill is a monk—at St. Meinrad.

We were not permitted to smoke cigarettes, although a pipe or a cigar was all right. However, even that privilege was occasionally withdrawn for disciplinary reasons.

I had a narrow escape from disaster one afternoon. I was standing under the basement steps, near our lock-boxes, and decided to sneak a cigarette. I put one in my mouth, but, just as I was about to light it, I felt a sneeze coming. I put the cigarette in my pocket, and sneezed away. And, as I was blowing my nose, the Rector walked by.

Once, when they took away the smoking privileges in the recreation hall, we decided it was only decent to give tobacco a nice burial. There were three pool tables in the recreation room, so we made a catafalque out of one. We put six cues on each side, then spread out empty cigarette packs and pipes and tobacco pouches in the center—a fitting funeral. When the Rector saw it, he added two weeks to the smoking ban.

I saw quite a bit of my brother Jerry during my first year in the seminary. He had already received all of his major orders except that of the priesthood itself. He had received the diaconate, the next to last step, the previous May, and was to be ordained the following June.

When we got together, we talked mostly of home or the priesthood. Now that I was actually at St. Meinrad, Jerry opened up more than he ever had when I was in high school. He told me what to expect in the years to come, and kept encouraging me to work hard so that nothing would go wrong.

The end of my first year at St. Meinrad marked the beginning of a new era for me. We were facing six years in the major seminary, and a curriculum far more difficult than during our one college year. Now, we would take a high concentration of studies leading directly to the priesthood.

We would be introduced to homiletics, the scriptural studies. These included the background, interpretation and history of the Bible, and the contemporary history of the times. For the first two years in the major seminary, our main subject would be philosophy, followed by four years of majoring in theology, including moral and dogmatic theology. One was the interpretation of the moral value of human acts; the other the interpretation of the teachings of the Church.

It was a big jump from a curriculum revolving around English, Latin, mathematics and science. No longer boys, we were about to become men.

I had two jobs in Indianapolis when I went home for the summer after my first year at the seminary. On Friday and Saturday nights, I made good money stuffing papers at the *Indianapolis Star*. We got seventy-five cents an hour, and on Saturdays I worked thirteen hours. I'd be through at six in the morning, so I would go to Mass on my way home, then sleep until midafternoon.

During the week, I worked for the city recreation department. I was in charge of a playground at the corner of Kansas and Meridian streets, in the south end of town. A number of the seminarians had similar jobs. We got sixty dollars a month for overseeing the grounds and watching over the children. It was pleasant work, and I stayed with it for five summers.

My first two years in the major seminary at St. Meinrad were uneventful. I studied and worked and prayed and meditated, and was happy and contented. I had no doubts about my future, and, at the end of my second year, I looked forward with calm anticipation to receiving the first of the minor orders.

CHAPTER 2

DURING THE FIFTH YEAR at the seminary, we learned the administration of Baptism, using a doll baby for practice, and the distribution of the Holy Communion. We also took part in Solemn Masses as deacon and sub-deacon.

The next year, we began practicing the saying of Mass. We had moved out of the dormitory and into smaller rooms in the major seminary. The last four years we had private rooms. In common with my classmates, I had an altar in my room. Daily we practiced saying Mass at these altars. They were called straw Masses. Not being priests, we could not validly perform the act of consecration. This part is the actual *transubstantiation* which is brought about by the words of *consecration*, but is only possible through a validly ordained priest. Transubstantiation signifies that the substance of bread and wine actually becomes the Body and Blood of Christ.

The Rector of the major seminary was Father Albert. He was a short, thin man, very strict and exacting, not only with others but with himself as well. While I was at the seminary I harbored occasional resentments toward him because of this strictness, and it was not until much later that I learned to understand him. Today, Father Albert is a wonderful friend, profuse in his encouragement of me in my work.

In his third year—actually, in my time, the fourth at St. Meinrad, counting the one year of college—a seminarian receives his first of two sets of minor orders. Preparatory to them is tonsure, when his hair is cut in the form of a cross. This, actually, is nothing more than an introduction to his life as a cleric. Then, in accordance with ancient custom which dates back to the earliest days of the Church, the seminarian receives the first set of minor orders when he is made porter and lector. The porter took care of the door. The lector read the Scriptures during the Mass.

I received my first minor orders in 1926. Actually, they barely served to make me feel much closer to my goal, because they are not particularly important. They simply constituted, for me, another step along the way, like entering Cathedral High, or going into the seminary for the first time. There was nothing irrevocable involved. When you receive minor orders, you still are not bound to anything. You are just as free to leave the seminary and enter lay life as you were before.

By the time I received my first minor orders, my brother Jerry was teaching at St. Mary-of-the-Woods, a convent and women's college near Terre Haute, Indiana. After his ordination, Jerry had been sent to Rome, where he obtained a Doctor of Sacred Theology degree.

In the summer between my third and fourth years in the major seminary, I went over to Terre Haute, about seventy miles west of Indianapolis, to see Jerry. During the course of our conversation one day, one of us mentioned a priest we both knew well.

"I've heard rumors that he's drinking quite a bit," I remarked.

"They're true," Jerry said. "It's too bad, because he's a fine fellow. But I'm afraid he's an alcoholic."

He looked at me a minute, then said slowly, "Ralph, did you know there's a history of alcoholism in our family?"

"I heard something about it," I said, "but nobody ever explained it fully to me."

"Well," Jerry said, "don't ever mention alcohol around Mom. It upsets her terribly. We've never had alcohol in the house. She's so dead set against it that it's almost an obsession."

I reminded Jerry of Mom's reaction to one of my first jobs. As long as I can remember, I have been a baseball fan. When I was in high school, I used to hang around the Indianapolis ball park when the Indians were in town. I finally got a job as an usher.

One day, a big, red-faced Irishman whom I seated in a box asked me if I'd like to work for him, posting baseball scores for the customers at his saloon when the club was on the road. I was delighted to accept, for this meant that I'd get the scores hot off the wires before anyone else did, and it would be fun being the first one to pass along the news.

I kept the job for a few weeks, then my mother found out about it. That was the end of the saloon for me. Mom couldn't stand the idea of my being that close to people who were drinking. She had no use for alcohol nor for anyone who used it.

"Do you think alcoholism is hereditary?" I asked.

"I don't know," Jerry said. "I've often wondered."

"If it is," I remarked, "one of us could be an alcoholic, I suppose—you or me or Vic or Ed or any of us."

Jerry smiled.

"Have you ever taken a drink?" he asked.

"No."

"Do you have any desire for one?"

I shook my head.

"Then I wouldn't worry about being an alcoholic if I were you," he said. "You're nearly twenty-one years old. If you were an alcoholic, you'd have wanted a drink long ago."

"I wonder if I ever *will* want one."

"Maybe," Jerry said. "It's no disgrace to take a drink once in a while. After you're ordained, occasionally you'll find that people will be offering you drinks when you go into their homes. Of course, with Prohibition, you can't drink publicly, but people who want liquor don't seem to have any trouble finding it.

"You've got to be very careful when people ask if you'd like a drink. If you can handle the situation, that's fine. Just be sure you can handle it. Now, poor George evidently couldn't. That's why he's doing so much drinking now."

"I wonder if I ought to take some sort of pledge," I said thoughtfully.

"If you want to, I don't see what harm it could do," Jerry commented. "Make your own decision when you're ordained."

Shortly after that, when I saw him again at St. Mary-of-the-

Woods, I asked him a question that had been vaguely bothering me since our first talk.

"How do you know whether you're an alcoholic or not?" I said.

"I really don't know," he replied. "All I do know is that alcoholics drink all the time—morning, noon and night. Most people drink in the afternoon or the evening, but not in the morning. So I suppose if you don't take a drink before noon, you'll never have to worry about being an alcoholic."

I didn't think about it again for some time. In the meanwhile, I had enough on my mind.

In 1927, I received my second set of minor orders, acolyte and exorcist. This completed my minor orders, still leaving me free to do whatever I liked. I would not receive major orders, the sub-diaconate and the diaconate, until the following year.

In our diocese, you are ordained sub-deacon and deacon on successive days, although in some places, they come as much as six months apart. These are binding orders, a point of no return. Even if you go no farther, you may not marry after your sub-diaconate.

As I entered my fifth year at the major seminary, the year that would be climaxed by the diaconate, I felt no qualms. Now, my goal was in sight. My only desire was to get the last of the preliminaries over with so that I could reach it.

That year, the Rector of St. Meinrad gave the five-day retreat for candidates about to receive sacred orders. I went to it quite convinced that all was well. I anticipated no snags of any description.

On the opening day of the retreat, the Rector's conference was based on the text, "I am prepared and I am not disturbed."

There was something about this text that suddenly bothered me. The Rector began talking, and I tried to concentrate on what he was saying, but I found it impossible. The only thing that whirled through my mind was the text.

"I am prepared and I am not disturbed."

Prepared? Was I truly prepared? What did being prepared mean?

You had to be worthy to take the tremendous step that I was facing.

Was I truly worthy?

I closed my eyes, and leaned back. The Rector's voice was coming at me, but I could barely hear him.

Think of the things you have done wrong in your lifetime. Think of the people you have hurt. Think of the lies you have told, the pain you have caused, the work you have shirked, the prayers you have missed.

Does this make you worthy?

Think of your mother who bore you and brought you up and trained you for this life you have chosen. Or did you choose it? Didn't she choose it for you? And don't you resent her for choosing it? And don't you show your resentment whenever you see your mother?

Does this make you worthy?

I tried to review my life as I sat in the chapel while the voice of the Rector served as a backdrop for my scattered thoughts. And, even as I tried, I knew the very thing I was doing was wrong.

Listen to the Rector, Ralph Pfau. He is talking to you.

I listened, but I didn't hear.

"I am prepared and I am not disturbed."

Where was all my confidence and hope and faith and contentment now? Was it possible that I was not yet ready to accept orders a hairline short of the priesthood itself?

"I am prepared and I am not disturbed."

Before the Rector had finished his conference, my mind was in a turmoil. *How can the plans of a lifetime be disrupted in less than an hour? Do I doubt? Is this possible?*

I stood up with the others, and walked out of the chapel in a daze. I was utterly confused on all but two counts:

I was not prepared. And I was very much disturbed.

All day, I tried to find solace in prayer and meditation, but I couldn't concentrate on either. My mind was a confused jumble of unhappy doubt that I could, or should, go on any farther.

Shall I turn back now? I have gone so far. Is this a time to stop?

I watched some of my classmates, wondering if they, too, were assailed by doubts. I studied them as they walked, as they stood, as they sat, as they knelt. I looked into their faces and watched to see if their hands were trembling or their knees shaking.

What are they thinking?

There was no way of telling. They all appeared to be composed, relaxed—and ready.

But what are they thinking?

I wished I could ask one of them, but I couldn't bring myself to do it. I wanted to know if others were as unprepared and disturbed as I.

How can I find out? This must happen to everybody. All seminarians are assailed by doubt at times, aren't they? Why should I be upset because it happens to me?

This is a phase I'm going through. It will be over by morning.

But it wasn't over by morning. I had trouble concentrating on evening prayers, and later, as I knelt beside my own bed, I could not make myself believe that this was only a phase.

I barely touched my evening meal. And when I went to bed I was more wide awake than when I had arisen that morning.

As I lay for hours, aware and envious of my classmates sleeping in their rooms, all of the flaws of a lifetime flashed through my troubled mind.

Can a child who told fibs grow into a man with priestly qualities? Can a child with a quick temper, a child who talked back to his mother and disobeyed his teachers grow into a man with priestly qualities? Can a child who once stole an apple off a passing pushcart grow into a man with priestly qualities? Can a child who made his mother weep because she could not afford to buy him a sled grow into a man with priestly qualities? Can a child who had fist fights with other children grow into a man with priestly qualities?

How can I go through with this? A priest must be a holy man, and I am not a holy man.

And with the approach of dawn came a new and terrible doubt.

Did I really want to become a priest? Was this, after all, meant for me? Wasn't it all my mother's idea?

All hopes that the phase I was going through would be over by morning were gone when morning actually came. I arose dead-tired and more confused than ever. Over and over, as I prayed and meditated, as I ate and walked about the grounds, as I went in and out of the church, as I carried out all the simple routines of the retreat, I reviewed the flaws which, I was sure, *must* keep me from going on any farther.

And the more I thought, the larger loomed the small mistakes of my troubled childhood.

I went around in circles, and I always arrived back at the same conclusion.

I am not ready. Perhaps I'll never be ready.

I couldn't eat and couldn't sleep and, after a while, I couldn't even think. The second day of the retreat was worse than the first, for I kept piling doubt on doubt, compounding my troubles into a horrible nightmare. If I slept at all the second night, it was only in fits and starts, forced by utter exhaustion.

It didn't seem possible, however, that I had as much as a single hour of uninterrupted sleep, for I spent the whole night going over and over my old problems, and even developing another terrible new one.

I thought of my talk with Jerry, when he told me that Mom was so dead set against having alcohol in the house. I remembered suggesting the possibility that one of us brothers might be an alcoholic, if alcoholism actually was hereditary.

Except for my two short talks with Jerry and my vague fears as a child, I had never thought one way or the other about alcohol. I had never had the slightest desire to try anything stronger than Coke. I hadn't even been around people while they were drinking, except when I worked posting baseball scores in a saloon. And then, with *everyone* around me drinking, I didn't have the slightest desire to join them.

Such frantic thoughts as these kept me awake for the remainder of the night.

When I arose on the third morning of the retreat, I knew I couldn't go on like this. I had to talk to someone. I recoiled at the thought of approaching any of my classmates. But, for the moment, I was so confused that I didn't know where to turn.

I was so exhausted that I could hardly drag myself to chapel for morning prayers.

Please, dear God, help me find someone who can tell me what to do.

As I walked out of the church, I saw Father Anselm. I waited for him outside.

"I've got to see you, Father," I said.

He looked at me, the quiet smile playing about his lips, the deep-set eyes resting like blue rivets on my face.

"Come to my room with me," he said.

I poured out my heart to him. I told him of my fears and doubts and resentments, and of my feeling of absolute unworthiness. I told him I was too much human being, too little saint, to become a man of God. I told him about my mother, and her brothers and sisters who had entered religion, and her own determination that I should, too. I told him about my own brothers, and how I had resented them, even Jerry, because they were all older and wiser than I. I told him that, after six years in college and seminary, I hadn't made any spiritual progress, so how could I be a priest?

And I told him about the alcoholism in my family, and my own fear that it would be passed along to me.

He listened to my long, rambling, sometimes incoherent recital without comment, and he sat silent for several minutes after I had finished.

Then he said, "You have nothing to worry about. This is just a matter of scruples. It happens to all of us at one time or another. We are so busy thinking of the little things we've done wrong that we can't see anything else.

"Do you think you are the only man who hasn't felt worthy? We all have felt that way; I still do, and I'm sure you will when you have been in the priesthood as long as I. Are you worried because you don't think you're a holy man? If you're a holy man by the time you're dead, you'll be doing well.

"Go back and finish the retreat. Go back and pray, and meditate, and mingle with your classmates. Forget your doubts.

They're only temporary. During the retreat, come and see me again, if you like. There will still be time before the sub-diaconate. But I'm sure you'll be all right."

I made a General Confession, thanked him, and rejoined the others. Father Anselm had certainly helped. It was comforting to know that there was nothing unusual about my feelings of inadequacy, and more comforting still to know that he understood them. His assurance that I'd be all right gave me confidence —at least for a few hours.

But again I tossed and turned at night, and my appetite was gone. I found it impossible to relax, or to concentrate on anything. The only improvement was an occasional feeling of relief in the knowledge that I had someone to share my secret with, someone to whom I could go back whenever I wanted.

And I went back again and again.

"Father, I don't know what to do," I said. "I try to ignore the doubts, but they keep cropping up. And I can't get my mind off the mistakes I've made in life."

He talked to me for hours, assuring me that I would be all right, that I was going through a phase that would pass and that I should try to think of my coming sub-diaconate in positive, rather than negative terms.

I saw Father Anselm every day—sometimes twice a day—during the remainder of the retreat. I pestered the poor man to death, repeating over and over my set of doubts, and hearing over and over his patient repetitions of assurance.

Each time I left him, I felt better, but it only lasted for a few hours. Then the fears would creep back, and the only way I could keep them from smothering me was to go back and see Father Anselm again.

Two nights before the sub-diaconate, I went to his quarters.

"Father," I said, for the twentieth time, "I'm afraid. I don't know whether I'm going to make it or not."

And for the twentieth time, he answered, "It's only a matter of scruples—a perfectly normal reaction. You aren't the only one going through this. It will clear up."

"Then why hasn't it by now?" I asked.

"Because you haven't let it. You're allowing it to hang too heavily on your mind. After this is over, you'll be glad."

I looked down at my feet. Then, with tears in my eyes, I faced him and said, "I can't go on, Father."

He didn't say anything for a long time. Then, very softly, he said, "There is no obligation for you to receive the sub-diac-onate, Ralph. You are free to leave, if you like. But somehow I'm sure you will be all right, so pray for help and try to forget this feeling of hopelessness. But you are letting yourself lose the fight. So, if you insist, perhaps it would be better for you to talk to the Bishop and tell him you would prefer not to go on."

That frightened me. To go to the Bishop would be a final move. It would release me from all obligations, and that would be the end.

But anything was a final move at this point. No matter what I did, I was facing a decision. The next forty-eight hours would be the most critical of my life.

I went back to my own quarters and prayed for guidance and the strength to make a decision. A decision was essential. I couldn't live with these gnawing doubts much longer.

I slept fitfully again and, as usual, I awoke dog-tired.

I can't go on. I've got to do something. I've got to make up my mind before I go crazy.

After breakfast, I went back to my room. Time was running out, and I still hadn't made up my mind.

What do I want?

Suddenly, without reason, but simply because it was a positive move, I decided to see the Bishop and tell him I was quitting. I could not receive the sub-diaconate.

Bishop Chartrand had come down to St. Meinrad from Indian-apolis the day before for the various ordinations, which began Sunday with tonsure and minor orders, and were climaxed with the ordinations to the diaconate and priesthood on Tuesday.

When I arrived at his office, I was met by Monsignor Joseph E. Hamill, Ph.D., who was Chancellor of the diocese.

"What is it you want?" he asked.

"I should like to see the Bishop," I said.

"Is there anything I can do?"

I shook my head.

"I *have* to see him," I said.

"The Bishop is resting," Monsignor Hamill told me. "I can't disturb him now."

My bitter disappointment must have been evident for the Monsignor gently touched my shoulder, and said, "Perhaps you'd better come in."

He held the door wide open, and I followed him inside. He led me to an office, closed the door and said, "Tell me, Ralph. What's wrong?"

I sobbed a moment, then looked at him and stammered, "I don't think I should be ordained."

"Why?" he asked quietly.

I tried to tell him, but only a few disjointed sentences came out. Then he said, "It's natural to be nervous and doubtful at a time like this. Everyone goes through this sort of thing. This is just scruples. You're all right. You should be ordained."

He talked for a few minutes more, then stood up and ushered me to the door. I muttered my thanks and left. And I went right from there to Father Anselm's room.

"I tried to see the Bishop, but he was resting," I said. "Then I talked to Monsignor Hamill. And he told me the same thing you told me."

"To go through with the ordination?" asked Father Anselm.

"Yes."

He stroked his chin thoughtfully. Then he said, "There must be some reason for this—some reason beyond our comprehension. You should go ahead now."

"With all these doubts?"

"Yes, with all these doubts."

He looked at me, his blue eyes boring into mine.

"God may have special work for you some day," he said.

God may have special work for you some day. How many times have I thought of those prophetic words?

We talked for half an hour, covering much of the ground that was so familiar. Then Father Anselm said, "Ralph, I think you really want to go through with everything. You have the spiritual strength and the moral understanding. This conflict of yours may also be due to some physical ailment. Why don't you see a doctor when you get home?"

"Perhaps I will, Father," I said.

I went back to my quarters, and tried to rest. I lay down, but sleep wouldn't come. As always when I tried to close my eyes, my life passed in review. I hardly dared lie down any more, for fear some new sin I hadn't thought of before would crop up.

Jerry arrived that day, the day before the sub-diaconate. I hadn't seen him since Easter. He was busy at St. Mary-of-the-Woods, and I couldn't leave St. Meinrad. I saw him only for a moment, and had no chance to talk to him. I wasn't sure I wanted to. He would have laughed the whole thing off if he had known my doubts.

By now I realized that this was no ordinary thing I was going through. I had been a nervous wreck for almost a week, and there was no sign of improvement. I was losing weight so fast I didn't dare step on the scales. As Father Anselm had pointed out, I also now needed medical attention.

Once again, I went through an almost sleepless night of tossing and turning and worrying and reviewing. I didn't need the bell to wake me. I must have been awake for hours when it sounded at 5:25 in the morning.

This was the morning of May 28, 1928, a morning different from all the other mornings, different from the mornings of school and college and seminary and retreats. This was the morning of the sub-diaconate. This time, when I went to church, I would do far more than pray.

I woke up this morning with no final obligations. I could go home, and nothing would happen. But I was not going home.

I would go to bed this night invested with one major order, and tomorrow night with another. And then I would be a deacon of the Church, bound to a vow of chastity I could never renounce.

When I stepped inside the church for ordination, the first person I saw was my brother Jerry sitting in one of the pews.

He looked at me and smiled. I tried to smile back, but couldn't. Seeing Jerry there, and knowing that he was unaware of my misgivings, scared me more than ever.

Then I began vesting for the sub-diaconate. First, I put on the amice, the white linen shawl. I touched the amice to my head before slipping it over my shoulders, then tucked the top around my neck and tied the bottom around my waist. The amice is a "Helmet of Salvation," which, when touched to the head, symbolizes protection from idle or evil thoughts at Mass. I then put on the alb, a loose-flowing white robe signifying purity of body and soul.

Now, it was time for the cincture, or cingulum. This is a thick cord, with tassel ends, and it symbolizes the priest's life of celibacy. At the sub-diaconate, it takes on a special significance, for it represents a priestly vow. It is tied around the waist to secure the alb.

As I was putting mine on, it broke.

I almost fainted. Now, I was sure I wasn't going to make it.

For a few awful moments, I stood rigidly still, the broken cingulum gathered around my feet. I broke out into a cold sweat, shivering inside and out. My hands felt clammy, my legs wobbled and my head ached.

I heard someone ask what the matter was, and I mumbled, "Nothing."

Then I stooped to pick up the cingulum, tied it together as best I could and slipped it around my waist. This time, I secured it without mishap.

Somehow, I went through the sub-diaconate that day, and the diaconate the next. I had to push myself, for I had the feeling I would collapse if I were not careful.

Jerry embraced me when it was all over.

"How do you feel?" he asked.

"All right," I said.

"You look a little pale," he said. "Are you *really* all right?"

I nodded.

He patted me on the shoulder.

"I'm very proud of you," he said.

For a few moments, I felt warm and happy. But my spirits drooped again after he walked away.

At a time when everyone was congratulating everyone else on completing the next to last step on the road to the priesthood, I was so depressed I wished I were dead.

CHAPTER 3

THE NEXT WEEK, I went home to Indianapolis.

It was stiflingly hot. I hardly remember riding on the train or arriving at the railroad station, for I was in a semi-stupor. I doubt if I had a clear thought in my head. I didn't even realize that I was over the diaconate hurdle. When I thought at all, I was vaguely aware of a feeling that I shouldn't have gone this far and couldn't possibly go any farther.

When I got home, it took me a few minutes to summon up the courage to walk into the house. I was still dressed in street clothes—in our diocese you do not put on the Roman collar until you have actually been ordained—and my wilted shirt was open at the throat. I set my grip on the sidewalk in front of old Doc Fleming's drugstore, and wiped my face with a handkerchief.

How can I face my mother? What can I say to her? She'll ask questions. How can I answer them?

I picked up the suitcase, and slowly entered the house, desperately hoping that my mother wouldn't hear me. I shuffled up the steps, taking one at a time like an old man on his last legs instead of a youth of twenty-three.

When I reached the top, I stumbled into the hallway, and stared at my grip as I carefully placed it on the floor. I heard a quick step, and raised my eyes.

My mother, her lips parted in a slight smile, was standing at the doorway. But when she caught sight of my face, the smile was replaced by a look of deep concern.

"Ralph! Ralph! What's the matter?"

I didn't move. I stood rigid for a few seconds, then bent my head and began sobbing. I moved heavily past her into the living room, where I sank down on a divan. Then I buried my face in my arms and cried until my whole body shook.

I don't know how long I stayed there—it could have been two minutes or two hours. I finally became aware of my mother's gentle touch on my shoulders. I sat up and let her wipe my streaming face with a damp cloth.

Then she said, in a voice deep with compassion. "Tell me, Ralph. What's the matter? Maybe I can help you."

I shrugged.

"Don't you want to go on?"

I couldn't speak. I only nodded.

"There is not too much to life," she said softly. "You make of it what you can. You can make a life for yourself in the priesthood. You can be happy in it."

She spoke for several minutes, and I let her talk, for it made me feel better. It wasn't what she said that affected me, but the way she said it. She was trying to understand me. She had never done that before. And, for the first time in my life, I got the feeling that she was more interested in me than in my career.

It was as though a lifelong stranger had become a lifelong friend. Sick at heart as I was, I felt closer to my mother that day than I ever had before.

The next afternoon Bishop Chartrand phoned me.

"How would you like to spend the summer at St. Mary-of-the-Woods?" he asked.

He doesn't know. Monsignor Hamill didn't tell him.

"I'd like that," I said.

"When can you go there?" he asked.

"Any time."

"Fine. Report to Monsignor Rawlinson tomorrow."

"Thank you," I said.

I hung up, more relieved than surprised. Many seminarians

get a summer assignment after the diaconate. Others help in their home parishes. I was glad I was going to St. Mary-of-the-Woods, where I had visited Jerry so often.

But I felt the need of more spiritual help before leaving. I called a classmate, and asked if he could suggest a confessor. He mentioned Father Amicus, a priest whom I knew casually. I went to see him.

I poured out the whole story, starting with the Rector's text on the first day of the diaconate retreat at St. Meinrad. After I had finished my long, unhappy recital, I said, "So you see, Father, now I just can't go on, and I don't know what to do."

"How do you know you can't go on?" he said. "You are a human being, and you are going through an intensely human experience. It is something that you will get over and be the better for. Have faith in God. Pray to Him and to His Blessed Mother. And remember—you are no more than human."

No one had ever put it just that way to me before. It made me feel better.

But, as usual, the feeling didn't last. By nightfall, I was as bad as ever. I went to bed, and did well if I slept as much as an hour.

The next day, when I went to Terre Haute to begin my assignment at St. Mary-of-the-Woods, I was scared stiff. I didn't want to talk to anyone. Jerry had gone to Fordham University for the summer, and I was just as glad he wasn't around. All I wanted was to be left alone.

I stayed at St. Mary-of-the-Woods two days, during which time I ate almost nothing and barely slept. Then I went to see the chaplain, Monsignor Rawlinson.

"I'm ill, Monsignor," I said. "May I have permission to go to Indianapolis and see a doctor?"

He gave me permission, and I left at once.

"My nerves are gone," I told the doctor. "I can't keep going like this. You've got to help me."

"How long has this been going on?" he asked.

"About three weeks."

Then I gave him a brief version of the story I had told Father Amicus. When I had finished, he said, "I don't think there's anything to worry about."

He examined me, then said, "You're all right. This kind of thing often happens to people in your position. I have a brother who's a priest, and he went through the same thing. I imagine every seminarian does."

"Does it last this long?" I asked.

"Sometimes. Anyhow, take these pills—one after supper and one just before going to bed. They'll make you sleep."

"What are they?"

"Nembutal."

That was my introduction to barbiturates.

I went back to St. Mary-of-the-Woods the same day. And that night, I began taking the sleeping pills. They helped temporarily. For the next few weeks, I slept a little better and my appetite picked up some. But it didn't last. By late June, I was as bad as ever. I phoned the doctor, and he told me to double the dose. That didn't help much either.

I was right back where I started from.

My work at St. Mary-of-the-Woods should have been interesting and rewarding, but instead it was a nightmare. Unhappily for me, I was closely associated with a visiting priest so painfully serious-minded that he couldn't see the light side of anything. Even if I weren't still in the throes of a nervous collapse, he would have depressed me. As it was, he drove me frantic.

No matter what happened, he reacted in the same way.

"*Cui bono?*" ("For what good?") he would say. After a while, I found myself echoing him. A month with him practically convinced me that everything *was* hopeless. "What's the use?"

I wanted to talk to someone, but there was no one I felt free to approach at St. Mary-of-the-Woods. I prayed around the clock. Every waking moment found me asking for help.

I carried on an active correspondence with Father Anselm, who had a summer parish in Cannelton, Indiana, and it saved me from falling apart altogether.

"I'm terribly upset," I wrote him early in July. "It seems to be the same old story. I can't make up my mind what to do. I have lost twenty pounds since the diaconate retreat, and there seems no end to my trouble. I'm not happy here, and I don't know if I'd be happy anywhere. I hardly ever talk to anyone. I feel like a hypocrite when I do, for I have no real interest in anyone else. And I look so bad I'm sure someone will ask me what's wrong, and I won't be able to say."

"Your best tonic is fresh air, and the removal of the cause of your trouble—worry," Father Anselm replied. "As long as you continue to brood over your case you will scarcely find relief. If you can take your mind away from your trouble, forget all about the past, and, perhaps, take to some hobby, you would soon feel better. . . .

"You say you are almost forced to play the hypocrite with the others there. If anyone asks you what's wrong, tell him the truth—that you don't feel well—and let it go at that.

"In the meantime, don't forget that there is a divine, benign Providence that desires not our ruin, but our salvation. Get your mind propped up by good resolves; look to the future and steer more or less clear of the past.

"May God bless you and give you a peaceful and tranquil heart."

I answered that letter with a rambling note, again emphasizing my doubt in the wisdom of going on to the priesthood, and a few days later he wrote:

"In regards to your doubt as to your vocation, let us grant, just for a moment, that you received major orders without a genuine call. St. Augustine says somewhere: 'If you think that you are not called, make yourself worthy to be called.' St. Alphonsus asks the question: 'Is one who has missed his vocation to be considered lost? No, for if he uses all the means at his disposal, God will supply the genuine vocation, though he may have greater difficulty than others.'

"Thus you can see, even supposing the extreme case, yours is not one that should make you despair. If you do what lies in you, you will have the grace to overcome your difficulty and to perform the duties incumbent upon your state, and especially to fulfill God's Will for you. . . .

"Whatever you do, do not wear yourself out and make your-self unfit for your seminary work in September. I on my part am remembering you in my prayers and Masses daily."

His letters were helpful. In early August, he repeated two

important points that he had brought up at the seminary—the possibility that God may have some special work for me, and the need for me to seek medical attention.

"When your trouble began last retreat," he wrote, "I certainly did not in any way dream that it could possibly turn out to be so stubborn. In the plan of Divine Providence, there must be a reason for it. A wholesome stirring up? An occasion for penance? A basis for something higher? *Perhaps God even has some special work cut out for you and is using this as a basis to prepare you for some future years.*

"Do not worry now in regard to a possible repetition of this year's retreat trouble next May when you will be ordained priest. Before that, you will have reached a definite decision one way or the other.

"The unfavorable interpretations which you are prompted to put on all prayers and texts [which I had mentioned in a previous letter] are a result of your state of mind. If you could read *Comfort of the Faint-Hearted*, by Louis Blosius, O.S.B., you might find some relief. Again I say it must come partly from physical aid. *Do not reopen your case again with any other priest.*"

It was badly needed advice. I had reopened my case with too many people already—and each time I repeated my story I did myself more harm than good.

"How can I make a decision, Father?" I wrote later. "I keep thinking of the past, in spite of myself, and trying to reconcile it with an uncertain future. It hardly seems worth while to return to the seminary at all. I'll be better off either remaining a deacon and returning to the lay world or going into a strict order, where I can retire from the world altogether.

"Help me, Father. Tell me what I ought to do."

His answer, dated August 7, read, in part:

"As to your past, I still feel you over-emphasize it. The past is gone, but the future is yours.

"In regard to your decision, I do not feel that I should make it for you. The first plan—remaining as a deacon in the world—is no doubt impractical; the second—religious life in a strict order—would imply great sacrifice and should come altogether from your own volition; the third—return to the seminary—is what everybody would advise you, but in your present state of mind you would not be contented. Hence, you must pray, and again I say pray for light and guidance."

I went home from St. Mary-of-the-Woods in the latter part of August, with my mind still in a turmoil and my heart heavier than ever with indecision. And, once again, I was facing a crisis. In two weeks, I was due to report back to St. Meinrad.

Then Father Anselm invited me to spend a few days with him in Cannelton.

I couldn't get there fast enough.

I arrived on a Saturday morning, and I felt better the moment I saw him. As he took both my hands in his and looked at me with those wonderfully expressive eyes, I felt at ease for the first time in months.

He will do it. He will get me out of this terrible mess.

I followed him around like a puppy as he went about his routine duties. We talked only of inconsequentials, but I was perfectly content simply to be in his presence.

After our evening meal, we sat in his study at the parish house.

"You're a deacon now, Ralph," he said. "How about preaching tomorrow?"

"Me? Preach?"

"Yes. You give the sermon."

"But, Father—"

"I think you can give a very good sermon," Father Anselm said.

"All right. I'll try."

My mind was in a turmoil again. *How can I preach in my condition?*

I was on my knees a long time that night. Then, after I got into bed, my mind whirled with ideas.

What shall I preach on?

It was within the Octave of the Assumption, and, after long hours of restless soul-searching, I decided to preach on the Virgin Mary. I got up and jotted down an outline, then went back to bed and fell into a troubled sleep.

The next day, I preached the first sermon of my life. When

it was over, Father Anselm said, "That was excellent. You have a very fine delivery, Ralph."

I was very pleased, and told him so. But after lunch, I was depressed again.

"Father, tell me what to do," I pleaded.

"You should know what to do," he said. "You can preach, and you will make a fine priest. Isn't it obvious what you should do?"

"But I can't go on like this," I said.

"You'll be all right when you get back to St. Meinrad."

"I'll be there less than a year," I said. "How far can I get in a year?"

"You can get very far in a year if you want to," he said. "All you have to do is make up your mind."

"But, Father, that's my whole problem," I said. "*I can't make up my mind.*"

"But you don't have to make up your mind this minute or this week or this month," Father Anselm said. "You still have plenty of time. You won't be ordained priest until next May.

"Set a date sometime in the middle of the year. Make up your mind now that *on that date* you will come to a final decision. You'll be surprised how easy it will be when the date comes. And, in the meantime, with the urgency eliminated, your mind will be much more at ease."

I thought about that for a while. *Set a date to make a decision. Why not?*

We talked the rest of the day, and I finally decided to make my decision on December 8. This is the Feast of the Immaculate Conception.

And, when I left Father Anselm to return to Indianapolis, I felt better again.

But I still couldn't sleep, and my appetite was poor. I had another physical checkup, this time by a different doctor. He found nothing organically wrong, but he took me off the Nembutal, and gave me bromides, which he said would have the same effect and would be much safer. Then, with at least a secondary decision made, I returned to St. Meinrad for my last year.

Back in the seminary, I put myself on a strict schedule. I set a time limit for everything—study, recreation, prayer, meditation—and I followed it faithfully.

It helped—for a while. So did the bromides—for a while. But a week or ten days after I arrived at St. Meinrad, the same trouble began to crop up.

Successive entries in my diary—and this was the only time I ever kept a diary—between September 30 and October 16 shows how badly my nerves were frayed.

On September 30, I wrote: "It seems that on reflection I am slipping almost imperceptibly back to my old ways. Although I cannot notice it clearly, yet there is some change, ever so slight. Today, I seem far from what I ought to be."

And on October 1: "Today I am very discouraged. It seems to be a haze, of something I can't explain. There seems to be something slipping, ever so little, but yet ever so sure. Everything seems so useless, so impossible, so hopeless. This is the beginning of the month of the Holy Rosary. It is a special month of Mary. Oh, God, because of Mary, Thy Mother, give me a big bargain, I who am always looking for bargains, especially this month."

The bargain I wanted was peace of mind. It didn't come. On October 4, a diary entry reads: "Terribly discouraged at the difficulties to be overcome. How long, O, Lord, how long?"

My strict schedule was slipping. I couldn't keep to it. Father Anselm had always told me that, no matter what happened to me, I should never miss my breviary, never miss my meditation. I couldn't concentrate on either.

On October 8, my diary read: "I have neglected so much my faith, the sacraments, my home, parent, friends, brothers. Yet in the depth of my failure, my spiritual poverty, I dare call on the depth of God's mercy."

On October 13: "I am still very discouraged. The continual struggle makes everything seem so hopeless. I would have given up long ago, but God alone is carrying on the fight now."

I hit the depths of depression on October 16: "What am I to do? I need not tell You, O, God, my condition. I was ordained to the diaconate. It is too late to retrace my steps—hence that surely is not Your Will. Either You want me to remain as I am or to be ordained a priest.

regrets "*I feel that had I to do it over again last May, I should not have gone on.*

"It is true that Your Ways, Your Judgments are not ours, but doesn't it seem that I should not continue? Or is it the cowardice which I have always had which repels me from Your Work?

"At present, I am praying to Your Holy Mother, Mary. Each day, I shall make this novena, for fifty-four days. I know that She will obtain for me that grace from You which is most conducive to my sanctification and salvation. In answer to these prayers, I am begging that You will grant, through Her intercession, for me the grace to decide on December 8th, the glorious Feast of Her Immaculate Conception, which road I shall decide to take.

"Grant me the grace so that I shall not err. I will decide on that day, and I ask Your Grace to guide me. I shall spend the intervening days preparing myself by prayer and mortification. By trying to fulfill all of my duties faithfully, I shall fast on the vigil of Her feast in Her honor.

"I ask you, Dear God, because of Your great mercy, to help me."

The fifty-four-day novena to the Blessed Virgin was suggested by Father Anselm during a talk I had with him on October 16.

"Instead of waiting until November 30 [nine days before the Feast of the Immaculate Conception], start now," he said. "Pray for the right decision on December 8."

The novena gave me real encouragement. On October 25, I wrote in my diary:

"It seems that I am resting better, but I am still somewhat discouraged."

And the next day: "The melancholy and the discouragement are confined to the morning hours. The afternoons and evenings are fairly peaceful. Thanks be to God."

The bromides the doctor gave me may have been helping, too, for I slept a little better during the late autumn weeks. There were still frequent nights when I tossed and turned so much that

I had to get up and pace my room or try to read, but at least those terrible all-night sieges were gone.

Day after day, I continued to make my novena, and on November 9, barely a month before my day of decision, there is a notation in my diary that reads: "Still some melancholy. Still a little discouraged. But it seems to be growing better."

I saw Father Anselm several times a week during that period. As he continued to encourage me, I felt increasing peace of mind. And, when December 8 came around, my decision came with astonishing ease.

I went to Father Anselm that day, and said, "I am going on."

Then I wrote in my diary: "The day has arrived. What have I gained? Have I drawn closer to God? Yes, I feel that God in His Mercy has answered my prayer as I traveled along my road of sorrow. Eternal Father, I thank You for all that I have, all that I am, all that I ever hope to be.

"I, Ralph S. Pfau, today solemnly promise, on the advice of my confessor, to proceed to the priesthood, to do my best to obtain as much sanctity as in me lies. I place myself under the special protection of the Blessed Virgin Mary."

That night, for the first time in months, I went to bed without taking anything to make me sleep.

And the next morning, I wrote: "I slept soundly last night. Thanks be to God."

My troubles seemed to be over. Now that I had made the decision, I took Father Anselm's advice and forgot about it. Instead of worrying about the future or fretting over the past, I concentrated on the present. I plunged into my work at the seminary with new zeal and devotion, determined now to let nothing interfere. And, for the time being, nothing did. My appetite returned and my sleeplessness disappeared.

When I went home for Christmas, I found my mother in failing health, but delighted to find me happy and relaxed. My assurance that I'd be all right seemed to perk her up, although only temporarily. She was a sick woman, and she showed it. I wondered if this were to be her last Christmas.

Just prior to returning to St. Meinrad, I went to the Trappist monastery at Gethsemani, Kentucky, for a two-day retreat with the Vicar-General of the Nashville diocese, where my uncle was Bishop. There, a great feeling of peace and well-being descended over me. I spent almost all my time in prayer and meditation.

On January 2, 1929, my second night at Gethsemani, I wrote, just before retiring:

"My room is the room of Saint Placid. This day was spent in thanksgiving for the many graces received these past months, and in petition for the continued protection of God throughout the rest of the days of my life. This has been one of the happiest days of my life."

I went back to St. Meinrad, prepared for the final stages of my seminary career. My mother's condition took a turn for the worse two months later, and we were all called back to Indianapolis, but she pulled through, although she was dreadfully sick.

From then until May 20, the night before my ordination to the priesthood, my life proceeded without incident. Then I suddenly came down with a 104° temperature.

They called a doctor from Ferdinand, and he gave me a combination of medicines designed to drive the fever down quickly. I perspired so much that the sheets of my bed had to be changed several times. Bishop Chartrand was in and out of my room until late that night, assuring me I'd be able to take part in the ordination rites.

In the depths of my fever, I was hardly aware of all this activity. But later in the night, when my temperature had subsided somewhat, I was assailed by a terrible fear of impending disaster.

I'm not going to make it. After all I've been through, I'm not going to make it. Why couldn't this have happened last week, or last month, or last year? Why does it have to happen now, when ordination is only hours away?

"I am prepared and I am not disturbed."

But I am sick.

Why?

I was well on my way to working myself up into a serious state when the Bishop allayed my fears. Early in the morning, he came into my room with a Brother Infirmarian and said, "Get a chair for this man. He has to be ordained, and we'll see that he is. Get a chair. He won't have to kneel or stand during the Mass, but he must be present and take part."

So, with a high fever, I was ordained priest sitting in a chair, while my classmates said Mass with the Bishop.

My mother was too ill to come to St. Meinrad. So, as soon as the ceremonies were completed, I sent her this telegram:

"My first blessing. May the blessing of the Almighty God, the Father, the Son and the Holy Ghost, descend upon you always. Ralph."

CHAPTER 4

LATER THAT DAY, Father Anselm came in to see me.

"How do you feel, Father?" he asked, smiling. "May I have your blessing?"

I smiled back, and gave him my blessing as he humbly knelt to receive it.

"It's wonderful," I said. "I'm sick, but I feel wonderful."

We talked for some time. Then I said, "Father, you know I don't drink, but I've often thought about the history of alcoholism in my family. Do you think it might be hereditary?"

"I don't know. You have a nervous temperament. Perhaps, it would be better for you not to drink. It's a decision you should make for yourself."

I pondered a moment.

"Suppose, Father," I said, "I decide not to drink for a year. What do you think of that idea?"

"An excellent compromise," Father Anselm said. "You can decide when the year is over. You can give it some more thought."

So I made up my mind not to drink for one year from the date of my ordination.

I was sick for several days. I said my first Mass at St. Philip's the Sunday after I returned to Indianapolis. My mother attended it in a wheel-chair. She had cancer, and the doctors told us she could not live much longer. That was the last time she left the house.

After spending the summer helping out in various parishes

around the city, I got my first appointment on September 13. I was sent to the Old Cathedral in Vincennes as an assistant pastor, and teacher in Gibault High School, which was connected with it.

I plunged into my work with a zeal that was almost patho-logical. I set up the same sort of rigid schedule I had planned at St. Meinrad, only this time I stuck to it. My Office, my medita-tion, my bookwork, my classwork, my schoolwork, my church work—everything I did—came at a specific time each day.

I never deviated. And I worked practically around the clock. I guess I averaged about six hours' sleep a night, not because I couldn't do better, but because I wouldn't. I was in bed at eleven and up at five, and I begrudged even those six hours as time wasted.

There is no question that I was asking for trouble, but trouble didn't come. I was not aware of nervousness or pressure. I enjoyed everything, particularly the teaching. My schedule con-sisted of four hours of Latin and one of religion every day. I also had missions on Sunday, and I guess I did more than my share of routine work around the parish.

On October 9, less than four weeks after I arrived in Vin-cennes, I was called home. My mother was dying. Before the day was over, all five of my brothers were in town, going in and out of the old home on North Rural Street—Vic, my oldest brother, and his wife, Teresa; Ed and his wife, Alice; Ray, who lived in Milwaukee; and Harold, who was still home.

Jerry came over from St. Mary-of-the-Woods the same day I returned from Vincennes.

First, we paid our respects to Bishop Chartrand.

"Go to St. Philip's," he said, "and ask Father Noll to give you all the necessary things for the Mass. Then go home and say Mass in your mother's house."

We got all the articles necessary for saying Mass at the church and took them home with us. There, we set up an altar on a table in the front living room, situated so that my mother could see it from her bed in the next room.

We anointed her and gave her Holy Viaticum.

From then until the day she died, my mother proudly watched

as her two priest sons said Mass every morning, first Jerry, then I. And each time her eyes lit up and I was glad, for her pride in us both, I'm sure, helped to sustain her through those last few painracked days.

At midnight on October 13, her respiration suddenly slowed perceptibly and her breathing became heavier. The doctor came out of her room, and said, "I'm afraid it's almost over. I doubt if she'll live through the night."

We gathered around her bed—Vic and Teresa, Ed and Alice, Ray, Harold, Jerry and I—and looked at Mom. Her eyes were closed, but she was still breathing. Once, with an effort, she opened them, and I'm sure she recognized us all, although she didn't say anything.

There was no sound in the room except her breathing, which was increasingly labored. We stayed there for a long time—it must have been two hours—but there seemed no change.

Then Jerry beckoned to me to follow him into the front room.

"We can begin Mass an hour before dawn," he said in a low voice.

Dawn lasts for varying times from day to day. We got out the almanac to check the morning of October 14, 1929. It showed that dawn would begin at four-fifteen. The liturgy of the Church at that time permitted Mass to be said any time between one hour before dawn and twelve o'clock noon. That meant we could begin Mass at three-fifteen A.M. It was then two o'clock.

Jerry and I went back into Mom's room, and joined the rest of the family in saying the Rosary. After a while, we went back into the living room.

We looked at our watches. It was five minutes to three.
Twenty minutes to go.

"You say the Mass, Ralph," Jerry whispered. "I'll answer the prayers. Mom would want it that way."

I began vesting for the Mass. I put on the amice, touching it to my head before slipping it over my shoulders, then the alb. My hands trembled as I tied the bottom around my waist. Then I belted myself with the cincture, arranged the maniple around my left arm and put on the stole.

I vested rapidly, for I didn't want to waste a second. I wanted to be ready promptly, so I could say Mass in time to give Mom Holy Communion once again.

On the dot of three-fifteen, I began. Overwhelmed with emotion, I took a deep breath.

"*In Nomine Patris, et Filii, et Spiritus Sancti . . .*" ("In the name of the Father, and of the Son, and of the Holy Ghost . . .")

My voice was low, but it seemed clear and steady.

Jerry answered the prayers. I thought I detected a bit of emotion in his voice. It made me wonder if I showed any in mine.

At the Consecration of the Mass, I consecrated a particle for my mother, and also several other particles for members of the family wishing to receive Holy Communion.

At communion time, I gave Holy Communion to my mother. I looked down at the bed. Her eyes were open. She gazed at the Host as she received Christ into her heart.

She spoke six words, her last. "I-want-to-go-to-Mass," she said. *She knows.*

Then her eyes closed. I left the bed, and returned to the altar in the front room.

Now, I was approaching the post-Communion.

"Grant, we pray Thee, O Lord," I began, "that Thy faithful people . . ."

I heard a stir in the other room.

". . . may ever rejoice in the veneration of all Thy Saints . . ."

Now there were sobs.

". . . and may they ever be guarded by their perpetual intercession."

It was all over, but I did not stop.

I turned to face the bedroom, murmuring, "*Dominus vobiscum.*"

"The Lord be with you." *Mom died*

The nurse was pulling a sheet over my mother's face.

I completed the Mass, and took off the vestments.

"Now, I will say Mass," Jerry whispered to me, his eyes brimming, "and it will be the first Requiem Mass for Mom."

Everyone had left the bed, and the family was now gathered in the front room. Jerry, vested, began Mass, and I answered the prayers. Except for our tremulous voices, there was no sound in the room but for an occasional sob, or a deep-throated intake of breath.

"Eternal rest grant unto her, O Lord, and let the perpetual light shine upon her."

A week later, I was back in Vincennes, buried deeper than ever in my work schedule.

Outside of Mom's death, it turned out to be a happy year for me. I had no problems, no worries, no fears and, despite my frantic routine, I maintained my health. I loved the work I was doing, and rarely stirred out of Vincennes.

At Christmas vacation, Jerry and I visited at Vic's when we went home to Indianapolis. He was the oldest brother, and his house became the family headquarters after Mom died.

The first anniversary of my ordination into the priesthood, May 21, came and went without incident. My one-year abstinence from liquor was over on that date, but I saw no reason to renew it. I had not been bothered by any temptation to drink, and I now felt that liquor would never be a problem to me. I could, I was sure, take it or leave it alone.

In late May, I asked permission to take graduate work at Fordham University. Gibault High School had applied for recognition by the State of Indiana, but needed licensed teachers. I couldn't apply for a license because, even though I had obtained all the necessary credits at St. Meinrad, they were not accepted for credit by the State of Indiana.

I selected Fordham, a Jesuit university in New York City, because that was where most of our priests went for summer courses. Besides, the city was so big that there would be plenty of work for a priest to do. Someone was always needed to fill in during the vacation period.

The Bishop approved my request, so, when school at Vincennes ended, I went to New York.

It was the first time in my life I had ever been on a train overnight; in fact, except for Gethsemani, which was in Kentucky, and Milwaukee, where I had once visited my brother Ray, it was the first time I had ever been out of Indiana. I was excited over the prospect of seeing New York for the first time, and really looked forward to this new phase of my career.

I arrived at Grand Central Station at about seven o'clock in the evening, and went right to the rectory where I was to live. It was in Washington Heights. There, I was met by one of the priests, who showed me to my room. After changing into fresh clothes, I got on a rubberneck bus, and spent the next three hours touring the city.

I met the rest of the crowd in the rectory the next day. The pastor was beyond middle age, but the others—four or five priests, all going to Fordham summer school—were young. I had little chance to mingle with anyone that first day, since I was busy putting my things away, checking in at the university and generally getting settled.

During the next week, I was so busy getting organized at Fordham and acquainted with the other priests at the rectory that I had no time for any outside activities. But one afternoon, three of us went to the ball game at Yankee Stadium. As we were walking out, a well-dressed man of middle age, who looked vaguely familiar, stopped me.

Holding out his hand, he said, "Pardon me, Father, but aren't you from Indianapolis?"

"I am, indeed," I said, smiling.

"You don't remember me," he said. "My name is David Batterly. I'm from Indianapolis, too."

I looked at him quizzically.

"It's always a pleasure to meet someone from home," I said.

"I don't blame you for wondering who I am," he said. "We've never been formally introduced. But didn't you used to post baseball scores—?"

"—in a saloon," I finished. "I certainly did. My mother made me give up the job."

"Because of all those drinking bums, I'll bet. Well, Father, I was one of those bums."

"You certainly don't look like a bum to me," I said.

"I'm not. I wasn't then. I just used to stop by for a drink occasionally, on my way home from the office. What are you doing in New York?"

"I'm taking courses at Fordham," I told him.

"Why don't you join me for dinner?" he said.

"I can't. I'm sorry, but I have to get right back to the rectory."

We talked for a few minutes, then exchanged phone numbers. David was a lawyer and, judging by his appearance, a pretty prosperous one.

"Come for dinner soon," he said.

I thanked him, and went on my way. I didn't expect to hear from him again. The dinner invitation sounded too casual.

But he called me a couple of days later.

"Can you come over for dinner tonight, Father?" he asked.

"I'd be delighted."

David lived in a spacious apartment on Riverside Drive, not too far from Washington Heights. A maid met me at the door. As soon as she opened it, I had an impulse to express my regrets because I was obviously not the only guest. There seemed to be a number of people in the living room, and I was shy about meeting them.

But before I could move, David himself appeared at the end of the hall.

"Welcome, Father," he said. "I'm glad you could make it."

"This sounds like a party," I said. "I don't think I'd better come in. I might cramp someone's style."

He laughed.

"It always sounds like a party around here," he said. "Come on in. You won't cramp anyone's style."

He led me into the living room, where there were half a dozen couples. After he had completed the introductions, he said, "How about a drink, Father?"

I shook my head.

"No, thanks," I said. "I don't drink."

"A little wine, perhaps?"

"No, nothing, thanks," I said.

I looked around. All of the men and some of the women were drinking, but no one was drunk, or even really noisy. It was just a gathering of friends and, as I settled back on one end of a divan, I was glad that David had invited me to join them.

"Have you been here long, Father?" asked the man beside me.

"Only a week or so," I said.

"How do you like New York?"

"Fine—what I've seen of it."

He took a sip from his glass.

"You don't drink, Father?"

"No."

Pressure

He held the glass up and looked meditatively at it as he slowly twisted it around in his hand.

"Drinking is fine if you know when to stop," he said. "Now—take me—I never have more than two at one sitting."

"It sounds like a safe idea."

"It works all right for me."

"Where do you get the liquor?" I asked, naïvely. Prohibition was still in effect.

"Oh, that's no problem," he replied. "There's more liquor around New York now than there ever was."

David came over and stood beside me.

"Sure you wouldn't care for a drink, Father?" he asked.

"No, thanks."

"Ever tried?"

"No."

"You know," said the man on the divan beside me, "you're very wise."

I smiled.

"It isn't a question of wisdom," I said. "It's just that I've never had any desire to drink."

Later, we went in for dinner. Mrs. Batterly, a fine-looking woman in her mid-forties, obviously liked to have everything just right. There was more than a touch of formality about the meal. The table was carefully set, with shining silverware and china, and snow-white napkins at each setting.

"Would you care to say Grace, Father?" she asked, after everyone was seated.

It was only later that I noticed a wine glass in front of each person, including me.

The food was excellent, and beautifully served by the maid who had opened the door to let me in. Shortly after we sat down, David opened a bottle of wine, and began passing it around.

My neighbor, a rather pretty brunette woman, eventually handed it to me.

"Wine, Father?" she asked.

"No, thanks. I don't drink."

"Not even wine?"

I felt a little foolish.

"Not even wine," I said.

I passed the bottle along.

This is getting ridiculous. Every time I turn around, I have to make excuses for not drinking.

After dinner, the women went into the sun parlor to play cards, while the men gathered in the living room. Someone remarked that it looked as if the Yankees were on their way to a pennant, and I joined in the general baseball discussion that followed.

Then David said, "Well, boys, who's ready for another drink?"

He started around the room taking orders.

I began to feel foolish again. I was the youngest man in the room, and the only one who didn't drink.

These fellows must think I'm holier-than-thou in my attitude about drinking, just because I'm a priest.

What am I worried about? I can drink if I want to. I'm not an alcoholic. If I were I'd have started drinking long ago.

Of course, I can get along without alcohol. I don't need it. But do I have to make a fetish of not drinking? Do I have to act as if I'm a little better than anyone else? These are obviously decent people. They don't drink to excess. They simply enjoy a sociable highball. And why shouldn't they? There's nothing wrong with it. If there were, I'm sure they wouldn't do it.

Perhaps this is a challenge for me. Is there any reason why I should avoid it?

What harm can a drink or two do me? I'm not an alcoholic. I've already proved it.

Now David was looking at me.

"Father—"

He stopped, then smiled.

"Sorry," he said. "I forgot—you don't drink."

A few minutes later, I went over to talk to him.

"You know," I said slowly, "if I were to take a drink, I wouldn't have the slightest idea where to start."

"That would hardly be a problem," he said. "You just try something and if you don't like it, try something else. Sooner or later, if you really want to drink, you'll hit on something."

If you really want to drink.

"What do you drink, David?"

"Bourbon."

"Why?"

He shrugged.

"I don't know," he said. "I just like it better than anything else."

"What else have you tried?"

"About everything. Scotch—rye—rum—gin. But I don't care for any of them. Bourbon suits me."

"I wonder which would suit me," I said, half to myself.

He looked sharply at me.

"Don't tell me you're weakening, Father," he said.

"Not weakening—just curious. It does seem sort of silly—my not drinking. I've been thinking that maybe I ought to try."

"You might not like it," David said.

"Well, if I don't like it, I can quit."

That's right. If I don't like it, I can quit. But how am I going to know whether I like it or not if I don't try? And why shouldn't I try?

I walked over to the table where the liquor was. David followed me.

"Mind if I try a little of that bourbon?" I asked.

"Go ahead, Father," he said.

With elaborate casualness, I poured two fingers into a glass, added ice and ginger ale and stirred it with a spoon.

Then I raised it to my lips and took a generous sip.

"How do you like it?" David asked.

For a moment, I didn't answer. I felt a gradual, and pleasant, sensation of warmth in my stomach.

I looked around the room, then smiled self-consciously.

"Not bad," I said. "Not bad at all."

first sip is the hardest

PART II

CHAPTER 5

THE FIRST HIGHBALL of my life was shortly followed by a second, but I thought nothing of either at the time. It was a warm summer's night, and anything with ice in it tasted good. I believe would have been just as happy without the bourbon. And straight ginger ale would have had no different effect on me.

I felt neither gay nor giddy. After the second drink, I had no desire for more. By eleven o'clock, I was ready to go to bed. said my farewells, went home to the rectory and immediately retired. I slept soundly, and was up and ready for my day's work at my usual hour.

David called me a night or so later and invited me over again. There were several other people there when I arrived, and he introduced me around. I had a couple of drinks, and when I got up to leave, he saw me to the door.

"We have open house here practically every night, Father," he said. "Drop around whenever you feel like a drink. And if you don't feel like it, drop around anyhow."

I thanked him and went on my way. Two nights later, I walked in on him. He was delighted to see me, and so were his friends.

These were good, congenial people. I liked them, and they apparently liked me. When David once again pressed his standing invitation on me, I decided to take advantage of it more often.

From then until I left Fordham to return to Vincennes in late August, I dropped in at David's almost every night, and each time I was there, I had two drinks. If they did me any harm, I wasn't aware of it. All I know is that I enjoyed myself.

In the meantime, I did a great deal of work, even though not much was called for in my formal studies. I was attending the school of education and taking only teaching courses—things like the philosophy of education and teaching techniques—subjects designed for credit toward a Master of Education degree.

But I worked hard on my teaching schedule for the coming year. I brushed up particularly on Latin. I needed work in the high school curriculum. While I had had five years of Latin including the seminary course, and many of our books were printed in Latin, I was not as sharp as I wanted to be in Caesar, Cicero and Virgil, the three basic authors in high school Latin.

I purchased half a dozen books on the teaching of high school Latin, and studied them until I knew them almost by heart. I looked forward with pleasure to returning to Gibault, and had made up my mind that I wanted to be a teacher on a permanent basis. In order to get the credits I needed, it would be necessary to come back to Fordham, but that did not pose a problem. The Bishop was aware of my desire to teach and was perfectly willing to help me.

One Sunday in July, I was removing my vestments after Mass when I suddenly realized that I had neglected my fifteen minutes of prayer beforehand. This was a routine I had always followed. Ever since my ordination, I had never missed prayer before Mass.

But the realization that I had missed this time did not bother me particularly. It was not compulsory, but simply something that I had got into the habit of doing, on the original suggestion of Father Anselm. I simply had neglected the prayer, and that was that. It was not a sin, so I had nothing to worry about. I thought no more about it. But from then on, I was haphazard with it; sometimes I was careful in my preparation for Mass and sometimes I wasn't.

The whole summer passed without my noticing that I was either cutting down or eliminating my daily periods of meditation. This was one of the things Father Anselm had always impressed upon me.

"Never miss your Office," he used to say, "and never miss your meditation."

The Office, a series of psalms and prayers contained in a book called the breviary, is compulsory for every priest, and it is a serious sin to miss it. But it is only neglectful to miss meditation. Father Anselm had pointed out, however, that I would be a better priest if I gave daily time to meditation; that it was not only necessary for priestly virtue, but an excellent way of maintaining peace of mind.

I even got a little careless about saying my Office. I never missed it, but more and more often I found myself hurrying over the words without thinking of their meaning. In the past, I had always faithfully concentrated whenever I said my Office.

When summer school was over, I prepared to return to Indiana. I went to one last ball game at Yankee Stadium, and took one last look at the city, for which I had developed a real affection. I was sorry to leave, and I looked forward to returning.

I said good-bye to my friends the day before departing, since the train for Indianapolis was scheduled to leave Grand Central early the next morning. I planned to get all packed that night, so I wouldn't have to waste any time getting started after Mass in the morning.

I went to my room, and spent an hour or so packing my things. But after I had finished and gone to bed, I couldn't sleep. A vague discomfort kept me tossing and turning.

Something's missing. What is it? I can't leave without it. Strange—I have everything I came with, and all the books and things I bought while I was here.

But something's missing.

I was puzzled.

Then, suddenly, it came to me.

Liquor.

Of course! You can get all the liquor you want in New York. But who knows where you can get it in Indiana?

Bootleggers were always leaving their cards at David's door, and he had a favorite whom he patronized. I went downstairs and phoned him, since I knew he never went to bed before one or two in the morning. He gave me a number, and told me I could call it on the spot. I identified myself as a friend of David's, and gave the man the street address, without telling him it was the rectory.

"Can you send up a case of liquor right away?" I asked.

"What kind?"

"Uh—" I hesitated. *I ought to get something good; something I surely can't get in Vincennes—I've got it:* "Scotch," I said. "I'm going to Indiana, and I'm sure I can't get any there."

"What kind?" the man asked again.

"Name a couple," I said.

I didn't know one from the other.

"I can give you a dozen quarts of Johnnie Walker for sixty dollars. It's the real thing—right off the boat."

Since I had saved practically all of my small salary, because my living expenses were taken care of, I had the money.

"O.K.," I said, "send it up."

"Right away."

It wasn't easy to jam a dozen quart bottles into a valise, but I managed to do it. I unpacked everything, and started all over again. I put the bottles in places where they wouldn't break, fitting them in around clothes. I did have to make a major shift. Both the bottles and the books wouldn't fit, so I made a separate package of the books. It was bulky and hard to carry, but I figured it was worth it.

Now, the vague discomfort was gone. When I went to bed this time, I went right to sleep and didn't wake up until morning.

I stayed at Vic's in Indianapolis a few days, then reported back to Vincennes. There, just as I had the previous year, I helped as an assistant pastor at the Old Cathedral, and taught at Gibault High School.

I set up the same strict schedule for myself, and worked even harder than I had the year before. I taught five hours a day, helped with instruction and handled other parish duties. I missed neither meditation nor preparation for Mass, and when I read my Office, I did so with the old concentration and enthusiasm.

The dozen bottles of scotch were stowed in a desk drawer in the small office which I used as a study. During the entire autumn, I didn't even pick one up. But every so often, I checked to make sure it was all still there.

During Christmas vacation, I went home to Indianapolis, taking two bottles with me. I gave one to Vic and the other to Jerry. Neither they nor I gave these gifts a second thought.

I had been drinking regularly for six weeks in New York, but never more than two drinks in an evening. And when I returned to Vincennes, I had stopped drinking.

Obviously, I wasn't an alcoholic. I was sure of that now. So were my brothers. I could take my liquor or leave it alone.

There were some family parties during Christmas vacation, and liquor was always available. I had a highball here and there —never more than two—but that was all. And, after vacation was over and I returned to Vincennes, I plunged right back into my work and forgot all about liquor.

I didn't drink again until I went home for Easter. I again brought along a couple of quarts to give away, and did a little sociable drinking, but very little.

Back in Vincennes, I found myself wrapped up in my work. There was a great deal of parish work to do that spring, and before I knew it, it was time to return to school. But we were so busy in Vincennes, I didn't feel I should go. Instead of returning to Fordham, I spent the summer of 1931 helping out at the Old Cathedral.

I could return to Fordham whenever I wanted; the Bishop assured me of that when I asked him about it.

I still wasn't satisfied with my Latin. I bought as many books as I could find, and worked hard on them. Jerry could speak the language fluently—the result of his stay in Rome. I wanted to do the same.

During that third year at Vincennes, I didn't touch a drop of liquor except when I was home for vacations. Alcohol was no problem. I was exactly like everyone else. I had a drink when I felt like it, but rarely felt like it.

I still hadn't opened any of the scotch I'd brought from New York for my own use. I had several bottles left in the drawer of my office, but no occasion to touch it. There was nobody to drink with, and I couldn't drink alone.

Only alcoholics drink alone.

Jerry had told me that once, and I had read it somewhere later. So, it wasn't simply that I didn't *feel* like drinking alone.

I was afraid to.

Now it was the summer of 1932. I had spent three years at Vincennes, and was well launched on a teaching career. But I still needed credits for my Indiana license. This time, with things quieter in the parish, I decided to go back to Fordham.

Another priest drove with me to New York. He was working for his doctorate while I was still seeking my Master's degree.

We returned to the rectory where I had lived two summers before. All of the priests I had known were still there. For the first couple of weeks, I spent my spare time with them. We'd go to ball games in the daytime when we weren't busy, and sit around talking at the rectory until bedtime.

I had no particular desire for a drink; I didn't even think about it.

Then, one afternoon, David phoned.

"Hello, Father," he said, "I just heard you were back in town. How are you?"

"Fine," I said.

"I'm having a little party tonight," he said. "The whole gang will be here. How about dropping around?"

"Thanks, David. I'll try to make it."

I did make it—that night and the night after and the night after that. It was easy to fall back into the old routine.

At first, it seemed the same as it always had. But, after a week or so, there was a change—a change which I didn't notice at the time, but realized only when I looked back on it years later.

Two drinks weren't enough. toleration

I don't remember exactly when I poured myself a third, and sometimes a fourth. But periodically—not every night, just every so often—I would reach for a bottle after I had downed two highballs.

One morning, Larry, a member of David's crowd, called and asked me to join him and two other men for lunch. I met them downtown, and we went into a small restaurant in the Forties. Larry told the waiter to get us some setups—Prohibition was still in force—then turned to me and said, "What's your preference, Father? You can have anything you want here."

I looked at my watch. It was twelve-thirty.

"Anything wrong, Father?" someone asked.

"No," I said, grinning a little sheepishly. "I just wanted to make sure it was after twelve. I never drink in the morning."

Then I turned to Larry.

"I'd like a little bourbon and ginger ale," I said.

I drank slowly, taking a swallow here and a swallow there, sometimes toying with my glass, sometimes not touching it, and I felt much as I always had while drinking. There was the first quick, warm glow, then not much of anything. Liquor had never really affected me. It didn't seem to be affecting me now.

The waiter came around, and we gave him our luncheon orders. While we were waiting, we all accepted Larry's invitation to have a second drink. This seemed quite natural, just as natural as taking a second drink in the evening.

But just before our food arrived, I became aware of a strange sensation. I didn't feel sick, but my stomach started churning in a sort of jumping motion. My head was perfectly clear, and my eyes focused properly, but there seemed to be something wrong.

I toyed with my food. I had been hungry when we first sat down, but now I lost my desire to eat. I couldn't figure out what the trouble was. One minute I had an appetite; the next it was gone.

I don't think I realized it at the time, but the only thing wrong was that I wanted another drink and didn't dare ask for it. _denial_

The strange sensation stayed with me all afternoon. I went about my routine duties with a vague feeling that something was missing. I was extremely jumpy. The day went by with me groping for something I didn't get—a drink—and my appetite was still skimpy by dinnertime. I ate very little.

I didn't feel quite right until the evening, when I dropped over to David's for a nightcap.

I had four.

I decided not to drink before lunch again. When I drank at night and went right to bed I felt no effects. But when I drank at noon, the liquor had all the rest of the day to work on me.

I confined my drinking to the evenings, and had no further trouble all summer.

The same priest who went to New York with me accompanied me back to Indianapolis. Before leaving town, I bought a case of bourbon, and stowed it under a blanket in the back seat of the car.

I still lacked credits for my Master's degree, so I looked forward to another return to Fordham, possibly the next year.

Back in Vincennes, I carefully packed the liquor in my little office. No one ever came in there to see me. When parishioners or visitors wanted to talk to me, we used another office.

I was looking forward to teaching. Of my five daily teaching hours, four were in Latin. I could have added another hour easily, for it was no chore to me, and I enjoyed working with the boys in the school.

As one of the assistant pastors at the Old Cathedral, I could have found plenty of other work to do if I had looked for it. But I was now used to the idea of being a teacher, and any of the other duties I might have had around Vincennes seemed secondary to me.

The day after I arrived in Vincennes, I was about to go to the pastor to ask for an extra teaching hour when he came in to see me.

"I meant to tell you yesterday," he said. "Brother —— [the principal of Gibault High School] and I have decided not to have the priests do any more teaching."

"What—what did you say, Father?" I stammered.

"We've got all the teachers we need among the Brothers without burdening the priests," he said.

"But it's no burden for me," I protested.

"It will be better this way."

"But why, Father?" I asked. "I don't understand."

"There's nothing to understand," he said, a trifle impatiently. "We've simply decided to relieve the priests of teaching."

"But I *want* to teach."

I was nearly frantic.

"There are plenty of other things for you to do," the pastor said.

I was crushed.

Not teach? How can I get along without teaching?

Teaching is my life. That's why I went to Fordham—so I could get a teaching license.

Now, I won't need one.

But I've got to teach!

I went to the pastor's study.

"Father," I said. "Forgive me for bothering you on this matter, but I've got to ask you to let me continue teaching."

"I'm sorry," he said. "We've made this decision, and we're going to stick to it."

"Hasn't my teaching been satisfactory?" I asked, plaintively.

"Of course it has."

"Then why can't I continue?"

By this time, the pastor was very much annoyed.

"Father Pfau," he said coldly, "I must ask you to accept our judgment in this situation. This is a big parish, and there are plenty of duties for a man in your position to perform."

I dragged myself back to my own office. I sat heavily at my desk, and stared into space.

My head was aching and my stomach was jumping, and I was angry and upset.

Not teach?

I sat there for some time. Then, slowly, I got to my feet, and went into the pantry for a glass. Back in my office, I opened the drawer where I kept my bourbon, and pulled out one of the bottles.

I set it on my desk, and looked at it for several minutes. I wanted desperately to open it and pour myself a stiff drink.

But I can't drink alone. ~~told himself fate~~

Only alcoholics drink alone, and I'm not an alcoholic.

I put the bottle back in the drawer.

After dinner that night, I phoned Bob, a lawyer friend of mine in town.

"Are you busy tonight?" I asked.

"No."

"Would you like to drop by for a drink? I have some very good stuff that I brought back with me from New York."

"I'd be delighted," he said.

By the time Bob arrived, I had the ice and setups in my office. I mixed a couple of highballs, and passed one to him.

"Here's to you," I said.

We touched glasses, and I took a couple of gulps. The stuff tasted good going down, and I felt a little better. I leaned back in my chair, and the two of us chatted.

We didn't drink too much—three or four highballs—and Bob left at about ten-thirty. When I saw him to the door, he said, "Thanks, Father. I enjoyed that."

"There's plenty more where it came from," I said. "Come around any time. I don't go out much."

"You're always welcome at my house," he said.

I felt good after he had gone.

Now, at least, I have someone to drink with.

I slept very badly. I was worried about not teaching, and angry and resentful both at the pastor and the teaching Brothers, who had taken over my favorite job. My thoughts bounced back and forth in a confused jumble, and I couldn't get them organized.

All I knew clearly was that I couldn't teach any more.

I've got to do something about it. If I can't teach, I'm beaten. What can I do?

After breakfast, I came to a sudden decision.

I'll see the Bishop. He'll help me.

I got into my car which I had purchased when assigned to Vincennes and drove to Indianapolis. I got there at about one in the afternoon, and went right to the Bishop's house.

Just before I arrived there, I got cold feet.

What will he say? He'll probably get mad and send me right back to Vincennes. Maybe I'd better go back without seeing him.

I was standing at the entrance to the Bishop's house when a new thought came up. Father Amicus, my confessor in Indianapolis, was stationed at the Cathedral. He lived at the Bishop's house. I'd ask his advice first.

He was glad to see me, and we talked about inconsequentials for a few minutes. Then I said, "Father, they won't let me teach any more."

"Why not?"

"I don't know. I can't understand what's behind it."

"Well, what did the pastor say?"

I told Father Amicus the whole story. When I had finished, he said, "The pastor must have a good reason for making this decision. You've got to accept it."

"But I *can't* accept it," I said desperately. "That's why I came here. I thought maybe the Bishop—"

Father Amicus stopped me with a wave of his hand.

"On the basis of what you've told me, the Bishop won't do anything," he said. "On the contrary, he won't like it that you came here at all. If I were you, I'd forget all about it."

"What can I do if I don't teach?"

"There are a lot of things for a priest to do in a big parish like Old Cathedral," said Father Amicus. "You can make calls, give instruction, hear confessions, hold yourself in readiness for emergencies—there is just as much work as you want to make for yourself."

"But I won't be happy just doing routine parish work," I said. "I've got to have more than that. And if they won't let me teach, what can I do?"

"Why don't you take up a hobby?" Father Amicus suggested.

"Like what?"

"Well, you can try writing."

I laughed mirthlessly, then said, "I couldn't write three lines if my life depended on it."

Father Amicus put his hand on my shoulder.

"Ralph," he said, "you're a priest. You have to accept things you don't like from time to time. You know that. Now, go back to Vincennes and bury yourself in parish work. You'll be surprised how much you'll enjoy it. The time will go by fast enough—don't worry about that. And, for the moment, forget about teaching."

I thanked him, and walked out. Then, resentful and frustrated, I got into my car and started for Vincennes. I didn't even stop at my brother Vic's.

So it was a wasted trip. There's no sense going to anyone else —Jerry or Father Anselm. As soon as they hear what happened, they'll tell me to do the same thing Father Amicus told me. Nobody wants me to teach. Why?

The more I thought about the situation, the more resentful I got. And the more resentful I got, the more determined I became to teach or do nothing.

I couldn't teach.

So I did nothing.   no life w/o teaching

CHAPTER 6

As the weeks went by, I performed only those parish duties that I couldn't avoid—emergency calls that found me the only priest in the rectory when they came in. I said Mass daily, but I was praying for the impossible—to teach again—instead of accepting the inevitable, that it was the will of God, since my superiors had decided against it.

The pastor got sick, and one of the assistants took charge. When that happened, I loafed more outrageously than before. I had an excuse for everything. I spent my life ducking obligations, pleading illness, or too much work, or previous engagements whenever I was asked to do something. After a while, the other priests stopped asking me. It was easier to do it themselves.

Some of the time, I actually did feel sick. I had periodic headaches, and I was very nervous. Often, I couldn't sit still longer than a few minutes. I had to get up and walk around.

I completely eliminated my meditation and preparation for Mass, and I went through my daily Office like a man in a trance. As I read my breviary, the words were just words; I couldn't concentrate enough for them to have any meaning.

I drank regularly, but never really got drunk. I continued to maintain a certain amount of control; I never drank alone and never drank before noon. I was simply a social drinker, but I was always looking for someone to socialize with. Sometimes, Bob came to the rectory and sometimes I visited at his house. I had other friends in Vincennes, and I often stopped by to see them.

They all drank purely for social purposes. So did I. I never passed out or got sick. I simply enjoyed congeniality, just as my friends did.

About a month after I returned to Vincennes, I ran out of liquor. I pulled a bottle out of the drawer, and discovered it was the last one I had.

That night, I was at Lou's, a friend who had once lived in Indianapolis. We often spent evenings together, and always had a couple of drinks.

"I need some stuff," I said.

"So do I," he said. "I know a guy in Jasper. Let's go see him."

Everyone in that area knew a guy in Jasper. It was the bootleg headquarters of southern Indiana. Dozens of bootleggers in the area south of there were using small restaurants and filling stations as blinds while their real income was derived from the sale of corn liquor.

"Have you a shirt I can wear?" I asked.

"Go as you are, Father," he said. "If this fellow doesn't happen to have anything, we'll have to see someone else. It'll help if you have your collar on."

Lou tossed two empty gallon jugs into the back seat of my car, and we drove the fifty-five miles to Jasper in a little more than an hour. Lou directed me to a tiny restaurant and filling station at a crossroads. I pulled the car up, and a man came out.

"How are you, Joe?" Lou said.

The man peered into the car, then smiled and said, "Oh, hello, Lou."

"Can you take care of Father and me?"

"Got anything with you?"

Lou reached in back and pulled out the two gallon jugs.

"Come back in an hour."

We drove into town, and stopped in a restaurant for coffee. We talked for a while, then Lou, after looking at his watch, said, "O.K., Father. Let's go."

Back at the filling station, the man quietly hoisted the jugs, now full, into the back seat, and Lou paid him. Then we drove back to Vincennes.

"What is this stuff?" I asked.

"Bourbon—corn liquor," he said. "It's green, but it'll be real good after three months. And if we're in a hurry, we can drink it sooner."

"What do you do with it?"

"Just put it in a charred keg by the radiator. It'll age by itself."

"I guess I should have brought a jug of my own," I said. "I've got a radiator in my study. I could leave it there."

"One of these is for you," said Lou. "And Jasper isn't so far away that you can't go there whenever you feel like it. And now you know whom to see when you get there."

We had a mission in Petersburg—a church which had no resident pastor and had to be served by the Old Cathedral. Petersburg was about thirty-three miles south of Vincennes, and Jasper was another twenty-two miles beyond that. Somebody from the Old Cathedral had to go regularly to Petersburg, so I sort of worked myself into the job. I made the mission to Petersburg every other week. And, whenever I ran low on liquor, I just went on down to Jasper to see the man at the filling station.

At the Old Cathedral, I also did most of the filing. This was routine work, which had to be done more or less in seclusion. I was alone most of the time. The job was a test of patience, rather than intelligence. It was easy enough, yet had to be done carefully, since a mistake might someday cost someone else hours of unnecessary work.

Now I began to think in terms of drinking by myself, since I couldn't have a drinking partner with me while I worked, and I liked to have a couple of shots in the afternoon.

Never drink alone. Only alcoholics drink alone.

But isn't there a difference between drinking alone and being a lone drinker?

A lone drinker sits by himself and drinks himself into a stupor.

But if I drink while I'm working, I'm not a lone drinker, am I? I have to concentrate on my job, don't I? And if I'm nervous, how can I concentrate?

excuses

A drink here and there will settle my nerves.

Therefore, there's no reason why I can't drink while I'm filing; in fact, I should drink then.

That doesn't make me a lone drinker, does it?

So I rationalized myself into a new phase. Now, every afternoon, I would mix myself a highball, and take sips of it from time to time as I worked on the files. I didn't drink a great deal—perhaps two or three each afternoon—and, as far as I could see, the liquor had no effect on me.

I never got drunk, never passed out, never blacked out, never got sick, never lost my equilibrium, never fell down on my job.

I still held a deep resentment against the pastor. I never forgot that he had taken my teaching duties away from me. He had had a prolonged illness, and I had seen nothing of him for months. I took my orders from one of the other assistants who had been designated acting pastor. He rarely checked up on me. I could do as I pleased and go where I pleased without interference from him.

My afternoon drinking had no bearing on my evening drinking, which I continued on a regular basis. Actually, I considered the afternoon and evening practically two different days. My afternoon drinking was medicinal, since it settled my nerves while I was working. My evening drinking was for social pleasure.

Between the two, I was averaging almost a quart a day. But I was not a drunk in any sense of the word. I could hold my liquor like a gentleman, and I was very proud of my capacity. Whenever someone else passed out or got sick, it was always Father Pfau who took care of him.

"I wish I could drink like you, Father," Bob said, one day. "You've certainly got a marvelous capacity for liquor."

"Never seems to hurt me, does it?" I said, smugly.

Actually, I never did become a drunk, in the popularly accepted sense.

It wasn't until years later that I learned you don't have to be in order to be an alcoholic.

I drank my way through the winter of 1932 and the spring of 1933 without incident. I did my filing in Vincennes, my mission work in Petersburg and my buying in Jasper. I did my drinking wherever anything drinkable happened to be available.

But I never drank in the morning. There was always that fear that to do so might make me an alcoholic.

With the exception of close friends, I never drank in the presence of parishioners. As far as I knew, very few people knew I was much of a drinker; indeed, I didn't consider myself one.

My brother Jerry and I got together from time to time. He was still at St. Mary-of-the-Woods in Terre Haute, and he would either visit me in Vincennes or I'd run up to see him. We had become very close since my ordination.

Jerry, of course, knew what a terrific blow it had been to me when I was relieved of my teaching job, but he was glad to see that I seemed to adjust myself to my new duties. In late May, when I saw him at Terre Haute, he noticed that I was jittery, and asked what was wrong.

"This is about the time I'd be thinking about going back to Fordham," I said. "But now there's no need to."

"Do you want to go back?"

"Well," I said, "there's not much sense to it, even if the Bishop will let me. If I'm not going to teach, I won't have any use for teaching credits."

"Maybe you'll teach somewhere else some time."

I shrugged.

"If I can't teach, I don't want to go to Fordham," I said.

A few weeks later, he came to Vincennes.

"Have you been doing an unusual amount of drinking, Ralph?" he asked.

I stiffened.

"What makes you ask?" I said cautiously.

"Well, the Bishop's got wind of it."

I took a deep breath.

"The Bishop?"

"Yes."

"How do you know?" I asked.

"Because he told me so."

That scared me.

"What did he say, Jerry?"

"Well, I saw him in Indianapolis the other day. He pulled me aside and asked, 'What's the matter with Ralph? I've heard rumors that he's drinking rather heavily.'"

I didn't say anything.

"It's none of my business," Jerry said, "but the Bishop asked me if I wouldn't talk to you about it. I'm passing it along for what it's worth."

I shook my head.

"I can't understand it, Jerry. Somebody's got this thing wrong. Sure, I take a social drink here and there, but that's all. I haven't been drinking too much. I don't know where the Bishop got the idea that I was."

"It's not important," Jerry said. "I just wanted to let you know how things stand."

"Thanks for telling me. But there's nothing to worry about," I said.

So the Bishop knows.

I've got to stop drinking.

I had arranged to meet Lou to go to Jasper that night. I phoned him and broke the date.

"Would you rather make it tomorrow?" he suggested.

"No, thanks, Lou. I'm going to be tied up for a while."

"Anything wrong, Father?"

"Not really," I said.

"Well, if there's anything I can do, let me know."

I thanked him, and hung up.

I had nothing to drink that evening, and went to bed early. I slept fitfully. I was worried about what the Bishop had heard and what, if anything, he intended to do about it.

But if he intended to do anything, he'd have done it. He wouldn't have sent Jerry to warn me.

I woke up nervous and jittery. I not only didn't have a drink all day; I had no desire for one. But I had little desire to eat, either. And I went about my filing duties in a half-trance.

What's the matter with me? I can't seem to concentrate. What am I worried about?

The Bishop isn't going to do anything to me. There's nothing to be afraid of.

But I'm afraid.

Now, some of the old fears were coming back. That night, when I went to bed, I couldn't sleep at all. Every time I closed my eyes, my life passed in review.

You'll never amount to anything.

Mom said it. My brothers said it. The teachers said it.

You'll never amount to anything.

Well, I'm not amounting to anything.

I'm bitter, lazy, resentful. I'm a bad priest. I shouldn't have been one in the first place.

What kind of a priest gets angry when he's told to do something? What kind of a priest gives excuses every time he's given a chore? What kind of a priest gets so wrapped up in worldly affairs that he can't get his mind on the affairs of God? What kind of a priest hurries his Office and neglects his meditation?

What kind of a priest uses his Roman collar as a means of buying liquor? What kind of a priest ages it in his own study and drinks it while he's working?

The passing of the days made me worse instead of better. I still didn't want a drink. I was too scared. But I could feel myself slipping, just the way I had slipped at St. Meinrad before the diaconate, and at St. Mary-of-the-Woods after it.

I wasn't eating properly and I couldn't sleep. One day, I stepped on the scales and saw that I had lost eight pounds.

I've got to see a doctor.

The only doctor I knew in Vincennes was a parishioner. I went to see him in his office.

"I feel terrible," I said. "I can't eat or sleep or think properly. I'm afraid my nerves are all shot."

"Ever had this kind of trouble before?" he asked.

"Well, I've always been pretty nervous," I said.

"I'll give you a sedative. That ought to straighten you out. And it wouldn't hurt if you had a drink once in a while. It would relax you."

I shook my head.

"I'm not drinking, Doc."

I took the sedatives for a week or ten days, but they didn't help. Now, as I tossed around in bed at night, my head felt heavier than ever, and my thoughts raced with my nerves in a mad scramble.

Here I am right back on the griddle. I've had one nervous breakdown. Is this the beginning of another?

What a fool I am! I was a pretty good priest for a while. Why couldn't I stay that way?

After that first breakdown, I got into a smooth groove. I did all the things Father Anselm told me to, and everything was going fine.

How can I be a good teacher and a good priest one year and neither the next? Now I'm all messed up.

How in the world did I get this way?

St. Meinrad was an easy drive from Vincennes. I sometimes thought of going to see Father Anselm, but I was too ashamed.

He's had enough of me. I drove him crazy the last time. He's gone over this with me so many times he must be sick and tired of me. I can't bother him again.

It's that pastor here. If he had let me teach I'd have been all right. He knew what teaching meant to me. But he took it away from me.

Now look at me! It's his fault.

But I'm a Catholic priest. I can't pick and choose my jobs like a layman. I have to do what I'm told.

This is all my fault.

How can I blame the pastor?

Sometimes, I directed my resentment against the unknown informer who told the Bishop about my drinking. I would lie in bed, ticking off the names of all the people I knew who had ever seen me drink, and trying to eliminate until I could pinpoint the culprit. Sometimes, I thought I knew who it was, and I would clench my fists and make up my mind to get even.

But then—

I'm wrong—I'm wrong—I'm wrong. I have no right to try to get even with anyone.

This is my fault—my fault.

The situation was getting out of hand. I couldn't hide my feelings any more. My troubles were reflecting themselves in the way I walked, the way I talked, the way I looked. I was glum with despair and self-pity, and I showed it. More and more often, people were asking me what was wrong.

I didn't dare tell them.

They always said I'd never amount to anything.

Well, I don't.

I finally went to the acting pastor.

"I'm sick, Father," I said.

"Have you seen a doctor?"

"He hasn't helped. He gave me sedatives, but they didn't do any good."

"Perhaps you'd better go to Indianapolis and see somebody there," he said.

When I got home, I went right to my brother Vic's. Jerry happened to be there.

"Good heavens, Ralph, what's wrong with you?" he asked.

"I don't know. I just feel terrible."

He called a doctor I didn't know.

"Go right to his office," Jerry said. "Do you want me to go along?"

I shook my head.

"I'll make it all right," I said.

The doctor was an elderly man, with a deeply lined face and snow-white hair. His eyes were light blue, and I felt more nervous than ever as he looked sharply at me.

"What seems to be the trouble?" he asked.

"Everything," I said. "My nerves are gone."

I stopped.

That's exactly what I told another doctor once.

"How do you know?" he asked.

"Well, I can't sleep, and I don't have any appetite. And my stomach jumps all day, and my head aches, and every nerve in my body is acting up. I can't sit still long enough to read a sentence in a book."

Even as I talked, I stood up and started pacing around the room.

"Take it easy, Father," the doctor said quietly.

I sat down.

"Now, tell me," he said, "do you have any evidence of other disturbances? Any blood disorder? Liver? Kidney? Heart? Anything at all?"

I shook my head.

"It's my nerves," I said.

"Take sedatives or bromides?"

"Only by prescription. A doctor in Vincennes advised me to try some, but it didn't do any good."

The doctor nodded.

Then—casually—"Do you drink, Father?"

I hesitated.

Then I said, "A little."

"How little?"

"Very little," I said. My voice took on a note of belligerence. "I don't drink much at all."

"A glass of beer here and there?"

"That's about it."

"But no hard liquor?"

"Well—maybe once in a great while."

"I see," the doctor said.

He gave me a thorough examination, then put me through a series of tests. When he had finished, he said, "There doesn't seem to be anything organically wrong with you, Father. I think this is just an emotional upset of some kind. I don't want to put you on sedatives again, since they don't seem to help. I'd rather you go to the hospital for rest and observation. I'm going to send you to St. Vincent's."

They gave me a private room, which suited me fine. I didn't want to see or talk to anyone. I knew I looked terrible, and I felt worse. People made me more nervous than I was before.

Besides, I was hurt and ashamed, and very, very sorry for myself.

And the longer I stayed in that little hospital room, with nothing but four white walls and a window to look at, the worse I felt. I had all the time in the world to pity myself. There was nothing to do but eat, sleep and worry. I didn't bother much with the first two.

Sometimes, I managed to lie flat on my back and stare at

the ceiling, my mind a perfect blank. Those were the good moments. But most of the time, it was the same old story—my life passing in confused review in a mind embittered by unhappy memories.

Everyone is disgusted with me—the Bishop, the doctor, the other priests at Vincennes, Jerry, my other brothers, my friends —everyone. Nobody has any use for me any more. Why should they? I'm an absolute failure. Everything I touch turns to mud. I've never done anything to inspire anything but disgust.

I'm no good to anyone—not even myself.

That was when I first began to think of suicide. If I could only figure out a way to do it and still have time to straighten things out first with God, I wouldn't hesitate a minute. And the more I thought, the surer I was that this was the only way out. I wanted to kill myself, and I spent two full days reveling in the idea as I lay alone on my bed at St. Vincent's Hospital in Indianapolis.

Suicide.

But how?

Here I am in bed. I'm in a hospital. Somebody's watching me all the time.

How can I kill myself?

I began weighing and discarding ideas with all the enthusiasm— but not much of the logic—of a laboratory researcher. First would come the idea, then the objection. I went over and over the same ground, trying to find the answer.

Suppose I were to throw myself out the window. Everyone would think it was an accident—that I went to the window and looked out, then got dizzy and fell. Who would think a priest would kill himself?

But I'm only on the second floor.

Suppose I didn't kill myself? Suppose I only crippled myself for life? What good would that do?

Maybe I could ask for a sharp knife to cut meat with. Then, when the nurse wasn't looking, I could jam it into my chest. It would be messy, but it might work, and leave time for me to call the chaplain.

But it would be pretty obvious. Everyone would know it was done purposely.

And that would hurt Jerry. I can't drag him down with me.

It might make sense simply to walk out in the middle of the night, and let myself get run over by a truck or something. Who would know whether it was an accident or not?

But how can I get out without being seen? And what if I get run over and don't get killed? I might get badly hurt—maybe crippled for life. And that would be no better than falling out the window.

I've failed at practically everything I've tried. I can't fail at this.

People would say, "That stupid Ralph Pfau—he can't even kill himself right."

I've got to make this look like an accident—or better still, a natural death. There must be some way to do it.

How?

I spent a whole afternoon trying to figure out how I could die a natural death.

By bedtime, I thought I had the answer.

Barbiturates.

I'll take an overdose.

That night, when the nurse brought me my sleeping pills, I said, "I keep waking up in the middle of the night. Would you please leave a few of those on my night table where I can get at them?"

"That won't be necessary, Father," she said. "Just call the nurse on duty."

"But I don't want to bother her just for a pill," I said.

"Don't worry. She won't mind."

Then she walked out.

So that's that. I wonder if she suspects. She looked at me kind of peculiarly. Everyone around here looks at me peculiarly. I guess they all suspect me.

Well, barbiturates probably aren't the answer anyhow. They're not sure enough. I imagine it would take a whole bottle to kill you.

I tossed around in bed, halfway between wakefulness and sleep, trying to figure out what to do.

Then I got another idea.

I've got to find out more about poisons. Tomorrow, I'll ask the nurse casually if she'll get me something to read. I'll tell her I'm interested in chemistry, and ask her for a book on the subject. I'll bet it will list all the poisons, and I can pick one out that will really work.

On that triumphant note I went to sleep—after a fashion.

Daylight brought me no solution to the problem. After sober thought, I realized that a book on chemistry wouldn't help. It might list the poisons, but it wouldn't tell how or where or in what form to get them.

Now if I should ask specifically for a book on poisons, I'd be better off. That would give me all the information I'd need. Then, perhaps, I could get someone to sneak some capsules to me.

I daydreamed for hours over that idea. Whenever I was alone, I thought of ways to ask the nurse for the book I needed. They sounded perfectly logical when she wasn't around. But the minute she walked into the room, I'd get tongue-tied. I couldn't imagine making myself sound convincing to anyone while asking for a book about poisons.

She'll ask questions.

And how can I answer them?

Suddenly, the thought of the sinfulness of my suicidal thinking shattered my insane reverie. I reached for the light cord. I pressed the button to call the nurse.

"Did you ring for me, Father?"

"Yes," I almost whispered. "I would like to see the chaplain."

"I'll see if he's in his room."

As the nurse left, I broke out in a cold sweat.

Not only have I been an utter failure, but now I have been guilty of the ultimate in hopelessness. I have been planning suicide. I, a priest . . .

There was a knock on the door.

"Come in," I managed to mumble in a shaky voice.

Father Bauer, the chaplain, came into the room and greeted me with his usual friendly smile.

"And what can I do for you?" he inquired cheerfully.

"I want to go to confession."

He heard my confession. I told him with great effort of my thoughts of suicide, of my discouragement, of my hopelessness. He listened patiently and then assured me that such trials come to all of us some time or another, that even Saint Ignatius had toyed with such thoughts. He bid me be of good heart and to trust everything to a merciful God. He gave me absolution, and then his blessing.

I said my penance after he left the room. Spiritually, I felt relieved; but, emotionally, I was still horribly depressed. And mentally, the merry-go-round of insane thinking continued to revolve —around and around and around. And on through the night, every attempt to regenerate hope was punctuated with:

But I'm different. I'm hopeless.

CHAPTER 7

I WAS IN ST. VINCENT'S HOSPITAL for a week, and each day was worse than the previous one. The old doctor with the snow-white hair and light blue eyes came by every afternoon, and we'd have the same conversation.

"How do you feel?" he'd ask.

"No better," I'd say.

"Still nervous?"

"Terrible."

"Eating?"

"Very little."

"Sleeping?"

"Badly."

He'd shake his head and mutter, "I can't understand it."

Jerry also came in every day. Nobody had to tell him I was making no progress in the hospital. He could see that for himself. Finally, he said, one day, "Ralph, we've got to get you out of here."

"That's all right with me," I said listlessly.

"I'll have a talk with the Bishop."

On the morning of my eighth day in the hospital, he and another priest I knew walked into my room. Both were smiling.

"Get dressed, Ralph," Jerry said. "We're leaving."

"All right," I said.

I didn't even ask where we were going. I wasn't interested.

I climbed into my clothes while Jerry checked me out of the

place. The other priest stayed in the room with me and tried to make small talk, but I wasn't very co-operative. I ignored his comments and answered his questions in monosyllables. I had no idea what he was saying, and didn't concentrate enough to find out.

By the time Jerry returned, I was dressed and ready to go. He took my valise, and the three of us walked along the corridor, then down a couple of flights of stairs and out the front door.

When we stepped into the street, we all stopped short for a moment. It was exactly like stepping into an oven. The heat overwhelmed us. The sun beat down with such blinding intensity that my feet felt hot through the soles of my shoes as I crossed the sidewalk.

The heat was the only thing that interested me.

"What's the temperature?" I asked.

"A hundred and four," Jerry said.

It felt hotter.

Jerry's car was in front of the main entrance. I got into the back seat, and the other priest sat in front beside Jerry. As soon as we started moving, I took off my collar and leaned back.

I closed my eyes and must have slept a little.

When I woke up, we were out in the open road.

Then, finally, I asked, "Where are we going?"

"St. Louis," said Jerry laconically.

I closed my eyes and pressed my hands to my forehead.

Did he say St. Louis?

I must have said it aloud, for Jerry said, "There's a wonderful hospital there. It's a nice place, where you'll have good food and a good rest. You should get away from everything, and this is just the spot for you."

Get away from everything. That's what I wanted to do at St. Vincent's.

"Who told you about it?" I asked.

"The Bishop."

The Bishop.

I'm no good to him, no good to the diocese, no good to anyone. I'm a failure—a flat, utter, one hundred percent failure. I've let everyone down.

worthless

Now, my head was resting on the back of the automobile seat, and my life was passing in awful review again. It was the same old cycle, spiked by the same old regrets. I remembered all the failures, forgot the little successes.

Why, I'm not even a good teacher. I couldn't hold my job at Gibault High School. That's why they made the rule that priests shouldn't teach there any more. It was on account of me. They wanted to get me out of there, and that was the only way they could do it.

If I had been a good teacher, the pastor would never have put the rule through. He'd have let me keep on teaching.

blame for all

No—it goes back farther than that. I shouldn't have been ordained. I shouldn't have received the diaconate or the sub-diaconate. I should have quit before it was too late.

But I didn't, and now I'm a burden on everyone—my brother, my Bishop, my diocese, my Church.

I'm no good. I'm a hopeless, flat failure.

We stopped, and I opened my eyes. We were in front of a restaurant.

"Come in with us and have some lunch, Ralph," Jerry said.

"I don't feel like eating."

"Oh, come on. A sandwich and a Coke or something will do you good."

"I'd rather stay here," I said. "It's too hot to eat."

Jerry shrugged.

"All right. Want us to bring something out to you?"

"I don't care."

I closed my eyes.

I guess I dozed off again, for the next thing I knew, we were back on the steaming highway. I could hear the drone of voices as my brother and the other priest talked, but I didn't know what they were saying, and didn't care.

Where are we going?

St. Louis.

A hospital. A place where I can get good food and good rest. A place where I can get away from it all.

What kind of a hospital?

"Jerry—"

My voice sounded as if it were coming out of someone else's throat.

"How do you feel, Ralph?"

Jerry spoke without turning his head. His eyes were glued to the road.

"No better. No worse."

"You slept."

"Jerry—what kind of a place is this hospital you're taking me to?"

"It's sort of a sanitarium. Run by the Alexian Brothers."

"The who?"

"The Alexian Brothers. They are an order of lay Brothers who specialize in hospital work. Wonderful people."

I closed my eyes again, and tried to sleep.

It didn't work. Crossing and recrossing my mind was a gallery of pictures of Ralph Pfau failing: failing at home—failing in school—failing at the playground—failing at St. Meinrad—failing at the sub-diaconate—failing at the ordination—failing at St. Mary-of-the-Woods—failing at Fordham—failing at the Old Cathedral —failing in everything, everywhere, under all conditions.

In self-defense, I opened my eyes.

"How much farther?" I asked.

"Thirty—thirty-five miles. Something like that," Jerry said.

Almost there. Less than an hour. Then I can rest.

wishful thinking

I hope it's cool there. I hope there's a nice long veranda— maybe one that goes all the way around the building. I hope they've got plenty of rocking chairs and hammocks where you can just lie back and close your eyes and take it easy. I hope there are lots of trees, with green leaves rustling peacefully in a gentle breeze. I hope there's a fountain, where you can watch the water spilling from a graceful spout onto wet concrete.

Wet concrete. What an odd thing to want to see.

But it's cool. And anything that's cool is better than this.

We went over a bump, and I was jolted from my position in the back seat. Now, I was aware of an ache all the way down my left side, and I realized I had been leaning my weight on it most of the way from Indianapolis. I tried to move my left arm, but it was asleep. I flexed the fingers while I rubbed the arm with my right. After a while, the circulation began to return.

It was dreadfully hot.

I reached into my pocket for a handkerchief, and wiped my streaming face. It did little good. Even as I drew the cloth across my forehead, beads of sweat replaced those I had wiped off. My clothes were saturated, my body sticky.

Now we were out of the farm country, well into an urban area. The sun ground into the pavement, the piercing bright rays softening tar on the street, cracking wood on the houses, sending clouds of steam up from the sidewalks.

"Is this St. Louis?"

My voice was far, far away.

"East St. Louis," Jerry said.

His voice was farther.

"Have you ever seen this Alexian Brothers Hospital, Jerry?"

It's a game—see whose voice can sound the farthest away.

"No."

His is farther.

"Do you think it will be cool there?"

Mine is farther.

"Cooler than here."

His is farther.

"Anything will be cooler than here."

Mine is farther.

Now we were on a bridge, crossing the Mississippi River.

What am I doing in St. Louis?

I don't belong here.

I want to go home.

"Jerry."

"What?"

"I don't like St. Louis. Take me back to Indianapolis."

"Take it easy, Ralph. You'll be all right."

Take it easy. Everybody tells me to take it easy.

Jerry stopped the car at a big intersection, and asked a policeman for directions. They talked a few minutes, then we started moving again.

"Put your collar on, Ralph," the other priest said. "We're almost there."

He was adjusting his own.

I sat up straight and fixed mine, almost choking myself in the process. The starched collar felt like a hot steel trap around my neck.

If the Alexian Brothers Hospital had a veranda with rocking chairs and hammocks, I didn't see it as we drove into the grounds. It looked to me like any other hospital—the main building setting back forty or fifty feet from the sidewalk, with a wide entrance in the middle, facing a driveway approach from the street. There was an iron fence along the sidewalk where we came in. I couldn't see the rest of the place.

The three of us walked up the steps and into a long, dark corridor. There was nothing extra bright about the place, but at least it was cool. Except for the sudden change from hot, bright sunlight to the natural gloom of hospital corridors, I was not aware of much of anything. I let the others lead the way, and I tagged along a step or two behind.

We went into an office where we were met by a Brother. He and Jerry went off into a corner and talked for a few minutes. After a while, another Brother walked in—a little old man with a fringe of white hair framing a bald head. He was no more than four and a half feet tall, and, with his wizened face and tiny features, he looked as if he were shriveling down to nothing.

He talked to the other Brother, then, without a word, signaled for us to follow him. He led us along the corridor, and stopped in front of a door fifty feet or so from the office. He took a huge bunch of keys from under his cassock, fitted one into the door and opened it, then stepped aside so we could walk in.

The room was almost bare. In one corner was a fairly large bed, and, on the other side, a chair and a table, with a newspaper on it. On the floor was a scatter rug, which covered about a quarter of the room.

Jerry held out his hand, and I took it.

"You'll be all right, Ralph," he said, kindly. "Take good care of yourself. We'll see you later."

I shook hands with the other priest, too, and managed to thank them both before they turned to walk away.

Then I threw myself on the bed, face down.

I didn't even hear the little Brother turn the key in the lock after he went out.

The same old story. Here I am back in a hospital again, being a problem, as usual. I've always been a problem. Ever since I was little, I was a problem to someone—my father, my mother, my brothers, my teachers, my confessors.

And what do these good Brothers here think they can do for me?

Don't they realize it's a hopeless job?

The collar chafed my neck, and I suddenly realized I hadn't even taken off my coat. I stood up and removed it, carefully hanging it on a hook. I took off my collar and put it on the table, and unbuttoned my shirt. Then I sat down on the bed, and stared at the floor.

Pretty soon I heard the key turning in the lock.

So I was locked in.

Were they afraid I was going to run away? Where did they think I'd run to?

"You locked me in," I said, petulantly, as the Brother's bald head came into view. He was followed by a short, fat, pudgy man, carrying a bag.

The Brother ignored my comment.

"This is the doctor," he said. "Tell him what he wants to know. He's here to help you."

Then he turned and walked out.

The doctor turned small, beady blue eyes in my direction. I didn't like his looks.

Before he could say anything, I asked, "When do I get out of here?"

"Pretty soon, Father," he said. "Sit down. Take it easy."

There it is again. Take it easy.

Everyone expects me to take it easy.

Do they think I can turn my nerves on and off like a phonograph record?

Take it easy.

I sat on the bed. The doctor took a pen and notebook out of his pocket, and sat on the chair by the table.

"Name, please, Father?"

"Ralph Pfau."

"Address?"

I gave him my brother Vic's address in Indianapolis.

"Age?"

"Twenty-nine."

When he had completed all the preliminaries, he asked, "When were you ordained?"

"May 21, 1929."

"Why?"

"Uh—pardon me?" I stammered.

"I asked why—why did you become a priest?"

For a few seconds, I said nothing. Then: "I guess—I just wanted to, I suppose."

"Um—"

He wrote down several notes. Then, turning back to me, he said, softly, "Tell me about it, Father."

So I told him. I talked for a long time, pouring out the same rambling story I had first told Father Anselm, and later Father Amicus, and later doctors and friends and other priests. It came easily now, for I knew it by heart and recited it by rote. The only difference between this and previous recitals was in the last part, for I brought it up-to-date.

The doctor scribbled furiously as I talked.

He didn't interrupt me. I guess he was afraid he'd break the spell.

He wrote on and on for fifteen or twenty minutes after I had finished, and I watched him with morbid fascination.

There's my life story. Isn't it a sorry business? But interesting. I hope you're having a good time writing about it. You'll have a picnic telling your colleagues, won't you?

"I had a priest once—a priest who didn't want to be a priest. Met him in the Alexian Brothers Hospital. Nerves were shattered. Unfortunate situation. Here's what happened—"

The doctor stopped writing, finally, and turned to me.

"Is there any history of mental illness in your family, Father?" he asked.

"None that I know of."

"Nobody ever had a nervous disorder—anything like that?"

I shook my head.

"And the first time you were aware of suffering one yourself was—" consulting his notes "—at the seminary?"

"Yes—just before I received the sub-diaconate," I said.

"I see. Take sedatives, Father?"

"When prescribed."

"Otherwise?"

"No."

"I see you smoke. Do you drink?"

I stiffened momentarily, but made a quick recovery.

"Not much," I said. "Just beer once in a while."

The doctor went to the door and beckoned. The small Brother came back into the room.

"I think we had better call his Bishop and see if we can't get a dispensation for him," the doctor said.

"A what?" I asked.

"A dispensation. Get you released from the priesthood."

I laughed mirthlessly.

"You're not a Catholic, are you, Doctor?"

"No."

"Well," I said, "I couldn't get released from the priesthood if I wanted to—which I don't."

"You're not happy in the priesthood."

"Not because it's the priesthood."

"Why, then?" the doctor asked.

"Because I'm a failure. If I weren't a failure, I'd be very happy in the priesthood."

"Then you want to continue as a priest?"

"Of course," I said. "But I want to be a good priest."

A few minutes later, the doctor and the Brother left. The Brother carefully locked the door after him.

I was scared.

This doctor doesn't know the right terms, but he knows what he means. Suppose he makes a recommendation to the Bishop consistent with what he's thinking about me? I might end up being laicized—released of all my functions as a priest and relieved of all responsibilities except the vow of celibacy.

I can't let that happen.

I've got to convince these people I'm all right, so I can get out of here as soon as possible.

But how?

I picked up the newspaper on the table, and idly glanced at the first page. Suddenly, my heart flipped.

Down in one corner of the page was a short item about a mission in one of the big downtown churches. It was being conducted by Father Peter Crumley, O.F.M.

Father Crumley was an old friend of mine. I had known him well at St. Meinrad, where he had conducted several retreats, including one during my last year there. He was a fine, understanding man, with a wonderful sense of humor.

If I can reach Father Crumley, he'll help me.

I banged on the door until the key started turning in the lock.

"Yes, Father?"

"May I make a phone call, please?" I asked. "There's a priest here in town who is a good friend of mine. I'd like to talk to him."

"Follow me."

The Brother led me to the office where we had first walked in, and pointed to the phone. I looked up the number of the parish where the mission was being held, and called it. A minute later, Father Crumley was on the line.

"Father Ralph Pfau," I said. "How are you?"

"Well, for heaven's sake. I'm fine. How are you?"

"Not so good, Father."

"What's the trouble, Ralph?"

"They've got me in the Alexian Brothers Hospital."

"Why, that's a mental hospital. What in the world are you doing there?" he asked.

"I'm in trouble, Father. I've got myself into a terrible mess."

"What kind of a mess?"

"I can't tell you over the phone, Father."

"I'll be right out," he said.

After we got through talking, the Brother returned and led me back to my room. He locked the door again, and I heard his footsteps dying away as he walked down the corridor.

Let him lock the door. I don't care. Father Crumley will help me. He'll talk to the Bishop, and make sure that doctor doesn't talk him into anything. Father Crumley will get me out of here. He knows I'm not sick.

Father Crumley was at the hospital half an hour later. The Brother let him in, then retired out into the hall. After our first greetings, Father Crumley sat beside me on the bed and said, in his deep, jovial tones, "Now, what's this all about?"

"I don't know," I said. "I've just had an attack of nerves, and here I am."

"Well, you look all right to me. Little thin. Have you been eating decently?"

"Not too well, Father. I've been pretty nervous."

"What's the trouble?"

I shrugged.

"I don't know," I said again. "Just—"

My voice trailed off.

"All right, Ralph. Tell me about it."

So once again, I went over the whole story. Father Crumley listened intently, nodding here, smiling there, and never taking his eyes off my face.

When I had finished, he said, "Well, it all adds up to one thing. Scruples. You've still got them, haven't you? This whole business goes all the way back to the days when you thought you weren't good enough to be a priest.

"Let me tell you something: I'm not good enough, you're not good enough, no priest is good enough.

"Ralph, I'm sure you've been as good a priest as any of us. You've been worried and scared, perhaps, but you've been a good priest. What you need now is activity—something that will keep you so busy you won't have time to brood and worry about yourself. You don't belong in this place. This is a mental hospital. You don't need the Alexian Brothers, and they can't help you, no matter how hard they try."

He stopped talking, and looked out the window. For a few minutes, he was lost in thought.

Then he said, "Did you stay at Fordham long enough to earn a degree?"

"No. I was only there two summers."

"Would you like to go back for a full year to complete your work for a Master's degree?"

"Why, that would be wonderful, Father," I said. "Only—" I looked around the room, and shrugged.

"Don't worry about that. We'll get you out of here. Just let me talk to the Bishop."

He started out the door, then turned back.

"That doctor who talked to you here—did he take many notes?"

"Pages of them," I said.

"I guess we'd better talk to the Brother here about them then. Now, you wait here. I'll be back in a few minutes."

He walked out, leaving the door ajar. It didn't remain that way. The Brother came right down the hall, gently closed it and turned the key in the lock.

Father Crumley was gone for quite a time. But when he returned, he had a wide smile on his round face.

"Get your things, Ralph," he said. "You're leaving."

"Right now?"

"Right now."

"But—I just got here. Where am I going?"

"New York," said Father Crumley. "Come on. I'll take you to the train."

"New York? Just like that? But, Father, where am I going to stay when I get there?"

"Where did you stay before?"

I told him. Then I said, "But that was just for summer school. That's started already. *This is for a whole year.* How do I know if they'll have room for me? Or any work for me to do?"

"There's always work for a priest," said Father Crumley. "But if it will make you feel any better, call up and see what the situation is."

So I phoned Father Frank Murphy at the rectory in Washington Heights. He was one of the assistant pastors.

"Can you find room for me if I arrive in New York tomorrow?" I asked.

"We'll work something out."

"Is there an opening anywhere?"

"The chaplain of the Holy Child nuns took sick yesterday," Father Murphy said. "The convent is only four blocks from here —140th Street and Riverside. You can take that job for as long as it lasts and live here at the rectory if you want to."

The next thing I knew, I was bidding good-bye to Father Crumley at the Union Station in St. Louis, and climbing aboard a train.

CHAPTER 8

I**T ALL HAPPENED SO FAST** that I didn't even notice the heat, which was still stifling. I didn't even have time to think until I got settled in the train. My berth was all made up, and I got into it, hoping that for once I'd be able to sleep.

Well, I'm out of that mess. How did it happen so fast? And how long will it be before I'm in trouble again?

I've got to be careful not to drink. Someone might turn me in, and then it will start all over again. I've had enough trouble to last me a lifetime.

But I'm afraid. I'll get into another jam. It's bound to happen. I was born for trouble. No matter how careful I am, I can't stay out of it. Something always goes wrong. I'm just no good, that's all. I'm nothing but trouble for everyone who comes near me. Now it was Father Crumley. Next time, it will be somebody else.

Sleep was impossible. As I lay in the berth, listening to the rhythmic click of wheels on rails, I went through the same cycle of hopelessness and regret and depression a hundred times. Over and over and over, my life passed in review, and each time I found a new mistake I hadn't thought of before.

Why can't I get off this merry-go-round?

What am I going to do? It's no use. Everything bad that's happened before will happen again. Maybe I don't need the Alexian Brothers this time, but I'll need them sooner or later.

I'm not normal.

I'll end up so bad that not even Father Crumley can get me straightened out.

Morning finally arrived, and I got up with the dawn, red-eyed and exhausted. I felt a little better after I had shaved and washed up, and I even ate some breakfast, but I was very shaky.

I tried to read, but couldn't keep my mind on the words. Instead, I kept staring out the window, wondering what was going to become of me. I was still wondering when we got into Grand Central Station.

At the rectory, I was assigned to new quarters.

"We have so many priests now that we don't have room for them all in this building," Father Murphy said. "You'll live next door, but eat here. I hope that suits you all right."

"It suits me fine," I said.

And that night, I sat around with the other priests, talking about one thing or another, and I felt pretty good. They asked no questions, although a couple of them remarked that I looked a little peaked. But they were glad to see me, and made me feel at home.

I slept fairly well that night, and when I woke up I figured that everything was all right. I had breakfast with the other priests at the rectory, then walked over to the convent on 140th Street, where I made all the necessary arrangements to replace the sick priest there as chaplain.

But for the next six weeks, while waiting for classes to begin at Fordham, I had little to do. I got up very early—five o'clock—because I had to be at the convent at six for Mass, but that just about completed my day's obligations, except for Benediction for the nuns later. I was back at the rectory for breakfast, and I had the better part of the rest of the day to think.

The evenings were better because I could enjoy the company of the other priests. I went to bed feeling all right, but I couldn't get more than two or three hours of sleep. Then I woke up, said Mass, had breakfast and started thinking again.

A week after I arrived in New York, I decided I'd better try to do something about getting more sleep. I went to a corner drugstore and got a bottle of bromides, for which I didn't need a prescription. I took a dose that night, but I didn't sleep long.

When I woke up and started tossing around, I took another dose, then fell into a drugged stupor. I woke up with a terrible headache, and dragged myself through a ghastly day.

That night I doubled the bromide dose before going to bed.

It worked. I slept well for the first time in weeks, and didn't feel too badly in the morning.

But three nights later, it was the same old story. The double bromide only put me out for a few hours. The rest of the night was murder.

I took a triple dose the night after, and that did the business for a while. But I was living in a fool's paradise. Within a week, I was fighting sleeplessness again.

I went back to the druggist and asked for something stronger. He gave me pentabromides, and told me I'd have to get a prescription for anything else. Somehow or other, I got by on them for the rest of the summer.

Stay busy

Things improved when classes began. Now I had something to do besides saying Mass in the morning and giving Benediction in the afternoon for the Holy Child nuns. The Fordham Graduate School was in the Woolworth Building. I went downtown right after breakfast for an hour of classes before lunch and another hour immediately after. I went from there to the convent, then returned to the rectory to study.

The subject of my thesis was: "History of Secondary Education in the Diocese of Indianapolis." Fortunately, it required considerable research. Between the convent, the library and the Woolworth Building, I had plenty of moving around to do, and I was busy working on my thesis at night. I didn't even have time to sit around with the other priests at the rectory.

And, when I was ready for bed, I was exhausted enough to sleep. I began cutting down on the bromides, and by Thanksgiving, I was back on single doses.

Two things happened in December that put me on edge again.

On December 5, the repeal of Prohibition took effect.

Three days later, Bishop Chartrand died.

I was badly hit by the passing of the Bishop. I had known him all my life, and had a deep personal affection for him. Beyond that, his forbearance and understanding had meant everything to me. Without it, I might have gone off the deep end altogether. He had always been good to me, and I knew I would miss him.

I debated about going to his funeral, but it would have meant flying to Indianapolis and back. In 1933, that would have been unusual. People didn't take flying for granted then as they do now. But I decided to do it, and reserved a round-trip ticket.

Two hours later, for reasons that I will never know, I decided to cancel it.

The plane crashed into a mountain in Pennsylvania. There were no survivors.

I hadn't taken a drink since my arrival in New York. I was afraid to. I didn't know how much they knew about me at the rectory, or if anyone had been instructed to watch me. I didn't dare take any chances.

For that reason, I had never phoned David Batterly. He didn't even know I was in town.

Repeal brought on a rash of publicity and advertising, both in and out of the daily newspapers, on the virtues of liquor. Now, you could legally enjoy cocktails before dinner, wine during it and cordials afterward if you liked, to say nothing of as many highballs as you wanted during the evening.

I couldn't walk down the street without passing a liquor store or cocktail lounge or barroom. Where once you had to make surreptitious phone calls or roundabout trips to out-of-the-way places in order to get liquor, now it was practically thrown at you. Seven-course dinners, liquor included, for as little as three dollars were advertised regularly in the daily papers. Everywhere I went, I heard people rave about this or that drinking establishment, or this or that scotch or rye or bourbon or rum or gin.

And I wasn't allowed to enjoy any of it.

By Christmas, I was feeling pretty sorry for myself. However, I didn't feel I should spend the money to go home. The other priests at the rectory took care of all the parish services, so there wasn't anything for me to do around there. I was working on my thesis, but classes were temporarily suspended.

I had too much time on my hands.

I turned to the movies for diversion. I went from one local film palace to another, and after I had gone through everything in the neighborhood, I checked the newspapers for pictures I hadn't seen, and went to them. And, when I finished that list, I started all over again.

On Christmas morning, after Midnight Mass, I went back to the rectory, but couldn't sleep. I doubled up on the bromides, but that did little good. I tossed around all night, finally fell into a fitful sleep and woke up feeling miserable at nine o'clock.

I got dressed and went to a morning movie in Times Square. When it was over, I had lunch, then went to another movie in the afternoon. After a lone dinner, I went to a third movie that evening.

I emerged from that show at about ten o'clock. Then, suddenly, I was overwhelmed by a surge of homesickness, so I went into a phone booth, and called Vic's house in Indianapolis. But, in order to save money, I put through a station-to-station call. Vic's nine-year-old youngster answered the phone, and I couldn't make him understand who I was or what I wanted. I finally hung up in disgust.

This is it. Nobody wants me. Why should I bother to try to do the right thing?

I need a drink.

But suppose I get caught? Suppose somebody hears about it in Indianapolis? Who's going to protect me now? The Bishop is gone. His successor isn't going to put up with me if I don't behave myself.

I didn't have the drink. I was still too frightened. Instead, I went back to the rectory and worked till I was exhausted.

Somehow, I weathered the Christmas vacation, and things got better again when it was over. Classes were resumed and I had a lot to do. I threw myself back into a busy work routine and, for the next few months, I was able to cut down on the bromides.

I finished my thesis in March. Now, I had nearly three months to kill. By this time, the regular chaplain at the convent had returned, so I didn't even have to go there. I asked the pastor if he could find me a job. He told me about a vacancy in a Harlem parish. One of the assistants was ill, and they needed a tempo-rary replacement.

That job was a lifesaver. Aside from the fact that it kept me busy, it also provided me with some badly needed laughs.

The funniest incident involved an old Negro, who came up to me one day and said, "Father, can you spare me a dime so I can pay a few bills?"

I gave him half a dollar and said, "Here, take this and get yourself ahead a little."

After a few weeks, I felt considerably better. I spent a good deal of time in the parish, and enjoyed the company of the other priests at the rectory during the evening.

The new Bishop of Indianapolis was to be installed a couple of months before I would get my degree at Fordham. I was de-lighted when it turned out to be my old confessor, Father Ami-cus, who knew me almost as well as Bishop Chartrand had. I went back for his installation, then returned to New York in my car which had been in storage since July.

I received my Master of Arts degree on Wednesday, June 13, 1934. I intended to return to Indianapolis, but the pastor in Har-lem asked me if I could stay until the regular assistant returned. I got permission, and remained in New York after Commence-ment.

Signs of hope

I'm all right now. I'm happy, and these people are happy with me. I can be a good priest, and I'm proving it.

I'm not going to get sick again. I have full control of myself. And I'm not afraid.

The next day, I phoned David Batterly to say hello.

"Back for summer school, eh, Father?" he said. "Well, it's wonderful to hear from you. Come for dinner tonight."

I didn't bother to correct him on the summer school part. It was just as well that he didn't know I had been in town all year. So I simply said, "Thanks, David. It'll be nice to see you again."

David had the usual crowd for dinner, and I was glad to see them all. I forgot my recent difficulties with alcohol in these pleasant, friendly surroundings. I had a cocktail before dinner and a cordial afterward. Later that night, after we had returned to the living room, I drank one bourbon and ginger ale. When it was time to leave, David smiled, and said, "I know you're busy, Father. But plan to see us often. We still have open house almost every night. We'll be delighted to see you."

Then, with a chuckle, he added, "And the liquor's much better since repeal."

"So I notice," I said, smiling.

I didn't bother to tell him that it was my first drink in a year.

Back at the rectory, I slept soundly, and woke up refreshed and ready for a good day's work.

I can drink. It doesn't do me any harm.

But I'll be careful.

I won't have more than one or two—or maybe three at the most—at a sitting.

That was neither a resolution nor a promise. But, for the remainder of the time that I was around New York, I lived up to it. Practically every night found me at David's, but I had full control of the situation. I usually stopped at two drinks. On rare occasions, I had a third.

Now, I was no longer afraid, no longer worried about getting caught, no longer concerned over the possibility that I was being watched. I could handle my liquor, and I wasn't drinking too much of it.

Besides, I felt good. I was eating and sleeping well, and keeping busy in the parish. I wasn't even taking bromides any more.

In early August, the Bishop wired that he was appointing me pastor of St. Rita's Church, a Negro parish in Indianapolis. Since I had been working with Negroes in Harlem, this was perfectly agreeable to me. And, in fact, as the time to return to Indianapolis approached, I felt a thrill of anticipation. After all, this would be the first parish of my own.

I left New York in August of 1934, and drove home alone. This time I carried no liquor in the car. I knew I could get a drink whenever I wanted. After arriving in Indianapolis, I could buy a bottle to keep in my room.

I didn't drink at all during the trip, and, even though I got the bottle, I had no particular desire to drink when I got home.

I reported immediately to the Bishop.

"We're making a change, Ralph," he told me, "but you're staying here in Indianapolis. Only instead of sending you to St. Rita's, I'm assigning you to St. Anthony's as assistant pastor."

My first reaction was mild disappointment at not having my own parish, after all, but it lasted only for a moment. I was familiar with St. Anthony's and was quite willing to go there.

"Incidentally," the Bishop said, "I have additional work for you. I'm appointing you chaplain of the insane asylum."

So, for the next year, I spent the Thursday before every First Friday of the month giving Communion and hearing Confessions for inmates who were able to receive the Sacraments.

While I was unable to teach at St. Anthony's, I found another interest fully as absorbing—sports. I became the athletic director of the parish. Indianapolis had a Catholic sports league, and St. Anthony's was represented with teams in football, basketball and baseball. I had always loved sports, and I was very happy to be working with the boys in the parish.

Our teams did pretty well. We didn't have much in football, but we went to the finals of the basketball championships, then won the baseball title.

Shortly after I began working at St. Anthony's, two young men came around to ask information about Sunday Masses at the lakes in northern Indiana, where they were planning to spend their vacation. In the course of the conversation, we got on the subject of sports. After a while, the boys invited me to their home.

The two were Jack O'Neal, Jr., and his brother, Bob. Their father, Jack, Sr., was on the Indianapolis police force, and later became its chief. There was another brother, Jim, and two sisters, Margaret and Mary Elizabeth. Mrs. O'Neal was a charming lady, and she and her family made me feel so much at home on my first visit that I often returned. Bob helped with the coaching of the football team.

The O'Neals became my closest friends in the parish. I was in and out of their home as much as my own, and, after a while, they took it perfectly as a matter of course that I have holiday dinners with them. For years after that, the O'Neals were my hosts at Thanksgiving, Easter and Christmas.

This was a far different relationship from the one with the

110 **P R O D I G A L S H E P H E R D**

Batterlys. An occasional drink was incidental in the O'Neal household. At the Batterlys', drinking was practically a way of life. I had visited David's home in a sort of frantic desire to get away from it all, and had been there almost every single night. I went to the O'Neals' perhaps once a week, and I was with them almost as part of the family. It was sort of a headquarters for me when I wasn't at the rectory.

My friendship with the O'Neals was—and still is—a strong, heart-warming, healthy relationship. My connection with David was transitory and, because of the amount of drinking I was encouraged to do, very unhealthy for me.

Partly because of the O'Neals, but mostly because I was busy and contented, I had a wonderful year at St. Anthony's. The people in the parish were my friends and the athletic work was rewarding. I even enjoyed the monthly visits to the insane asylum.

I was too occupied to do very much drinking. I had an occasional highball, but only while visiting in someone's home. One of my friends liked whiskey sours and hated to drink alone, so I joined him occasionally. I accepted a drink when it was offered, but I never happened to be anywhere where people were drinking heavily.

All during the time I was at St. Anthony's, the bottle in my room remained unopened. I took it with me intact when I left there.

In July of 1935, I was transferred to St. Augustine's, in Jeffersonville, Indiana, a thriving city of about seventeen thousand, directly across the Ohio River from Louisville. My job was assistant to the pastor, Father Joseph Bryan, a wonderfully friendly priest whom I had known in Indianapolis.

We were both new to Jeffersonville. Father Bryan had spent the previous twenty years as pastor of St. Rita's, the Negro parish which I had been originally scheduled to take. He and I got along fine, and I was delighted at the prospect of working with him.

Father Bryan was a generous man, so anxious to please that he let me do anything I wanted. I took over the athletic program in the parish, not only running it, but coaching the football, basketball and baseball teams as well. Since the seasons in these sports overlapped each other, I was busy all the time.

On top of that, of course, I had my routine parish duties, which I performed with conscientious enthusiasm. Father Bryan was so easygoing and so thoughtful that I never wanted to let him down. I helped him in every way I could, and was much too busy to think of anything but my work.

The football season was uneventful, but we had a remarkably good basketball team. It did so well that I decided to stage a state parochial school basketball tournament at the end of the season. I got some of the merchants around town to co-operate, and pretty soon we had a good collection of individual and team prizes for the winners. The high school agreed to let us use its gymnasium, and the newspapers helped with publicity.

By the time the tournament was played, on March 12 and 13, 1936, we had ten teams entered, and the whole town was pretty well steamed up about it.

By this time, the St. Augustine boys had won twenty-four of their twenty-six games. Our kids were small, but they were fast and skillful, and they had a wonderful spirit. When they won the title, I felt a real glow of satisfaction. This was my team, and I was very proud. I was proud, too, of the success of the tournament, which attracted attention all over the area. It was fully covered by the *Jeffersonville Evening News*, in its March 15 issue:

"Battling against great odds from the first toss-up, Father Ralph Pfau's fighting St. Augustine Saints whipped the classy St. Joseph's quint of Jasper Friday night, 15-10, at the Jeffersonville High School gym and copped the first Parochial School meet. . . .

"Mayor Allen W. Jacobs awarded the trophies at the conclusion of the tournament. Capt. Bobby Constantine, midget forward, received the *Evening News* trophy. The runner-up trophy went to Captain Yaggi of the Jasper five. Howard Weber, a member of the St. John's team of Loogootee, received the sportsmanship trophy, and Ernie Gedling, ace scorer of the St. Augustine's five, received the medal offered the most valuable player."

There was more of the same, and I got a huge thrill out of it.

And, when the basketball season was over, I went right to work on baseball. We won no titles, and, in fact, didn't even come close, but I enjoyed the work and was sorry to see the season end.

Throughout this period, my drinking was occasional and relatively unimportant. As the year progressed, I made new friends, who invited me to their homes. Sometimes they offered me a highball, sometimes they didn't. It made no difference to me. I could take my liquor or leave it alone. I never drank in the parish house, and often went for weeks without taking anything.

These were much like my early days at Vincennes, when I was plunged in the sort of work I loved. But at Jeffersonville, I also had a close personal friendship with the pastor and happy relationships with parishioners, as well as their children.

I didn't have the time to worry. For the same reason, I never had occasion to feel sorry for myself. I had something that filled my whole life. During the summer, I continued my work with the parish teams. The boys were my friends, and they came around regularly.

Life went on without incident or personal problems—and only a moderate amount of drinking—until January of 1937.

Then came what the *New York Times* later described as the "heaviest volume of flood waters in the history of the Ohio Valley."

CHAPTER 9

It HAD BEEN A COLD WINTER, with several snowstorms, especially in the area north and east of Jeffersonville. But in mid-January, the weather suddenly shifted, and it became unseasonably warm.

On Thursday, January 14, we had a heavy rainstorm. It poured, all up and down the Ohio, all the way from Pittsburgh to Cairo. Jeffersonville, in common with everything else within hundreds of miles, was drenched.

But this was only the beginning. The rain continued on Friday, and there was no sign of a letup Saturday. Now, there were reports of floods in other sections of the valley. Jeffersonville, an old hand at floods, began bracing for trouble. So did Louisville, across the river. The flood record there was a high water mark of something over forty-six feet. By Saturday night, the river was up over thirty-five feet.

The rains continued, in varying degrees of intensity, through Sunday and the first half of the following week. By Wednesday, the water in Louisville was at forty-five feet and still rising. In Jeffersonville, the situation was correspondingly threatening.

Yet, while we were sick and tired of all the rain, we weren't terribly upset at the church. St. Augustine's was located on high ground in town, in the 300 block on Locust Street. While neither Father Bryan nor I had ever had any experience with floods, the people of our parish weren't scared. They had lived with floods for years. Flood warnings had been routine in Jeffersonville for as long as anyone could remember.

There was a dike down by the river, several blocks from the church, and it had never broken. We could see it from the second floor of the parish house, and we got into the habit of looking out at it every night just before we went to bed, and in the morning after we arose. Even though the water was getting higher and higher, the dike looked safe, and seemed to be an adequate shield for us all.

But with the rains pouring down and the snows from the mountains melting and swelling the waters of the Ohio River, we weren't so sure just how safe the city was. It didn't seem possible that the dike could hold forever. All day and all night, the radio was blaring news of the flood, and the daily papers were full of it.

By Thursday, the twenty-first, the water had gone over forty-eight feet at Louisville to break a record that had stood for more than half a century. And that night, we were told that there was a definite question how long the Jeffersonville dike would hold out.

Father Bryan, the housekeeper, Miss Ryan, and I were in the parish house that night, talking about the flood and listening to the radio. We checked the dike from the window every so often, but we couldn't see very much. The only sound was the splashing of the everlasting rain, now in its eighth straight day, against our windowpanes and on our roof.

The next morning, we went over to the church to say Mass, and later returned to the parish house. Before I left the church, I talked for a moment with the janitor, who had reported for work, as usual.

"Good morning, Father," he said. "It's getting worse—if that's possible."

I nodded.

"Good morning, John," I said. "I wonder how long it will last."

"It has to stop sometime," John said. "It always does."

Before going back to the parish house, I asked John if he thought he'd better come along. He didn't think it was necessary. He told me he had work to do in the church, and said he intended to stay there all day. He did assure me, at my insistence, that he would come right over to the parish house if the situation became critical.

Miss Ryan met me at the parish house.

"Father," she said, "I just heard on the radio that the dike is weakening. Where can we go?"

"I think the best thing for us to do is stay right here," I said. "We're on the highest ground in town."

"I'm scared, Father," she said.

"Don't worry," I said. "We'll be all right here."

I went upstairs. Father Bryan was getting ready to come down.

"Is everything all right in the church?" he asked. "I'm worried about the dike."

Even as he spoke, we heard a distant roar. We both rushed to the window. Instead of the reassuring sight of ugly gray concrete, all we could see was water. There were solid sheets of it, spurting in giant jets from along what had once been the dike, and rolling in huge waves toward us.

Father Bryan headed for the stairs.

"Where are you going?" I asked.

"To get the Blessed Sacrament out of the church," he cried, over his shoulder.

"Father—you can't make it."

I ran down after him, and we both reached the side door at the same time. He flung it open, but before he could go out, the way was blocked by a couple and two teen-aged children, a girl about sixteen and a boy of thirteen. I recognized them as the Greenes, parishioners who lived just beyond the church, and on lower ground.

"We're trapped," Mr. Greene yelled. "May we come in?"

"By all means," Father Bryan said.

We opened the door wide, and looked toward the church, about one hundred feet away. The water, slowed slightly by the rise in the ground, was rolling steadily toward it.

Father Bryan started outside, but I grabbed his cassock.

"Stay here," I said. "It's too late now. You'll never make it."

I pulled him inside, then slammed and bolted the door. He

didn't argue. He knew as well as I that he would have drowned before he got anywhere near the church.

Later, Father Bryan was seriously criticized for not having saved the Blessed Sacrament from the church, but there was nothing he could possibly have done. The waters were moving so fast that he was helpless.

Now, we were all worried about John, the janitor. He was still in the church. I was sorry I hadn't insisted he come with me when I left there, but his experience with floods was greater than mine, and he seemed pretty sure that the dike would hold. If he remained in the church proper, he must certainly have been caught. Both Father Bryan and I prayed for him for some time. Later, he waved to us from the tower, and we knew he was all right.

The waters hit the side of the parish house like a tidal wave. We could hear them pounding with a roar, and, for a moment, we wondered if the house would stand up. Water was already streaming in, and we were ankle-deep before we realized what had happened.

Miss Ryan was already in the pantry, clearing the shelves of canned goods. All of us, including the Greenes, crowded in there to help her. Mrs. Greene remembered the refrigerator, and told her daughter to take as much as she could out of there.

Then, our arms loaded, we headed up the stairs.

"In the name of the Father, the Son, and the Holy Ghost—"
Miss Ryan was on her knees, starting her Rosary.

We all prayed with her.

"Our Father, Who art in Heaven—"
We could hear the water swishing around downstairs.

"Hail, Mary, full of grace. The Lord is with thee. Blessed art thou among women—"

When it was over, I started down the stairs again. The water had poured in at frightening speed at first, but now it was moving in more slowly. I had a long pole, and measured from the lowest step I could stand on without getting my feet wet.

The water on the first floor was five feet deep.

Back upstairs, Father Bryan had turned on the radio. We kept it on, listening for each new development, and wondering where all this was going to end.

All day, we alternately talked, prayed, listened and went downstairs to measure the water. John waved to us from the church tower in midafternoon. We were glad to see him, but he was there alone, without food or a radio, and too far away to talk to us.

By nightfall, the water was beyond the halfway mark on the first floor, and still rising. I went down to check, and when I returned, Father Bryan was saying his breviary. I joined him with exceptional fervor.

At midnight, with the water still rising around the parish house, Mr. Greene said, "We've got to do something. Father, why don't you call the radio station and tell them where we are? Maybe they can get help to us."

Luckily the phone was still working.

I called Station WHAS in Louisville. When the operator answered, I said, "I am a Catholic priest. There are seven of us, including two children and another priest, stranded at St. Augustine's parish house in Jeffersonville. Our janitor is trapped in the church tower near by. Can you send help?"

There was no answer.

I jiggled the receiver, but nothing happened.

I hung up, and turned to the others.

"Did they hear you?" Mrs. Greene asked.

I shrugged.

"The operator at the station answered," I said. "She must have heard something. I don't know how much."

For a moment, no one spoke.

Then: "*In the name of the Father, the Son, and the Holy Ghost—*"

We all prayed for a long time.

Then, over the radio, we heard the announcer say, "Attention, Jeffersonville! Two priests and five others, including two children, are stranded on the roof of St. Augustine's parish house on Locust Street. Anyone in a boat who can get over there, please go and take them off."

The message was repeated a few minutes later.

We didn't mind the slight inaccuracies. We weren't on the roof, but it didn't matter. Someone at the station had taken the trouble to look up the address before making the announcement. At least, some of our message had got through.

Later, another location where someone else was stranded was repeated over the radio, then another. Pretty soon, the announcer did practically nothing but give approximate locations of marooned parties not only in Louisville and Jeffersonville, but all over the area.

Everyone in town had picked up the idea that Mr. Greene had suggested to me. They were all calling the radio station for rescue boats.

We still had a long wait. We were up all night, praying and measuring the water. By morning, it covered the first floor completely and was lapping around our feet. Even the top step of the stairway was now below the surface.

We continued to pray.

By nine in the morning, the water had risen almost to the second floor of the parish house. Three hours later, it was even higher.

By this time, the electricity had gone off. We were now completely cut off from everything.

The rain, although still coming down, was lighter. It no longer pelted against the windows in huge drops. Instead, it had developed into a misty, steady drizzle. The visibility was so bad that we couldn't even see the church tower.

We were praying again, when suddenly I heard a voice. I was nearest the window, but could see nothing. I poked my head out.

"HALLOO! HALLOO!"

"Here!" I yelled. "This way!"

Everyone but Father Bryan crowded around the window, and began yelling. Pretty soon, we made out the outlines of a skiff, almost on a level with our eyes. There were six people in it.

"Thanks be to God!"

It was Miss Ryan. She was nearly hysterical.

The children climbed out the window and into the boat first. Then Mrs. Greene and Miss Ryan followed, then Mr. Greene.

I turned to Father Bryan.

"Go ahead, Father," I said.

"I'm not going."

"Not going? You've got to go! You'll drown if you stay here."

"I can go up on the roof if I have to," Father Bryan said. "But I'm going to stay here with my people."

"But your people are getting out."

"Not all of them," he said. "And if the water goes down, they're going to have to have a place to come to. I've got to stay here."

"Then I'll stay with you," I said. "I won't let you stay here alone."

"These people need you, Ralph. You go along with them."

"But what if the flood gets worse?"

"If it gets worse, I'll go," he said gently.

I climbed into the boat then. And the first person I saw was John, the janitor. He was smiling.

"They picked me up on the way," he said.

"Are you all right?"

He nodded.

"Sit down, Father!"

The voice was a gravelly, hoarse whisper, but there was authority in it. I sat down, then turned to look at the boatman who had spoken.

I couldn't believe my eyes.

He was a tiny man, hardly bigger than the Brother who kept locking me in my room at the Alexian Brothers Hospital in St. Louis. His face was weatherbeaten and deeply lined, and a pipe was sticking out of his tight mouth. His hands were gnarled and veiny, but they pulled the oars with a sure, strong stroke. The heavily laden boat glided easily along under his expert touch.

We moved rapidly toward downtown Jeffersonville, past islands of treetops and roofs. Here and there, we met other boats, some as loaded as ours, heading toward town, others comparatively empty.

In about twenty minutes or so, we arrived at American Legion Hall—or at least the second floor of the building, since the first was under water. There, crews of men were helping to unload other boats. We waited our turn, then climbed into an open window. I was the last one off our boat.

Before I left it, I said to the little oarsman, "There's another priest in the parish house where you picked us up. If the water keeps rising, will you go back for him?"

He nodded, but said nothing.

Later, I found out that Father Bryan had been taken off the roof of the parish house about twelve hours after we had been picked up.

American Legion Hall in Jeffersonville was only a transfer point. It happened to be the most spacious building in town that wasn't completely under water. One side faced our part of town and the other side faced the river. As fast as boats unloaded people into the Jeffersonville windows, other boats, operating from the opposite side, took them out and rowed them to the bridge so they could walk to dry land in Louisville. In the meantime, volunteers were serving coffee for people waiting their turn to get transportation to Louisville.

Since it was a cold, raw day I had on a wool shirt with a jacket over it. I was glad to have some coffee, although I wished it were something stronger. We had been marooned in the parish house about forty hours, although it seemed like weeks. I had had no sleep for two days, and my nerves were beginning to crawl.

I wanted a drink.

There was no place to get one.

Late that afternoon, I boarded another boat for the trip to Louisville. By this time, I had lost the others in the confusion at American Legion Hall. As far as I knew, they had long since been taken away from there.

Downtown Louisville was not under water—probably the only spot for miles that was dry. We ended up at the Tyler Hotel, on the corner of Main and Third streets in Louisville.

Seven of us were put into a room which evidently was normally used as a salesman's sample room. Coffee and sandwiches were available, and everyone was in good spirits. We were surrounded by water, and there was no way of knowing when we would get out of there, but nobody seemed to mind. For the moment, it was all something of a lark.

But it didn't remain a lark. It wasn't a lark when vandals began looting the downtown stores, and the U.S. Army, called in to keep order, was given instructions to shoot to kill. It wasn't a lark when smoking—even the lighting of matches—was declared illegal because of the fire hazard. It wasn't a lark when the waters stayed up at flood level for days. And it wasn't a lark when the food supply dwindled to a point where we stood in line every morning for the day's ration of bread.

As a priest, I was anxious to help try to ease the situation for others, but there was very little I could do. The army had charge of the city, and some of the volunteer organizations were trying to work out ways to help the thousands of refugees who had now poured into downtown Louisville. But while the water was so high that nothing but small boats could go in or out, there was little that anyone could do.

In the last three days that I was there, we all lived on bread and coffee, and only went through the motions of trying to sleep. I got an hour here and an hour there, but never put together more than three hours at a time. But I couldn't complain. Everyone else was in the same boat.

Nerves were frayed, but there was no panic. Sometimes, I had to try to answer questions for no other reason than that I was a priest, and the people around me knew it.

"How much longer, Father?"

"Not much."

"How much of this are we expected to stand?"

"It'll all be over soon."

I was talking off the cuff. I had no better idea than anyone else how much longer this would last. All I knew was that the water would have to go down sometime, and when it did the pressure would be off.

It happened quickly. The rain finally stopped about five days after I reached Louisville. The water began receding, but it was another two days before there was anything but boat traffic in and out of the city.

Finally, nine days after I was brought into town, I had a chance to get out. Buses had been operating to Cincinnati for a day or so, and now an indirect way to Indianapolis was open. I took the first bus I could get, and arrived home at about three o'clock on a Monday afternoon.

I went directly to the Chancery office to see the Bishop. He questioned me at great length, since I was the first priest who had been through the flood to reach Indianapolis. He told me that many of our parishioners from Jeffersonville had gone to an area of high ground north of town, and that they would probably have to stay there for some time. Jeffersonville was a mess of silt and debris, and it would be many weeks before the city was back to normal.

At the request of this group, the Bishop had sent a priest there to say Mass the previous Sunday. Now, he told me, "Go there as soon as you can, Ralph. They need a priest to say Mass on Sunday. Take up residence at St. Edward's Hospital in New Albany. You'll have to stay there until the parish house in Jeffersonville is ready."

The Bishop had not heard anything about Father Bryan, and couldn't tell me where he was.

After I left the Chancery, I got a room at a hotel. That night, I had my first highball in weeks. Then I went to bed and enjoyed my first full night's sleep since the flood.

The next day, I borrowed a car, and, just before leaving for New Albany, I bought a fifth of bourbon. Then I headed south.

When I arrived at the area north of Jeffersonville, almost the first person I saw was Father Bryan.

For a moment, I didn't recognize him.

His hair was snow white.

We greeted each other affectionately, then I stood back and asked, "Are you all right, Father?"

He smiled wanly.

"Yes—I'm all right."

He spoke slowly, groping for words.

"Have you been to a doctor?" I asked.

"I don't need a doctor, Ralph. I only found out yesterday that our people are here. We must set up a place to say Mass."

A Mr. Wathen, who lived in the dry area, offered his home.

Father Bryan took up residence there, and said Mass there on Sundays. We used it for some time. Because of the great amount of cleaning up to do around the flooded church property, both of us lived almost exclusively in work clothes. I kept the holy oils for anointing in the car.

It was fortunate that I did. One day, I was stopped on a back road by a man who said, "A man is dying and we must have a priest. Can you get one for me?"

"I'm a priest," I said.

We went to a near-by farmhouse. I anointed the dying man and heard his confession. He died with the Sacraments shortly after. I was under continual pressure, traveling around New Albany and Jeffersonville, doing what I could to help Father Bryan and living a makeshift life. I had a couple of drinks from the bottle I had brought from Indianapolis on my first day in New Albany, and I had at least two drinks every day thereafter. When I ran out of liquor, I drove twenty miles north to a package store to get more.

After a while, I increased to three, and sometimes four drinks a day. Occasionally, I would be driving along and, feeling the urge for a quick one, I would take a swallow right from the bottle and chase it with a Coke.

I never got drunk, but sometimes I felt jittery during the day. Then, to snap out of it, I had a glass of buttermilk, because someone told me it was good for your stomach if you felt you'd had too much to drink.

I didn't see much of Father Bryan. I had my own room at the hospital, and I could mix myself a highball there whenever I felt like it. No one was bothering me. I came and went as I pleased.

In late May, we got back into the parish house at Jeffersonville, but things were still far from normal. Father Bryan had aged terribly during those months. The flood had not only changed the color of his hair practically overnight but had taken something vital out of him. He was no longer the jolly, effervescent personality he had been before. He was still considerate and generous and kind, but now he rarely smiled, and he never cracked jokes as he had in the past.

He had no idea how much I was drinking. Except for an occasional glass of beer, he never drank himself. Now, he retired early, leaving me to myself during the evenings. Sometimes I would visit a friend and drink at his home; more often, I fixed myself a few highballs during the evening in the parish house. I would read, or listen to the radio, while nipping at my drink.

I had no feelings one way or the other about drinking alone any more. I simply took it as a matter of course that when I needed a drink, I should have it, whether there was someone to drink with or not.

I got into the habit of staying up very late, sometimes not retiring before midnight. This meant I would have a minimum of sleep, since we were always up at five-thirty for morning Mass.

Now it was early fall of 1937. Jeffersonville was still digging itself out of the flood debris, although the place was beginning to look natural at last. But nobody gave much thought to sports, so I didn't get together with the kids in the parish. Instead, I handled routine chores, taking as much as I could off the shoulders of Father Bryan.

And I kept on drinking. I was a little jittery every day, and averaging only a few hours of sleep a night, but I kept going on momentum. I wasn't aware of anything happening to my nerves. On the contrary, they seemed fairly steady.

I suspected that I might be drinking too much, but refused to admit it, even to myself. And I was very successful in keeping the knowledge that I was drinking from other people. My closest friends had no idea what was happening. When I was with others, I never had more than one or two. It was only after I left them that I would have any more.

CHAPTER 10

In early November, I was appointed pastor of St. Bernard's Church in Gibson County, Indiana. It was located, appropriately enough, in Snake Run. The appointment was to take effect on November 13.

I had never heard of Snake Run, but when I mentioned to another priest that I was going there, he told me he knew the place.

"What's it like?" I asked him.

"Oh, it's a place all right. Wait'll you see it."

"What kind of a place?"

"A corner."

"A corner?" I repeated.

He nodded.

"That's about it," he said.

"Far from here?"

"Maybe three hours."

"How about going over there with me tomorrow?" I suggested.

The next day was a bad time to go to Snake Run or anywhere else. It was dreary and dark and miserable. A misty drizzle turned the whole world into a gray screen.

We started out early, heading almost due west from Jeffersonville. We had been traveling something over two hours when we turned off the main highway onto a black-top road. Then, after we had gone three or four miles we turned again, this time into a gravel road that seemed to lead nowhere.

We bumped along for a mile or so before I finally said, "How much farther on this?"

"Four or five miles."

"All on gravel?"

"I'm afraid so, Ralph. You see, there isn't a smooth road within a radius of six miles in any direction from Snake Run."

It was still drizzling. I couldn't see much as we bumped along, but I knew we were going by one farm after another. Finally we came to a crossroads, with a house on one corner.

"Pull the car up to the side of the road," my friend said.

"What's the matter? Have we got a flat tire?"

"No. We're here. In Snake Run."

"This is Snake Run?" I said. "But there isn't anything here."

"Yes, there is. Look up the hill on the right there."

I could barely make out the outlines of a church. I turned up the hill, and when we got closer I could see that it was a typical country church, a white square building, with a spire in front. After we came to it, I saw that there was an ancient house beside it. It had once been white, but now was sadly in need of a coat of paint.

"Where's the parish?" I asked.

"All over the place. It extends for miles. Come on in and meet the pastor."

The pastor was only a little older than I, a tall, friendly farm boy who welcomed me with open arms when I told him who I was. He was delighted to show me around the place. I wasn't impressed. Having spent practically all of my life in cities and urban communities, this was hardly my cup of tea.

The parish house had no electricity, no heating system, no inside plumbing. There was a well near the side door and an outhouse near the back. I didn't know how to use one and shuddered at the thought of using the other.

"Why don't you have inside plumbing?" I asked.

"It's pretty expensive," the pastor said. "Besides, it's really not necessary."

"What do you do for light at night?"

"We have kerosene lamps."

"And heat?"

"There's a coal furnace," he said. "Now, let me show you the barn."

I hadn't noticed that there was a barn. It was in back of the house, but over near one corner. It was a nice barn, as barns go, but I didn't expect to see much of it. Besides, the pastor frightened me to death when he displayed his farm implements.

"You can raise just about anything you want here—corn, peas, beans, wheat, lettuce, cabbage—and you'll find that it pays," he said. "I keep what I need myself, and go into town every Saturday to sell the rest. This is a poor parish. The money comes in mighty handy. I don't know what I'd do without it."

I swallowed a couple of times. I didn't know a plow from a lawn mower. I couldn't raise an ear of corn if my life depended on it.

"What happens if I don't raise all this stuff?"

"You'll have to depend solely on pew rents and the annual picnic."

"Where's the nearest city?" I asked.

"Well, Fort Branch is six miles west of here, but I think you'll be too busy to go there much. Haubstadt is five miles further on. That's where I sell my vegetables. I think you ought to plan to farm, too, Father. You won't find it so hard, once you get used to it."

"Any towns any bigger?"

"Well," he said, "Evansville's the biggest. That's twenty-three miles southwest of here. And Princeton is twelve miles to the northwest. But you won't have any occasion to go to either place. I think you'll be too busy on the farm."

The pastor led me and my friend back to the house, then took us through it. One thing I wouldn't have to worry about—space. There was plenty of that.

We stayed about an hour and a half, then the pastor escorted us back to the car. I thanked him, and told him I'd take over the parish two Fridays later, if that was all right with him. We always took new assignments on Fridays, so that we could be settled in time for Sunday services.

"How big is the parish?" I asked, just before we drove off.

"About fifty families," the pastor replied. "Mostly German."

"That's good," I said. "I'm of German extraction myself."

He smiled, then said, "Don't worry, Father. You'll get along."

I wasn't so sure.

own Church But I felt better when I thought about it later. Snake Run was no bargain, but at least it was mine. I would be my own boss, do as I please, run the parish as I wanted. And, as far as I knew, I was the first member of my class at St. Meinrad to have a parish of his own. It was only eight years since my ordination.

I said my first Mass at St. Bernard's two Sundays later. Not long after that, we had a trustees' meeting in the parish house, so that I could get acquainted with the leaders of the parish.

We talked a while, then I said, "My most urgent need right now is an inside toilet. I can get one installed for twenty-one dollars."

"Twenty-one dollars?" repeated a farmer, with a strong German accent. "For a toilet? What's the matter with the toilet you got?"

"It's only an outhouse," I said, a little lamely.

"So—an outhouse you think is any more than we have?"

I changed the subject. Pretty soon I mentioned something about having to figure out a way to raise money.

"You have the farm," one of the men said. "You can make a living from that."

I shook my head.

"I'm afraid not," I said. "There's no sense in my even trying."

Some of the people were quite upset when I insisted that I couldn't keep the farm going. I told them I knew nothing about farming, and if I tried to learn I wouldn't have time for anything else.

"We'll find some other way to raise money," I said.

"Like what?" someone asked.

"We'll simply have to hold a bigger picnic," I said.

We talked for some time longer. After a while, I began to get some encouragement. Several of the trustees thought the picnic idea was a pretty good one. And, as we progressed, I was pleased to find that not all of them were unsympathetic to my problems.

The upshot of the meeting was that I was authorized to check further into the inside toilet situation, and make preliminary inquiries about getting electricity into the place. And, as I bade each trustee good-bye, each smiled and shook hands. Even the man who had first objected to the toilet said, "Excuse me, Father. I didn't realize that you come from the city. But twenty-one dollars for an inside toilet—"

He walked off, shaking his head.

I was pretty busy for the next six months. There was a question about piping water into the house because it might have been contaminated. I took a sample to Princeton, and it tested all right. I went to Evansville to see about getting electric wires run into the parish house. At first, they laughed at me, but finally agreed to look into it if I could get enough others in the area interested.

I got an astonishing amount of co-operation from the neighbors, both Catholic and non-Catholic. Most of them had never thought about having electricity. Now, when they realized that the more who took part, the less it would cost each, they were enthusiastic about the idea. I got the signatures of all but two families, and the electric company agreed to make the necessary installations.

We scheduled the picnic for early June. Things moved along smoothly enough, but, as the day approached, I worried more and more about the possibility of rain. Bad weather could ruin us. I was depending heavily on the proceeds from the affair.

One day, at a trustee meeting, I suggested we hire a tent.

"But a tent costs forty dollars, Father."

"It would be worth the investment," I said.

Several of the men whispered among themselves. Then one, with an air of finality, declared, "We can't afford a tent, and that's all there is to it."

I shrugged.

"All right," I said. "We'll get along without a tent. I just hope it doesn't rain, that's all."

"It won't rain," a trustee said. "It *never* does at our picnics."

I'm sure that he and the others who so violently opposed having a tent thought I prayed for rain from then on. I didn't, but I might as well have. On the day of the picnic, it poured.

We didn't make a dime. We were lucky to break even.

But later that summer, we had another picnic, and it was a howling success. This time we hired a tent. It was lucky we did, for it rained off and on all day. But everyone had a good time, and we made money.

busy = no drink

Between getting acquainted in the parish and arranging to get things done around the house, I had little time to drink when I first went to Snake Run. However, I didn't stop altogether, nor did I confine my drinking to sociable highballs with friends. I knew people in Evansville, but I couldn't go there often. Instead, I had one or two drinks every night before going to bed.

I was pretty well settled by April. My parishioners were hardy folk, very busy with their farms, and widely scattered. They attended Mass and came to confession regularly, but that about satisfied their spiritual needs.

They were glad to see me when I went to visit them, but they were just as glad to see me go. They retired early, and were not much on entertaining the parish priest or anyone else.

As far as they were concerned, it was enough that I was within reach in case they wanted me. They needed a priest, but simply didn't have any spare time to spend with him.

This left me with very little to do, and, after I got settled into a routine, an enormous amount of time to do it in.

Since the nearest place where I knew anyone well was Evansville, I began going down there a night or two a week. Soon I got into the habit of staying overnight with friends there from time to time.

Because the Snake Run parishioners were always very busy on their farms in the early hours of the morning, I said Mass at eight o'clock. But even that didn't attract many worshipers. Often, I said Mass by myself. I had no housekeeper and did all my own cleaning and cooking. After a while, I decided to skip saying Mass occasionally. When that happened, I was in no hurry to get back home if I spent a night in Evansville.

Then I started going farther away from Snake Run. Sometimes, I'd spend two or three days in Louisville, or wander up to Vincennes to see my old friend Lou. Once in a while, I would even go to Indianapolis to be with friends or members of the family. The longer I stayed at Snake Run, the less time I had for the parish there.

Gradually, and without realizing it, I was changing my drinking habits. Instead of two or three highballs at a time, I was taking bourbon straight, and chasing it with beer. Rather than see that this meant more drinking, I figured it meant less, because now I didn't drink every day. I'd go for several days, or even a week or more at a time without anything, then, after I was all dried out, I'd start in again.

I never had hangovers in the sense that most people have them. When the average person suffers a hangover, he doesn't want to look at alcohol. The very thought of a drink disgusts him. But after I had had a lot to drink—and sometimes even after I hadn't— I had the jitters so badly that I *needed* a drink.

I didn't know it at the time, but this is a prime characteristic of all alcoholics. They seldom have hangovers in the accepted sense of the word. They just get the shakes so badly that the only thing that relieves them is another drink.

The idea that I was becoming an alcoholic never crossed my mind. The reason was that, no matter how badly I wanted a drink, I never took one before noon. It was all right to drink alone. It wasn't all right to drink in the morning.

This obvious lack of logic made sense to me.

One night, shortly after the first church picnic, a friend from Evansville called and invited me to his house for dinner. As usual, I accepted.

"On the way down, Father," my friend said, "would you mind picking up Wally?"

"Not at all," I said.

I knew Wally well. He lived just outside Evansville, and I had to go right by his place in order to get into town. I reached his house at a little after five o'clock. We each had a couple of shots of bourbon, with beer chasers, then proceeded into town to our friend's house. There, we had several more drinks before dinner. Later, we kept right on going. By midnight, when it was time to go home, I had been drinking rather steadily for some hours.

Wally and I got our coats, said good-bye to our host and climbed into my car.

That was the last thing I remembered until ten o'clock the next morning when I woke up in my car on a macadam road twenty miles north of Snake Run.

I didn't remember dropping Wally off, or passing the turnoff to Snake Run, and I didn't have the faintest idea how long I had been sleeping in the car.

This never happened to me before. black-out

I turned the car around to drive back to the parish house. On the way I phoned Wally.

"How are you?" I asked.

"Fine," he said. "How are *you?*"

"I'm O.K. I was just wondering—did I seem all right when I left you last night?"

"I'd say you were in very good shape indeed, Father, particularly in view of the amount of liquor you drank."

"Well, did I act funny—or talk funny?"

"Not at all."

"And I—just dropped you off at your house without anything going wrong?" I said.

"Sure. Then you drove off. Don't you remember, Father?"

"Not really. That's why I called you."

"You looked all right to me," Wally said. "And you obviously didn't get into any trouble, so I wouldn't worry about it if I were you."

"Thanks. I won't."

And I didn't.

I'm all right. No question about it. If I weren't, I wouldn't have acted so natural with Wally.

The ten-hour blackout didn't bother me. I decided I was probably simply overtired from all the work in connection with the picnic.

I didn't think any more about it.

But I didn't have anything to drink for several days afterward.

I remained at Snake Run for another year. I got along fine with the parishioners, all of whom were finally reconciled to a city-bred pastor. As far as I knew, none of them suspected I was much of a drinker. When I visited at someone's house, I never was offered hard liquor. These were poor, hard-working people, and they had no money to spend on anything stronger than beer.

Actually, except when they came to Mass on Sundays and Holy Days and when I made First Friday calls, I didn't see much of them.

I slept pretty well every night and woke up in fairly good shape right up to the fall of 1938. I usually got to bed at about midnight, and was up around six-thirty. Then, after Mass and breakfast, I'd go about my few duties without any strain. When I was drinking, I'd have my first shot at about four in the afternoon, and keep on going until bedtime.

But then I began to notice increasing uneasiness when I got up in the morning. It started in September, but got worse as the autumn progressed.

One night, after I had had a great deal of bourbon to drink, I got into bed and woke up in the middle of the night in a cold sweat. I couldn't get back to sleep for a couple of hours and when I did, I only slept fitfully. When I finally had to get up, I was in a terrible stew.

Never in my life had I suffered so from the shakes. Every nerve in my body was screaming. My stomach was jumping and my head throbbing. My knees felt wobbly and there was a dull ache in my back. Even though it was a brisk October morning, I was sweating profusely.

I never felt this way before. I'm sick.

It had been months since I had taken the time for meditation, and I thought nothing of missing it again. But I wondered how in the world I could say Mass or my Office.

Somehow or other, I managed to do both.

I smoked half a dozen cigarettes before breakfast, then decided not to eat anything. Instead, I had a couple of cups of steaming black coffee and a few more cigarettes.

Neither did the slightest bit of good.

What's the matter with me? I'm so jittery I can't keep my hands still. I keep rubbing my face as if I need a shave.

I went over and studied myself in the mirror. Except for an occasional twitch and the fact that my eyes were slightly blood-

shot, my face seemed perfectly normal. I stepped back and sur-
veyed my body. Externally, everything appeared to be all right.

It's all inside.

I'm jumping like a kangaroo under the surface.

What's the matter with me?

I took a couple of aspirins, and lay down on the couch in the
living room of the parish house. I didn't stay there long. Instead
of making me relax, it tensed me up more than ever.

I've got to have something stronger.

I fixed myself some more coffee, had a bromide and a cigarette,
then went back and lay down again.

I still felt miserable.

I need a drink.

I walked into the kitchen, got out a tumbler and filled it half
full of bourbon. I sat at the kitchen table and looked at it for
several minutes, then turned and stared at the clock.

It was ten-thirty.

Too early for a drink.

I'll have to wait until noon.

I don't want to be an alcoholic.

I picked up the glass and put it on the kitchen cabinet under-
neath the clock. I could see them both at once that way. Then
I went into the living room and lay down again.

*An hour and a half. I can't have a drink for an hour and a
half.*

Otherwise, I'll be an alcoholic.

I lit a cigarette and took a few quick puffs. Then I put it out
and went back into the kitchen to get myself a bromide. I fixed
it with my back to the clock, only glancing at it as I walked
out of the room.

Ten-forty.

*This is terrible. I've got to stay out of the kitchen or I'll go
crazy.*

I managed to remain in the living room for quite a time. But
I needed a bromide, and I went out to get one. Before I was
through, I had two more bromides.

It was three minutes before twelve by the kitchen clock when
I took the last one.

Three minutes.

I went to the refrigerator and took out a bottle of beer, which I opened on the spot. Then I poured some into a glass and put it beside the bourbon on top of the kitchen cabinet.

Two minutes.

I walked into the living room, lit a cigarette, sat down, got up, looked out the window, puffed twice on the cigarette, pressed it hard into an ashtray and moved back to the kitchen.

It was one minute to twelve.

My mouth was bone dry. My tongue felt like raw leather and my throat was parched.

I took a quick look at the clock. It was exactly twelve.

Now!

I rushed to the cabinet, picked up the glass and drained it in three or four gulps, then took a quick swallow of beer. I stood still for a minute or so, turned and walked slowly into the living room and sat down on the couch.

My heart was pounding, but now my head was clearer, and my stomach had stopped jumping. And, in a few moments, I felt like my normal self. I was ready for a good day's work.

Now, I'm all right.

All I needed was that drink.

Wasn't it lucky I could wait until twelve o'clock for it?

Now I know I'm not an alcoholic.

Later in the day, when my nerves began to kick up slightly, I settled them with another shot, and, after dinner, I had several more. I went to bed feeling pretty well, and I slept very well.

A week or so later, the same thing happened. I woke up all nerves, wondering how I could possibly get through the morning without a drink. I wanted one terribly. I said Mass at eight o'clock—several people came to church that morning.

I couldn't wait for the people to leave. One or two wanted to talk to me after Mass. I listened to them and tried to act normally, but I couldn't tell whether or not they realized how jittery I was.

The moment the last of the parishioners was gone, I went to the kitchen to pour a drink. I placed it on the cabinet and stared at it for a long moment.

It's only nine o'clock.

I can't drink it now. I'll have to wait until noon.

How I got through those three hours I'll never know, but I did. I took several doses of ASA, a combination of aspirin, phenacetin and caffeine, made myself coffee and smoked incessantly. I never smoked a cigarette all the way down. I would light it, take three or four quick drags, then crush it out. And two minutes later, I would light another and do the same thing.

It was impossible for me to read or listen to the radio. All I could do was move restlessly from the couch in the living room to the cabinet in the kitchen and back, counting first the hours, then the minutes and finally the seconds.

denial

I went through a stretch of three days like that, drinking heavily at night, waking up with the shakes and fighting the morning battle with the clock until noon.

On the fourth morning, I woke up feeling worse than ever.

I want a drink.

But I can't keep going on like this. If I do, I'll get into trouble. Maybe I'd better not drink today.

I forced myself through the day without pouring a drink. The next morning, after a restless night, I felt a little better, and for a week or so after that I was all right.

But now I was on a sort of delayed treadmill. I could go for a week or ten days, but then I would visit someone in Evansville or decide I ought to have a drink while I was around the house, and there I'd be, back in the same groove again.

The next morning, I would drag myself through Mass and head right back to the house. If anyone came to church, I hoped he wouldn't want to talk to me about anything.

Yet, on the few occasions when anyone did want to see me, I always managed to handle the situation. The moment the bell rang, I put the glass of bourbon into the cabinet and walked slowly to the front door, taking long, deep drags of a cigarette as I walked. It really didn't help much. I still jumped all over the place inside, but at least I exhibited outward signs of composure.

As soon as my visitor left, I hurried to the kitchen to put the bourbon back on top of the cabinet where I could look at it.

The only good thing about these visits was that they helped to pass the time. When I was alone, the minutes dragged by; when someone was with me, my mind was off the clock.

The months went by, with the dry stretches fewer and fewer. I was going through a fifth of bourbon and smoking nearly three packs of cigarettes two days out of every three, yet not once was I theologically drunk. (Theological drunkenness is defined as willful drinking to the point where loss of the use of reason takes place.) Occasionally, I suffered a blackout, but never one like the night I was with Wally. I simply would lose an hour here and there. I didn't give this much thought.

The thing was to keep relaxed.

I lived this way until the summer of 1939, sometimes going for a week without a drink but always returning to an alcoholic, bromidic routine. I never drank in public places and I never drank before noon, no matter what it cost me in nervous exhaustion.

One morning in June, I woke up with an unusual taste in my mouth. I had not been drinking the night before, and I didn't have the jitters. When I went to brush my teeth, I saw that my gums were bleeding profusely. I took a mouthwash, rinsing well, but it gave me little relief. My gums, now a deep, dark red, continued to bleed all day.

That afternoon, I decided that a drink would probably kill whatever the germ was, so I had one. This, of course, was followed by another, and pretty soon I had finished a fifth. I went to bed, and woke up the next morning terribly nervous.

And when I got up, I saw there was blood on the pillow.

I went over to Princeton to see a doctor that morning. He gave me a strong mouthwash, and told me not to worry about it.

But I did worry. I worried enough so that I could hardly wait for twelve o'clock, when I could have a drink. And I kept worrying like that for ten days.

I drank every afternoon and evening, and took bromides every morning. And my gums kept right on bleeding.

Finally, I went to Indianapolis, and saw my doctor there.

"You've got Vincent's angina," he said.

"What's that?"

"Trench mouth. How long has it been this way?"

"About ten days."

"That's a long time, Father," he said. "This thing has become pretty serious. I'm going to put you into the hospital, so we can treat it properly."

So I went back to St. Vincent's Hospital. By this time, I was too scared to want a drink. I had lost a lot of blood, and the doctor was obviously concerned.

In those days, before penicillin was discovered, an advanced case of trench mouth was not easy to get rid of. The doctor tried giving me a powder first, but that didn't work. Then he began giving me shots. At first, that didn't work either, but then, after a couple of days, my mouth started to improve.

After one week in St. Vincent's, I was ready for discharge. I got dressed, and was just about to leave when the nurse brought in a special delivery letter. It was from the Bishop.

Here, in effect, is what it said:

"You are hereby relieved of your parochial appointment to St. Bernard's, Gibson County. At the discretion of the doctor, you are to report at the first opportunity to Father Ambrose J. Sullivan, pastor of Holy Rosary Church in Indianapolis, who will assign you to your duties as his assistant."

Setback

CHAPTER 11

I WAS FLABBERGASTED.

He's taken my parish away.

Why?

What have I done to lose my parish?

With tears of frustration and resentment in my eyes, I went right from the hospital to the Chancery office. All the way over, I rehearsed what I would say to him.

You can't do this to me. I've been a good priest. Why should this happen to me? You know me. You helped me when I was in trouble. Why do you hurt me now?

The Bishop received me as soon as I arrived. After I had greeted him, I blurted, "Why did you make this appointment?"

"I have reports that you have been visiting taverns," he said.

"I've never been in a tavern in my life," I replied belligerently.

"I've heard otherwise," he said.

"Well, you've been misinformed."

The Bishop stood up.

"This is your appointment, Ralph," he said quietly. "And that's all there is to it."

I was crushed.

There was nothing to do but mumble an apology and leave.

Now I've done it. He's found out about the drinking.

But he accused me of going into taverns. Where did he get that idea? I told him the truth. I've never been near a tavern.

He took my parish away because he thinks I've been drinking in taverns. I haven't been drinking in taverns. Therefore, he shouldn't have deprived me of my parish.

All right. I've taken a little drink here and there. Maybe once in a while, I had a bit too much. But I never neglected my parish duties. I said Mass regularly. I visited the people in their homes and welcomed them in mine whenever they wanted to see me.

I did everything a parish priest should do.

And now I'm being punished for something I didn't do.

Where in the world did the Bishop get the idea that I ever went into taverns in the first place? On account of the trench mouth?

It couldn't be that.

Someone must have told him.

Who?

I returned to St. Vincent's where I spent a miserable night alternating between resenting everybody I thought had ever done anything to hurt me and reproaching myself for throwing away another opportunity.

I'm no good.

I had my own parish and I lost it.

The Bishop was right in taking it away from me. I didn't carry out my duties. I wasn't sympathetic to the parishioners. They were farmers, and wanted me to become one. I wouldn't even try. If I had, I might have understood their problems better. All I thought about was my own comfort.

And I neglected my prayers. If I hadn't I wouldn't be in this mess.

That is the way it always is with me.

I should never have become a priest.

All night long, I rode my carousel of misery, reviewing my life in the same old way, and finding myself wanting at every turn.

I was right back where I started from in those ghastly days before the diaconate; right back where I left off in the Alexian Brothers Hospital in St. Louis.

I awoke the next morning, shaking and miserable and wanting a drink—but not daring to take one.

After a while, I decided to see Father Sullivan at Holy Rosary.

He was a nice fellow, and I knew I would get along with him, but I wasn't ready to start working yet.

"I'm glad to see you, Ralph," he said. "And I'll be delighted to have you with me."

"I've had quite a time, Father," I said.

"I know. But it's all over. You can start fresh here. You'll have a nice home in nice surroundings, and you'll like the people in the parish."

"Do you really think I can be useful here?" I asked.

"Indeed I do," said Father Sullivan.

"Have you talked to the Bishop about me?"

He nodded.

"Don't you worry," he said. "Everything will be all right."

"Thank you, Father," I said. "Now, I want to stay longer at the hospital. I don't feel quite right. The trench mouth isn't completely cured and I'm awfully nervous. I need medical care."

He patted my arm.

"Go ahead," he said. "And don't think about coming to work until you're ready. This opening will be here for you whenever you want it."

I thanked him again, and left. Then I went back to St. Vincent's Hospital, for a talk with the doctor.

"My mouth is better," I said, "but I'm not myself yet. What's the matter with me, Doctor?"

"You've been under a heavy nervous strain."

"Terrible. I can't sleep, and I'm shaky all the time."

"Well," he said, "I don't think you should go back to work yet. You need a rest. I suggest you go to the Sacred Heart Sanitarium in Milwaukee."

"That's all right with me," I said, "but will the Bishop let me go?"

"I'll call him and see."

The Bishop was perfectly willing for me to go to Milwaukee, and I took the train the next day, leaving my car at home. I found a window seat, and stared, unseeing, at the Indiana countryside as we sped toward Chicago.

I missed—I missed—I missed—

I always miss.

The wheels of the train clicked.

I missed—I missed—I missed—

Thoughts of suicide crept across my confused brain. I wanted to get up and walk back through the train until I got to the end, and then just keep on walking. It seemed so simple—such an easy way to finish everything.

They would say it was an accident.

But I can't. I'm a priest. Only God can give or take life.

Why am I such a failure?

Why?

I leaned my head back and closed my eyes, and the wheels clicked on.

Where am I going?

Milwaukee.

Milwaukee?

Click—click—click—

St. Louis.

Click—click—click—

That's it. St. Louis. I'm going to St. Louis, not Milwaukee.

Click—click—click—

Listen, Ralph—listen to Jerry and his friend. They're in the front seat, talking about you.

They're taking you to St. Louis—to the Alexian Brothers Hospital.

Click—click—click—

You're crazy, Ralph. They're taking you to the crazy house.

Crazy—crazy—crazy—

What's the use, Ralph?

Give up.

You're beaten.

Give up—give up—give up—

Click—click—click—

I had to change trains in Chicago. I picked up my valise and walked out of the station in a daze. I suppose I took a cab to the Northwestern Station—to this day, I don't remember how I got there. I stepped aboard the Milwaukee train, slumped into a seat, leaned my head back and closed my eyes.

No more.

I don't ever want to think any more.

But my mind raced faster than the train.

By the time I arrived in Milwaukee, I was limp from nervous exhaustion. I could hardly make it from the train to a taxicab.

"Sacred Heart Sanitarium," I told the driver. "Do you know the place?"

"Yes, Father. It's on South Twenty-seventh Street."

"Take me there—quickly, please."

I had only been in Milwaukee once before, but I had no curiosity about the place at the time. All I wanted to do was to get to where I was going so I wouldn't have to think any more.

They've got to give me something—something that will knock me out—something that will make me forget everything.

I wonder if I'm going crazy. doubts life

I felt a little better when I saw the Sacred Heart grounds. They were green and spacious and sweet-smelling. It was a warm summer day, and here everything looked cool and peaceful.

I breathed deep, and my head felt clearer as the taxi driver rolled up to the main entrance. After he let me off, I stood there for a moment, looking back over the lovely landscape.

Then I turned and walked into the building.

My doctor in Indianapolis had given me a letter for the doctor in charge at Sacred Heart. I took it from my pocket and handed it to the Sister at the Information desk. Then I sat down and waited.

The Sister returned in fifteen or twenty minutes, and I followed her into an office. She introduced me to a tall, bald-headed man, impeccably dressed and very severe-looking. He told me to sit down, then glanced at the letter from my doctor as it lay on his desk.

After a few preliminaries, he asked, "Is the trench mouth condition still giving you trouble?"

"Some," I said. "It isn't quite cleared up yet."

"We'll see that it's taken care of. Now, tell me, Father, have you been subject to nervous ailments of any kind in the past?"

"Yes. I've had trouble off and on for years."

Then I told him the whole story, a story I knew so well that I didn't even have to dredge my memory to make it come back.

It was all there on the surface, an ever-longer recital of fear complexes and frustrations, of failures and resentments. And now there was more—much more than I had told the last time—the trip to St. Louis, the year at Fordham, the strain of the flood in Jeffersonville, the unfamiliar living conditions in Snake Run, the demotion from my own parish to assistant pastor.

I told him everything—or, at least, practically everything.

I left out the part about drinking. I didn't think it was important.

deny problem

And when I had finished my dreary report, he asked, "Do you drink very much, Father?"

I shook my head vigorously.

"Oh, no," I said. "I don't drink much at all."

He looked out the window.

"I can't understand it," he mused, half to himself.

Then he said, "You got into all this trouble—you're still in it—and you don't drink very much. There must be something wrong with you mentally, Father. I think you're a manic depressive."

I didn't know what a manic depressive was, and I was afraid to ask. I simply sat and said nothing.

The doctor leaned back in his chair, and tapped his teeth with a pencil. His fingernails, newly manicured, glistened as a ray of sunlight caught them.

"Personally," he said, "I think you're hopeless. Everything points in that direction. But you have a good family background. From that, I suppose, we must assume that there might be a slight chance for you."

He stood up.

"Sister will show you to your room," he said. "We'll assign you to your routine in the morning."

Hopeless.

Just as I expected.

The doctor said so.

Then why do they bother with me?

But I felt a little better when I saw my room. It was large and airy and bright, well furnished and facing the cool, green grounds. When I looked out one of the windows, I saw a building on top of a hill which seemed to be within the same orbit as the sanitarium. I asked the nun what it was.

"That's St. Mary's, Father. It's our mental hospital."

"Isn't this a mental hospital?"

"No. This is a general hospital, with an emphasis on nervous disorders."

"Are you going to lock me in?"

She smiled.

"I hardly think that will be necessary."

Then she said, "Now, Father, make yourself comfortable. You had better get into bed. The nurse will be here in a little while to give you something that will make you sleep."

"Will someone wake me so I can say Mass in the morning?"

She nodded.

Later, I asked the nurse about saying Mass.

"You don't say Mass, Father," she said. "Doctor's orders."

"Oh."

The nurse patted me on the shoulder.

"Later, it will be all right," she said softly. "But not now."

Then she gave me a sedative, told me to ring if I needed anything and left.

I was awakened at seven o'clock the next morning after a restless night which found me ringing for more sedatives twice when I couldn't get to sleep. I got dressed and went to breakfast in a bright, spotless dining room in one corner of the building. There were six other priests sitting around when I got there. I murmured my name, and sat between two of them.

They were in a general discussion about sports, but I didn't join in. I was too busy with my own thoughts, wondering where I was going and how everything would end up. All I remember is that I ate a hearty breakfast. The food was excellent.

Later, I was directed to Doctor H. H. Blanchard's office. He was a smiling little Frenchman, with a dark moustache and jet-black hair. He invited me to sit down, and we talked easily for several minutes.

"Now, what seems to be the trouble, Father?" he asked kindly.

"Everything, I guess. Do you want the whole story?"

"Yes."

After I had finished almost exactly the same recital I had told the other doctor, he said, "That's everything, Father?"

I nodded.

"You haven't left anything out?"

"One thing," I said. "The doctor told me last night I was a manic depressive and that my case was hopeless. And I agree with him. I am hopeless."

Dr. Blanchard shook his head.

"You're not hopeless," he said. "Nobody's hopeless."

"Do you think I'm a manic depressive?"

I still didn't know what it was.

"The doctor in charge mentioned something about it," Dr. Blanchard said. "However, I wouldn't worry about it. There's only one thing to do now. Stay where you are, and do as we tell you."

Then he gave me my daily therapeutic routine. It consisted basically of daily conferences with him, massages and Wickel baths.

"You're to stay in the building for the time being," he said. "Later, you'll be permitted to walk around the grounds, and even outside, with permission. This is a sanitarium, not an asylum. Nobody here is committed, and anyone can leave when he pleases."

I didn't have the remotest idea what a Wickel bath was, but I found out the next morning. I was told to report to the dressing rooms in the basement. When I got there, I was ushered into a small room by an attendant, who said, "When you have removed all your clothes, go into the next room and sit down on the stool there."

"Naked?" I asked.

"Yes," he said. "Naked."

I stripped, and padded into the next room in my bare feet. I found myself in a sort of alcove, with walls that did not reach to the ceiling. I could hear voices all around me, where others were evidently getting the same treatment in similar alcoves. The only furniture in the room was a white stool and a low cot. I sat on the stool and waited.

Pretty soon, the attendant came in with a damp sheet under

one arm and a wool blanket under the other. He nodded to me, then rapidly spread the sheet on the cot.

"All right, Father," he said. "Lie down."

I got off the stool and went over to the cot. Somewhat gingerly, because I knew the sheet was wet, I started to sit down. But the minute my skin touched the cot, I shot right up again.

The sheet was ice cold.

The attendant snickered. I looked painfully at him. I didn't see anything funny.

"Sorry, Father," he said, "I should have told you. This isn't easy the first time you do it. But just lie flat on your back on that sheet. Hurry now. We don't want it to get warm before you get on it."

I threw myself on the cot, and lay shivering. Rapidly, the attendant drew the sides of the wet sheet around my body, then pulled the bottom up and tucked the top snugly around my neck. Then, with no wasted motion, he threw the blanket around me, tucking it in close so that every square inch of the sheet was covered.

In a moment or two, the cold shock turned to a comfortable warmth, and I began to feel quite relaxed. The attendant asked, "Feel better?"

"Much," I murmured.

"Good. Don't move. I'll be back."

I had no intention of moving, and, in fact, was quite willing to stay there indefinitely. I didn't fall asleep, but I came very close. I felt at peace with the world for the first time in months. Even my mind was a blank.

Later that morning, the same attendant gave me a Swedish massage, and that time I did fall asleep. I had another that afternoon.

After a few weeks, I felt a little better, but I still had trouble sleeping at night. I went to Dr. Blanchard's office every morning after breakfast, and he greeted me with a cheery "Good morning, Father. How are you doing?"

And every morning, I replied, "Not so good," and I would tell him how my fears and worries kept me from going to sleep.

But one morning, after I replied to his "How are you doing?"

with a routine "I feel terrible. I didn't sleep," Dr. Blanchard said sharply, "I didn't ask you how you felt. I asked you how you were doing."

"What's the difference?" I asked.

"There's a big difference. You can feel terrible and still go about your daily chores. People work day after day with a splitting headache or a jarring backache, even though there's nothing seriously wrong with them. These people are *feeling* rotten, but they're *doing* fine."

We discussed that idea for quite a while. And, from time to time, we discussed it in some detail in later sessions.

One day, the doctor said, "Father, I think you're doing well."

"I don't," I said. "I still can't sleep."

"What's the matter? Don't you like it here?"

"Well, I'm not getting any better," I said.

"I didn't ask you that."

"All right, Doctor. I don't like it here. Is that what you want me to say?"

"What's the matter? Are you afraid of something?"

I looked at him a moment, then said slowly, "Yes, Doctor. I'm afraid. I'm afraid I'm hopeless. I'm afraid I'll never get out of here."

He walked over to the bookcase and picked up a Bible. He came back to where I was sitting, opening it as he walked.

"You know," he said, "I'm not a Catholic, but this is a universal language that we can all understand. Listen, Father—"

Then, from the Psalms, he read: ". . . though I shall walk in the valley of the shadow of death, I will fear no evil, for Thou art with me. . . ."

He stopped.

"What do you think of that, Father?"

"Sure," I said. "I know. But the other doctor said I was hopeless. I've tried a hundred times, and it always comes out the same way. I end up a nervous wreck and have to come to places like this. It always happens this way."

"You're not hopeless, Father, and there's nothing to be afraid of. You're making much more sense now than you did when you first came in here."

I didn't say anything for a minute.

Then: "Doctor—"

I hesitated.

"Yes?"

"Do you think I'm an alcoholic?"

"What makes you ask?"

"Well," I said, "there was alcoholism in my family. I've always been scared to death that I might be an alcoholic."

"Do you drink much?"

I shook my head.

"Just once in a while," I said.

"Then don't worry. You'll never be an alcoholic if you don't drink much, Father."

I felt quite relieved.

Dr. Blanchard says I'm not an alcoholic.

So why should I worry about it?

And, for some time, I didn't.

After a while, except for the daily therapy and the fact that I was living in the sanitarium, I was doing much as I would have done anywhere else. The doctor permitted me to say Mass again, and my life settled into a routine that was much like normal.

Now, it was November, and I was really anxious to get away from there. I didn't want to be in a place like that for the holidays. Thanksgiving and Christmas were approaching. Everything seemed to be very much under control.

"I'm all right, Doctor," I said, one morning. "I want to get out of here."

"Are you sure you're ready, Father?"

"Well, I'm doing everything I'd be doing at home, so I might as well *be* home. I'm saying Mass every day, and I never miss my spiritual obligations or my meditation, and I'm coming and going practically as freely as I would if I were living in a hotel. I don't see why I can't go back to Indianapolis. I can do everything there that I'm doing here."

"Can you?"

"Can't I?" I said, a little testily.

The doctor looked out the window, and my eyes followed his for a moment. The spacious grounds looked as beautiful in early winter as in summer. There was a thin blanket of snow, and everything green had turned to white.

I looked back at the doctor. He finally turned away from the window, and our eyes met.

Then he said, "Father, you *can*, but you *won't*."

"So you aren't ready to let me go?"

"We'll see."

I nagged him every day for a week after that. I guess I wore him down, because one day he said, "All right, Father. You say you're ready and you seem to be living a pretty well-ordered life. If you want to go home, go ahead. But watch your step. You've been a sick man, and you don't want to get sick again."

I thanked him, and went back to my room to pack. Before I had gone through the process of checking out, a nurse came in with a small box of pills.

"Doctor says you should take one of these a night to help you sleep," she said. "You can renew the prescription twice. By then you won't need any more."

CHAPTER 12

I GOT to Indianapolis that night, and reported to Father Sullivan at Holy Rosary. He greeted me with warm cordiality.

"Welcome home, Ralph," he said. "You look fine. How do you feel?"

"Very good, Father," I said. "And I'm ready to go to work."

"Fine. There's a lot to do. I've got several ideas for you. Take what you think you can handle."

The Little Sisters of the Poor had only recently been placed under the jurisdiction of the Holy Rosary parish. These are the nuns who take care of elderly people. They were in need of a chaplain, and Father Sullivan asked me if I'd take it. I accepted because I thought it would give me a chance to re-identify myself with the spiritual life, and get readjusted in general. It meant going over to the Little Sisters', to say Mass at six o'clock every morning, which was important, since this would help me discipline myself. I walked the mile and a half between the parish house and the Little Sisters' every day.

Father Sullivan also asked if I would like to run part of the parish entertainment program, including various money-raising projects. This was the type of work I liked, and I was pretty good at it. Between that, my job with the Little Sisters of the Poor and routine parish duties, I had my hands full.

I plunged back into a stiff schedule, which kept me on the move a good part of the time. Father Sullivan was an easygoing, trusting man, and I got along as well with him as I had with Father Bryan at Jeffersonville.

Except for the first couple of months while I was working myself off drugs and bromides—I used some of the latter after I had finished the prescription renewals from the sanitarium—I slept pretty well. Even at best, I was never a heavy sleeper, but I got into about a six-hour-a-night routine, which was perfectly all right for me.

One evening, shortly after I returned to Indianapolis, while Father Sullivan and I were sitting in the parish house, I asked him, "Did the Bishop ever indicate the reason why he sent me here?"

"None in particular. He knew you weren't feeling well, and he thought you'd be better off here with me than alone down in Snake Run. And I'm delighted to have you."

"Well, Father," I said, "did you know he accused me of running around in taverns?"

"I heard something about it," said Father Sullivan, "but it's all over now."

"I don't have the slightest idea where I picked up that trench mouth," I said. "But I just want you to know that the Bishop was misinformed. I've never been in a tavern in my life."

"It's all right, Ralph."

We said no more about it. But from then on, regardless of what happened, Father Sullivan always stoutly defended me whenever I was accused of having done anything out of line.

I worked hard, and didn't even take a glass of beer for about ten months. I was in good physical condition, sleeping and eating well, happy in my job and enjoying a close personal relationship with my immediate superior. Things were going so smoothly that I forgot about my own problems, and tried to help others solve theirs. Nothing mattered except my duties, to which I attended with conscientious devotion.

Liquor didn't interest me. I didn't even think about the possibility of my being an alcoholic. I figured I didn't have to. I could take my liquor or leave it alone.

Which was why, when I dropped by at a friend's house and he offered me a drink one night late in 1940, I said, "Sure. Why not?" And, while we sat and talked, I slowly sipped a bourbon highball. When I had finished it, I got up, thanked my host and went back to the parish house.

That drink meant nothing to me. I didn't want a second, and I didn't worry because I had broken a dry spell of nearly a year. And I didn't have another drink for several days. Then, it was under almost exactly the same circumstances, except at another friend's house. I was offered a highball, and I took it.

At just about this time, with the holiday season approaching, we became very busy in the parish house. We had a small printing press, which we used for announcements of various church functions. Since this was my department, I always handled the job myself. It was long-drawn-out and tedious because, after we'd printed about two thousand announcements, we had to put them into envelopes and mail them all out.

I always worked on the press on Mondays and Thursdays, and I always worked alone. One Monday afternoon, a week or so after I had started drinking a little again, I was vaguely uneasy as I worked with the announcements. My nerves weren't exactly jumping, but I had a touch of the jitters. I didn't quite know what was wrong, but I knew what I needed to cure the condition.

A little drink won't do any harm, and it will relax me.

There was no liquor in the house, so I put on a hat and coat and walked down to the corner drugstore. There, I bought a half-pint of bourbon, as small a quantity of liquor as you can get in a bottle in Indiana. I took it back to the house, fixed myself a highball, then put the little bottle in my room.

That one highball lasted me all afternoon. I timed it perfectly. Just as I finished getting the last of the announcements into an envelope, I drained the glass. I took it back to the kitchen, rinsed it out and put it in its place on a pantry shelf.

The next morning, which was Tuesday, I skipped my meditation. But I resumed it on Wednesday and Thursday. On Thursday afternoon, I was back at the printing press again.

The same thing happened. Halfway through the afternoon, I felt a little jittery. I stopped working long enough to get myself a drink. And, when I went back to the job, I sipped as I worked.

I remember thinking to myself, "I must get more liquor. This isn't going to last very long."

I skipped meditation on Friday morning. And, that night, I visited a friend, and had two drinks with him.

I had trouble getting to sleep after I went to bed, so I took a bromide. It put me to sleep very nicely. And the next morning, when I woke up, I was only a little nervous.

The pattern was forming, but I still maintained good control of the situation. The big difference was that now I didn't stop after one drink at someone's home, because I always wanted a second. But I rarely took it on the spot. I usually waited until I returned to the parish house, and then fixed myself a drink just before going to bed.

Another priest came to live with us in January of 1941. A few days after he arrived, Father Sullivan came over to me and said, "The chaplaincy of the Little Sisters of the Poor would be perfectly fitted to our new priest. Don't you think it would be a good idea for you to give it to him?"

I had no objections, so the other priest assumed that job. Now, for the first time in a year or so, I didn't have to get up at five in the morning, and take that mile and a half walk. In fact, I suddenly seemed to have much time on my hands.

Not long before I turned the chaplaincy of the Little Sisters over to the other priest, I happened to be reading something in the newspaper about the John Herron School of Art in Indianapolis, a very well-known school in its field. I had always been mildly interested in art. Once, while at Fordham, I even got a brush and an easel in a hobby shop, but, after fooling around a few days, I dropped it.

Now, I wanted something to do. At the O'Neals' one night, I mentioned the idea of going to art school, and Jack thought it made sense. He was well aware of all my problems, and he agreed that it would provide me with badly needed diversion.

So I decided to enroll at the school. I took up oil painting, charcoal sketching, commercial drawing and sculpture. I was the oldest one in class; in fact, most of the other students were only recently out of high school. The instructor assumed that everyone had a basic understanding of the fundamentals of painting, so I had to plunge in from the middle.

Another student showed me how to set up my easel and tack on my canvas, and I started working on still-life drawings. I painted mostly vases and flowers. Every once in a while, the instructor came around, pointed out what I was doing wrong and showed me how to correct it. Then I was expected to start over again. At the end of every month, he took the best drawings and paintings from all the classes and put them on the wall to show.

For about three months, I worked hard with brushes and easel, going to school four days a week. I improved so much that I had a painting selected for display the second month I was there. In the meantime, I didn't neglect my parish duties.

When I began to attend art school, I stopped drinking altogether. This seemed to take the place of liquor. I still had part of a bottle—a fifth this time—in my room, but I didn't touch it. When I went out in the evening, I satisfied myself with a Coke while others had highballs.

Father Sullivan was aware of my painting activities, but he said nothing about them. He went his way and I went mine. We sat around with the other priest on evenings when we all happened to be home at once. The talk was always general, for Father Sullivan was too trusting to quiz either of us on what we were doing.

Then one day, the Bishop sent for me. He asked if it was true that I was attending art school. When I told him it was, he said, "Someone phoned here and said he didn't think art school was any place for a priest to be seen. I would rather you stopped going there, Ralph."

"I don't see what harm it does," I said.

"I'd just as soon you forgot it," he insisted. "Anyhow, at your age, I don't see how you can possibly accomplish anything. You couldn't have any talent."

"Oh, I don't know about that," I said. "The instructor seems to think I have."

I said no more, but that night I had a couple of drinks while I was mulling the situation over in my mind. I wanted to continue at art school, and I saw no reason why, because some busybody had called the Bishop's attention to my going there, I'd have to stop.

He says I don't have any talent.

Well, I'll show him. I'll let him see some of my work.

The next day, I put three or four of my best paintings into the car and took them over to the Chancery office. When the Bishop called me in, I had them under my arm.

"I thought you'd like to see some of my work," I said. "Just to decide for yourself if I'm getting anywhere or wasting my time."

I held them up, one by one, for the Bishop to see. He looked at each a moment, and when I had finished, he said, "Not bad, Ralph. You seem to have a talent, at that. Maybe you'd better keep going. If you'd like to continue, it's all right with me. But I don't want you to go so often that your parish duties suffer. You can enroll for a couple of hours a week."

I went home and had a drink. Then I had another.

So I can enroll for a couple of hours a week. Now, that's fine— real big of the Bishop.

A couple of hours a week! How much does he think I can get done in a couple of hours a week?

I poured myself another highball just before going to bed. And, after I had finished it, I took a bromide and retired.

Why bother?

I'll show the Bishop.

I won't go to art school at all.

And I didn't.

But now I began drinking steadily again. At first, I'd have a couple of highballs in the afternoon, then two or three more at night. But that didn't relax me enough, so I started drinking bourbon straight, with beer for chasers.

I did most of my drinking outside the parish house. I didn't want either Father Sullivan or my other associate to see what was happening. However, I did drink in my room late at night, when I was alone.

One day, Father Sullivan said, "Ralph, I heard something today that bothered me, but I just can't believe it's true."

"What's that, Father?"

"Someone told me—now, understand, I don't necessarily believe this, but I want to hear right from you that there's nothing to it—that you've been drinking a great deal lately."

"Nothing to it, Father," I said quickly.

"So I thought," he said. "You know, I told this person he is wrong, but he insisted. Even said you were an alcoholic."

I bristled.

"That's absurd," I said. "Someone's trying to hurt me."

"I'm afraid so, Ralph. *I* know you're all right. I just wanted you to know what I heard."

"Thanks, Father."

I cut down considerably after that, although I didn't stop drinking altogether. I was scared. I didn't mind what Father Sullivan heard, but I didn't want any more word about me to get to the Bishop.

I took a vacation in June—my first real one since entering the priesthood. I went with a group of friends, all laymen, to northern Minnesota, where they had rented a hunting lodge for two weeks. We went in two cars, one of which was mine.

I lasted two days, then left them to their own devices.

The reason was because everyone was drinking too much.

Ridiculous as this may sound, it was quite true. They all got drunk the two nights I was with them. I wanted to stay with them, but had no use for people who couldn't handle their liquor.

So I said good-bye to them, and went to another camp in Wisconsin, where I could rent a cottage for a few days and eat in a common dining hall. I wore a sport shirt when I checked into the place, and registered simply as "Ralph Pfau." No one there knew I was a priest. I hired a boat and fishing equipment and got settled.

"Getting settled" included the purchase of half a dozen fifths of bourbon and a small case of beer. There was a refrigerator in the cottage, and I was very comfortable.

Here began a curious combination of drinking and healthy outdoor recreation which, I thought, just about canceled each other out. I got up jittery every morning, and went right out in the boat without bothering with breakfast. I took my fishing stuff, a bottle of bromides, a thermos of water and a watch. I rowed some distance out on the lake, baited my hook, threw my line out and started fishing. When I got really nervous, I took a bromide. I worked my way in toward shore, keeping one eye on the water and the other on my watch, and always managed to arrive on the beach at about five minutes before twelve. Then, I went right to the cottage, got out the whiskey and the beer and, by that time, it was after noon and I could drink to my heart's content.

I ate neither breakfast nor lunch, but had a big dinner at night, which probably saved my life, for it was the only food I took all day. After dinner, I returned to the cottage to listen to the radio and drink until midnight.

I did that for five nights. Then I returned to Indianapolis.

Back at home, I cut down on my drinking again. Now, I was back on a social basis, drinking with friends, averaging perhaps two highballs a night. I continued to do this through the fall of 1941. In late November, I started drinking while working with the printing press, but only on the same basis as I had before. I would fix a highball in the middle of the afternoon, and time my drinking so that I finished it at just about the moment I was through with my work.

On December 7, I was with friends when the news of the Japanese attack on Pearl Harbor came through. We talked all afternoon about the outbreak of the war and, of course, we had to have a bit of sustenance to carry us through this trying day. I got back to the parish house at about eleven o'clock that night, neither drunk nor showing that I had been drinking.

"This is war, Ralph," Father Sullivan said, when I walked in. "And that means I'll have to go. I'm in the National Guard, and we've already been alerted."

A few days later, he told me he had his orders.

"I'm leaving next week," he said. "Before I go, I'm going to ask the Bishop to appoint you pastor."

"Do you think he will?" I asked.

"I certainly hope he will," said Father Sullivan. "You know the parish, you've done a good job and you're well liked. I'll do everything I can to convince him."

I was so grateful that I didn't have a drink for a couple of days. But then Father Sullivan told me, "The Bishop has other plans. He's going to name a permanent pastor here, and give me another parish when I get back. I'm sorry I couldn't swing it for you."

"That's all right, Father," I said. "You did your best, and I appreciate it."

It's the same old story. An opening like this comes up and I get by-passed.

What's the use? The Bishop doesn't trust me.

I was really upset. As soon as I could get away from Father Sullivan, I went to my room and poured myself a stiff drink.

Later, a young priest who had been only a few years ahead of me at St. Meinrad became pastor of Holy Rosary. We had known each other at the seminary and we got along fine.

One night in February of 1942, while I was out visiting, he phoned me.

"There's a special delivery letter from the Chancery here for you," he said.

Here it comes again.

Who told the Bishop this time?

"Open it," I said, trying to keep my voice steady, "and tell me what it says."

There was a pause at the other end of the line.

Then: "Congratulations, Ralph. You've been appointed pastor of St. Anne's."

"St. Anne's? Here in the city?"

"That's right."

St. Anne's was small but one of the nicest parishes in town—as large as Holy Rosary and in the Mars Hill section of the city.

Father Sullivan must have convinced the Bishop that I'm all right. And the Bishop gave me this because he must think he did me an injustice before.

Well, everything's fine now. I'll work hard, and show the Bishop he hasn't made a mistake.

As soon as I finished talking on the phone, I poured myself a fresh drink to celebrate my appointment. A week later, I moved into the St. Anne's parish house. I swore off liquor for Lent, which was just beginning. My resolution lasted ten days. Then I forgot it, and started drinking again.

My pastorate at St. Anne's lasted a little over a year, and ended disastrously. Yet, during the time I was there, I made many friends. Indeed, the trustees presented me with a plaque, with twenty-five silver dollars plastered on it, on the Silver Jubilee of my ordination in 1954.

We conducted many parties and functions for money-raising purposes, and the parish, which had been in the red when I got there, had money in the bank before my pastorate was over. I *did* work hard, and, from an economic standpoint, I accomplished a great deal. But from all other standpoints, I was a flat failure.

I started drinking heavily as soon as Lent was over. And I kept on drinking heavily all the time I was at St. Anne's.

One reason I got away with it for so long was because I had a housekeeper only two-thirds of the time, and she didn't live in the parish house. She arrived early in the morning and left after dinner at night. I had plenty of time to drink, both at home and elsewhere.

By December of 1942, I was back on the dreadful merry-go-round which had driven me out of Snake Run. I stepped up my diet of bromides, bourbon and beer until I practically lived on them. Day after day, I took ASA all morning and heavy shots of liquor and beer in the afternoon and evening. When anyone came to see me, I talked to him in the living room, and after he left returned to the kitchen, where I kept the liquor. Sometimes, I skipped dinner, something I hadn't done even at Snake Run. I became careless about when I drank. Drinking was a way of life for me again. My whole day revolved around the noon hour, when I could start, and it ended at about midnight, when I took the last shot before going to bed.

I picked my drinking companions with care, and tried hard to cover myself before strangers. Under any conditions, I didn't want to get drunk, but I didn't want to stop drinking, either. I read all the old wives' tales about antidotes for alcohol, and put one of them into practice every day. Sometimes, I drank buttermilk, a familiar remedy which I had used in my Jeffersonville days. I tried crackers and stale bread, olive oil, heavy shots of lemon juice, even greasy foods. And I chewed gum until my jaws ached.

I did everything but stop drinking.

The only thing I succeeded in doing—and that was through no efforts of my own, but only because I had an enormous capacity for alcohol—was to refrain from getting really drunk, in the popularly accepted sense of the word. No matter how much liquor I consumed, I never appeared to be under the influence. I always acted normally, sometimes without realizing it. And I never either got sick or passed out.

Throughout this period when I did my heaviest and most consistent drinking, the thought that I might be an alcoholic was so deeply buried in my subconscious mind that it never rose to the surface. In the first place, I never drank before noon. In the second, I never landed in the gutter, or had to be helped home or looked, acted or talked like a drunk. From everything I had ever heard on the subject, nobody could be an alcoholic as long as he avoided these pitfalls.

Some of the parishioners, of course, knew I would take a drink, because they drank with me on occasion. But, except for Jack O'Neal, who was worried about me almost from the start, none realized how much I drank. I did my heaviest drinking in the parish house, most of it alone. Since no one else was there most of the time, I felt perfectly safe.

But sooner or later, word was bound to get to the Bishop. I doubt if he actually had anyone watching me or checking up in any way. Father Sullivan had convinced him that I was completely straightened out, and the financial success of my pastorate at St. Anne's seemed to substantiate Father Sullivan's faith in my sobriety. But, no matter how discreet I was—and I wasn't always too discreet—I couldn't possibly drink so much so often and keep it a secret from the highest authority in my diocese for very long.

The blow fell in May of 1943, and once again it came by special delivery letter. This time, there was no subtlety or attempt to spare my feelings. The Bishop wrote, in substance, that my drinking had been called to his attention again, and that now he knew he was right in the first place, when he took away my parish at Snake Run. He ordered me to vacate the parish house at once and go directly to the Alexian Brothers Sanitarium in Oshkosh, Wisconsin, under pain of suspension if I refused, until further notice.

At the time, that particular sanitarium was known as a hospital for mental patients. Actually it really wasn't, although mental patients were sent there. Today it does not accept mental cases. But when you got sent there in 1943, you were supposed to be at the end of the line. To me, the Bishop's orders meant that I was consigned to a mental institution, very possibly for the rest of my life.

In the past, my first reaction on hearing bad news from the Chancery had always been one of fright. I knew I was wrong and that the Bishop, having caught up with me, was right in disciplining me. I swore off liquor and resolved to reform, hoping that, after he saw I meant business, he would give me another chance.

But this time I resented being punished, and I wanted to fight back.

I've done a good job. The Bishop has no right to remove me, let alone send me to a mental hospital.

What if I do drink a little? Is there any harm in that? I don't hurt anybody. I don't neglect my duties. I don't disgrace myself or the cloth I wear.

The Bishop can't do this to me.

I went right to the Chancery office, but the Bishop wouldn't see me. I tried to talk the Chancellor into letting me in anyhow, but he wouldn't listen to me. He had his orders to keep me out, and he wasn't going to disobey them. I never got into the Bishops's office.

Back at the parish house, I phoned one of my very few drinking companions and asked him to come over. We sat across the kitchen table from each other, separated only by a fifth of whiskey, and started working on it.

"I'm not going to Oshkosh," I said. "I don't care what the Bishop does to me. I won't go to Oshkosh."

"I don't blame you," he said. "But what are you going to do?"

"There's only one thing I can do. I'll load up my car, say good-bye to Indianapolis and head west. And I'll keep on driving until I get somewhere where nobody knows me."

"What about your priesthood and everything?"

"I'm just going, that's all," I said.

My friend left at two o'clock in the morning, and I went right to bed. I was up at six o'clock. I was unsettled and nervous, but I wasted little time. I gathered up all my personal belongings and loaded them into the car. I had a case of liquor, and twelve bottles fitted perfectly into my gladstone bag, six on each side. I put the bag in the front seat, where I could reach it easily.

Then, without even calling Jerry or Vic, my two brothers closest to me, I drove off, heading for Chicago. After that, I had vague ideas about continuing west, picking up Route 30 and, possibly, following it all the way to the Pacific Coast.

It was about ten-thirty or so when I left Indianapolis. I drove slowly, with one eye on the road and the other on my watch. Just before twelve, I pulled up at the side of the road, opened the bag and took out a fifth. By the time I got the bottle open, it was noon. I drank several swallows right out of the bottle, then placed it on the seat beside me, letting it rest against me so it wouldn't upset.

My progress to Chicago became even slower. I took my time, and frequently nibbled at the bottle.

Then I blacked out.

CHAPTER 13

I WOKE UP IN A ROOM completely devoid of furniture except for a chair, a table and the cot I was lying on.

"Do you want some breakfast, Father?"

I blinked my eyes. Standing in front of me, with a breakfast tray in his hand, was a Brother.

"Where am I?" I asked.

"You're in Oshkosh, Wisconsin."

"Oshkosh—?"

"At the Alexian Brothers Sanitarium."

Good heavens.

"How did I get here?"

"You drove."

"What day is this?"

"Friday."

I had left Indianapolis on Tuesday.

I watched the Brother as he set the tray down. Then, without another word, he left, closing the door behind him. He didn't lock it.

I looked around the room. It was much like the one in the Alexian Brothers Hospital in St. Louis.

What happened? Where have I been? I was headed west. How did I end up here?

I never found out the whole story of my strange odyssey. A nephew of mine—one of Vic's sons—who was stationed at an army base in Milwaukee, later gave me a fragment of information.

It seems that I phoned him from Chicago, and told him I'd be in Milwaukee the next day. And the next evening, we had dinner and a few drinks together. He knew I'd been drinking, but had no idea that I had blacked out. He did most of the talking, but I was perfectly rational in everything I said. I told him nothing about myself except that I was on a trip. After we said good-bye, he didn't see me again.

The rest of the trip is an absolute blank to this day.

I didn't feel like eating any breakfast. I had a little coffee, but didn't touch the food. I wasn't hungry and, except for an acute case of the jitters, suffered no ill effects from what must have been a rather heavy bout with the bottle.

I got out of bed, and started to get dressed, moving very slowly, like a character in a slow-motion movie. I was still putting my clothes on when a small, gray-haired Brother—not the one who had awakened me—came in and said laconically, "I'll see you in my office in half an hour" and walked out.

I said nothing. I was still trying to remember what had happened.

There was the letter from the Bishop, removing me from St. Anne's, and ordering me to Oshkosh. There was the argument with the Chancellor because he wouldn't let me see the Bishop. There was that drinking session in the parish house. There was the loading up of the car, and my leaving Indianapolis.

Only I was going to drive to the West Coast.

Why did I change my mind?

I didn't want to come here. And I don't intend to stay. This is too depressing.

I've got to get out of here.

I finished dressing, and went into the administration office, determined to tell the Brother that I wasn't going to stay. When I walked in, he said, calmly, "We expected you. You've been sent here by your Bishop."

I started to say something, but he held up his hand.

Then he said, "Of course, legally we can't hold you. If you want to leave, you're free to go. Naturally, that would result in your suspension."

"Are you the Superior?" I asked.

"At the moment, there is no Superior. I am in charge until a new one is appointed."

"Well, I want to get out of here."

"Are you sure?"

I hesitated.

What shall I do?

If I stay, I may never get out.

If I leave, I'll be suspended.

The Brother was speaking.

"—presume you've changed your mind about leaving. This is your routine. Mass in the morning, then breakfast—"

"Do I say Mass?" I asked.

"Oh, no. You don't say Mass."

"Well, I'm staying, so I'm not suspended."

"Father, you don't say Mass. The rule of the sanitarium is you do not say Mass until *our* Bishop gives you permission."

"Why can't I say Mass?"

Now I was pleading.

"I'm sorry," the Brother said, "but you will not say Mass, Father."

I got up and walked out without waiting to hear the rest of the routine. I dragged myself back to my room. My mind was fuzzy. I forgot what I'd gone in to see the Brother about. I forgot about wanting to leave the sanitarium, going west, running away, everything. Suddenly, all that counted was that I couldn't say Mass. It had become very important.

Why won't they let me say Mass?

I was deeply resentful. I felt put upon, taken advantage of. All I could think of was the Brother's refusal to let me say Mass.

I forgot completely that I hadn't been permitted to say Mass when I first went to Sacred Heart Sanitarium in Milwaukee either.

The only positive recollection I have of the rest of the day is an afternoon conversation with the Brother who was acting Superior. Apparently, I decided if I couldn't say Mass, I would leave and go somewhere where I *could* say Mass. I went to the Brother's office, and this time, as I was walking there, I noticed that the outside gates were locked.

"Aren't you allowed out?" I asked pettishly.

"With permission," he said. "You may go in town once a month if one of the Brothers is with you."

"What about saying Mass?"

"You will not say Mass, Father," he said patiently.

"What about my car?"

"You are not to use it. Your Bishop has given orders that you are never again to drive a car without his permission."

"What am I expected to do with it?"

"We can sell it for you," he said, "or, if you prefer, you may designate a friend to sell it. But you are not to use it yourself."

"What's the chance of seeing a doctor? I don't feel good. I'm nervous. My stomach is upset. I've been ill."

"We will arrange for a doctor to see you."

"Well, where do I see him?"

"We will arrange it, Father. He will call on you. Just go back to your room now."

"But when will he see me?" I persisted.

"Tomorrow," said the Brother.

The rest of the day is a blank, but I remember the night. Somewhere along the latter part of the evening, my mind cleared considerably. I was terribly shaky and desperately anxious for a drink. I lit one cigarette after another, and paced the floor hour after hour. Sometimes I sat on the chair, sometimes I lay on the cot and sometimes I just stood and stared out into the night from the darkened window.

I was deeply resentful, and almost all of my resentment was directed at the Bishop of Indianapolis.

He's the cause of everything. He sent me here. He'll keep me here. He won't let me say Mass. He won't let me drive my car. He won't let me lead a normal life. He won't even let me be free. I've lost my parish, my friends, my car, my liberty, my self-respect—everything.

And it's all the Bishop's fault. blame others

I paced and sat and lay down and looked out the window and smoked and stewed and worried. And, gradually, as the night progressed, my resentment turned to self-pity.

Everybody has it in for me—everybody wants to hurt me. I can try and try, and even succeed a little, but it doesn't do any good. I'm a marked man.

But I asked for it. It's my own fault.

I shouldn't have listened to Father Anselm. I knew I wasn't worthy of being a priest when I was a seminarian.

And I've proved it a thousand times ever since.

Over and over, my life passed in morbid review, just as it had so many times before. All the failures stood out in bold relief— St. Meinrad, Vincennes, Fordham, Jeffersonville, Snake Run, Holy Rosary, St. Anne's—and each attempt at rehabilitation seemed to be wasted effort.

I blamed everything in the world for my troubles—everything but alcohol—with the resentment aimed, in the last analysis, at myself.

I can't hold anyone else responsible. This trouble is all of my own making.

I can't stand prosperity. Whenever things are going well, I find some way to wreck the works. I do it all myself. How can I expect help or sympathy from anyone else?

Now I'm finished.

Here I am in a mental institution and I'll never get out.

By dawn, I was hopelessly convinced that there was nothing anyone, anywhere could do to straighten me out.

A Brother brought in my breakfast, but I didn't touch any of it except the coffee. I didn't even finish that. Two or three swallows of the steaming brown liquid only left me wishing it were something stronger. I pushed the whole business away. When the Brother came back for the tray, practically everything was still on it, and I was standing at the window, looking at everything and seeing nothing.

Later that morning, a youngish man, with a spry step, came in. He wore glasses and, except for a fringe of hair around the edges, his head was bald. He had a friendly smile on his face, and his hand was outstretched as he walked into the room.

I shook it limply.

"How do you feel, Father?"

"Terrible," I said. "Just terrible."

"I'm Dr. Bernard Hughes," he said. "Sit down."

I sank down on the cot, and Dr. Hughes pulled the chair up close to me.

"Now, what's your difficulty?" he asked. "Why did your Bishop send you here?"

"I don't know," I said lamely. "I guess he thought there was something wrong with me."

"Do you think so, too?"

I shrugged.

"How about the past, Father? Have you ever had trouble with your nerves before?"

"Often," I said.

"Tell me about it."

So, once again, I recited the long, unhappy story of my career, complete to the last up-to-date details that I could remember. It was a story easy to recite, for I had rehearsed it half the night. All I had to do was say aloud everything that I had been repeating to myself only a few hours earlier.

The longer I talked, the more I seemed to break with reality. *This is not me. This is somebody else—some other Ralph Pfau. It is he—not I—telling the doctor everything here in the Alexian Brothers Sanitarium in Oshkosh, Wisconsin.*

I feel very sorry for him. He needs help—badly. He has lost everything. I wish I could do something for him.

My flow of words didn't stop. I kept on saying one thing and thinking another. The words were automatic, coming from the mouth of a stranger; the thoughts were the real me.

When I came to the end, Dr. Hughes said, "Father, there were twelve full bottles of liquor in your bag. Do you drink much?"

Twelve full bottles?
How much did that other Ralph Pfau drink?
How much more did he have to buy to fill the bag with fresh bottles?

"Not much," I said.

I'm telling the truth. It's the other Ralph Pfau who does all the drinking.

"How much?"

"Oh, a little beer now and then." personality clashes

*That other Ralph Pfau really doesn't care much for beer. He
just drinks it for chasers.*

"No hard liquor?"

"No."

Not me.

"Did you ever drink to excess, Father—ever in your life?"

"No, Doctor. Not ever."

*It was somebody else who sat all morning, waiting for twelve
o'clock to come—somebody else who rushed back and forth between the kitchen and the living room at Snake Run—somebody
else who used ASA to ward off the horrible desire for a drink, so
he wouldn't become an alcoholic—somebody else who drank to
kill the jitters when he was filing at Vincennes and printing announcements at Holy Rosary—somebody else who blacked out
on the way from Evansville to Snake Run—somebody else who
walked that ridiculous treadmill between fishing and drinking at
the camp in Wisconsin—somebody else who headed for the West
Coast with a case of bourbon in his bag—*

"That was quite a large amount of whiskey you had with you,
Father. What did you intend to do with it?"

"Give it away."

"But not drink it yourself?"

"No—not drink it myself."

I'm not lying. I'm somebody else.

I was detached from everything. I had nothing to do with this
man who was asking me questions.

The doctor said something, but I didn't get it, so I asked him
to repeat it.

"I said, Father, that I think you're a schizophrenic."

"Is that so?"

I had never heard the term, and I didn't want to know what it
meant. I was afraid it was something very bad.

"Yes," the doctor said, "but I think we can help you."

"Nobody can help me."

"Father, we're going to try shock treatments."

Shock treatments.

They must be like those Wickel baths and wonderful massages
I had at Sacred Heart.

And I said, "Fine, Doctor."

He stood up, smiled, shook hands and walked out.

I spent the rest of the day looking out the window.

The next morning, a limousine came up to the front door of the sanitarium. I saw it from my window. A few minutes later, a Brother walked into my room and said, "There's a car here for you, Father."

"All right," I said.

He led me out of the building, and into the car. The only person in it was a uniformed chauffeur, who stared straight ahead and paid no attention to us. I got into the back seat, and the Brother climbed in beside me. Then we drove off.

"Where are we going?" I asked listlessly. I really didn't care much.

"I don't know, Father. The chauffeur has his orders from the doctor."

"Oh."

What have I got to lose, riding around in the back seat of a limousine, complete with chauffeur? This must be part of the therapy.

I settled back comfortably, and looked out the window. I had never been in that part of Wisconsin before, and the scenery was quite beautiful. We skirted Lake Winnebago for fifteen or twenty minutes, passing one lovely home after another. The fresh grass gleamed smoothly in the sunlight, and the water looked blue and cool. A breeze fanned us gently through the open windows on either side of the car.

If this is therapy, I'm all for it. I could ride around like this all day.

At length, we came to a long fence, surrounding what appeared to be a gorgeous estate. Through the trees, I could see a huge red-brick building. We turned off the main road, following the fence, and I could see other brick buildings.

Finally, we arrived at a wide gate, and, as the limousine slowly turned into it, I could read the sign slung over it.

It said: "Winnebago State Hospital for the Insane."

This is it.

This is the place you don't go beyond.

Insane ward

What's going to happen? Are they going to leave me here?

As we rode majestically up the driveway leading to the main entrance, I turned to the Brother beside me, and asked, "What's this?"

"I don't know," he said. "You'll see the doctor in a few minutes."

We reached the front entrance, and I followed the Brother out of the car. Without a word, we went inside, and he led me to a small conference room. There, waiting for us, was Dr. Hughes.

"What's this all about?" I demanded.

"We're going to give you a shock treatment."

"You mean *here?*"

"Yes," the doctor said. "They don't have the equipment at the Alexian Brothers. Everything has been arranged. We have called your Bishop, and he's given the necessary permission. The nurse will come for you in a minute."

We talked for a few moments, but my mind wasn't on the conversation.

Permission? What do they need permission for? What kind of a business is this that they have to ask the Bishop first?

Nobody from Sacred Heart in Milwaukee asked permission to give me a Wickel bath.

What is this shock treatment anyhow?

I voiced the last thought aloud.

"You'll see," said the doctor.

Now, a big male nurse poked his head in the door, and, at a nod from the doctor, beckoned me to follow him. He led me into another room, where he handed me a hospital "johnnie," a white, shapeless garment that fastens in the back, and said, "Take off your clothes, Father, and put this on. I'll be back for you in a few minutes."

He returned shortly, and told me to go with him. We got out into the corridor, and walked about thirty feet to another room. This one was small—about ten feet by twelve—and, because of the equipment and all the people in it, it looked smaller.

There was a table in the center, similar to an operating-room table, but wider and heavier. Within easy reach, with wires sticking out of them, were two attachments which looked a little like earphones. They were fairly stable, but swayed gently back and forth.

Dr. Hughes stood at the head of the table, with a woman nurse beside him. Halfway down the table were two of the biggest, most powerful-looking men I ever saw. They looked like black-smiths. Both stood well over six feet in height, and their muscles rippled in the glare of the light from above. Both wore shirts, open at the throat, with the sleeves rolled up.

I was petrified.

"Father, get up on the table, please," the doctor said.

I guess I tottered a little. The big man nearest me took me by the elbow and, with a surprisingly gentle touch, guided me to the edge of the table, then picked me up and sat me on it. In the meantime, the male nurse who had led me in from the other room stationed himself near the foot of the table.

"Lie down, Father. On your back."

The voice came from far away.

I stretched out, putting my head on an uncovered pillow. Somebody began rubbing grease on my temples, and somebody else reached for the attachments that hung from a box on the table. When the grease job was done, they were fitted over my head, one on each side.

They're going to electrocute me.

O, God, get me out of here.

I tried to get up on one elbow, but I couldn't move. One arm was pinioned by each of the blacksmiths. I tried to move my feet, but they wouldn't budge either. I found out later that the male nurse was leaning on them.

Terrified, I looked up into the eyes of the woman nurse. I tried to say something, but the words stuck in my throat. She was coming at me with something big and wide and white. It moved closer and closer to my face and I tried to pull away from it, but there was nowhere to go. It just came down—down—down—

It hovered over my mouth for a few seconds.

What are they doing to me?

Let me out.

I thought I was screaming, but I couldn't have been.

"Open your mouth!"

The nurse spoke sharply, as she poked the white apparition at me.

"Now bite!"

I clamped my teeth together.

I felt engulfed in a blinding white flash that seemed to consume me, inside and out, from head to foot.

That was the last thing I knew.

CHAPTER 14

I WAS SITTING ON A COT in a darkened room when I came to my senses. I shook my head for a few minutes, and looked around. The woman nurse was standing beside me, and in a corner of the room was the Brother who had come with me from the sanitarium.

"Where am I?"

"In the Winnebago State Hospital," the nurse said.

"Where?"

She repeated it.

"What am I doing here?"

"You're getting treatments, Father."

"What kind of treatments?"

"Electro-shock."

"Why?"

"You have mental anxieties," she said quietly. "The doctor is giving you shock treatments to make you more relaxed."

"How long do I have to stay here?"

"You won't stay here at all. You're going back to the Alexian Brothers Sanitarium."

"The Alexian Brothers?" I repeated.

"Yes."

"What city is it in?"

"Oshkosh. We're in Oshkosh, too."

What am I doing in Oshkosh?

"How do you feel, Father?" the nurse asked.

175

I shook my head again several times.

Then I said, "I guess I'm all right. Only, I don't remember anything."

"It will all come back. I'm going to leave you now. Get dressed, and go with the Brother here."

Then she walked out.

Later, in the limousine returning us to the sanitarium, a little light came through the fog in my mind.

The Bishop wouldn't see me. I wonder why the Bishop wouldn't see me?

And why did I want to see him?

Back at the Alexian Brothers', I was led to my room, but I didn't recognize it at all. My bag was in one corner, and my clothes were on hooks and hangers, but all the kindness and patience of the Brothers meant nothing to me.

Why wouldn't the Bishop see me?

"Get undressed, Father," the Brother said. "The doctor's orders are for you to go right to bed."

He must have given me a sedative to make me sleep, for I don't even remember taking my clothes off. I must have passed out on my feet.

When I woke up, the acting Superior was standing by my bed. He asked me how I felt.

"All right," I said vaguely.

I peered intently at him, then, from far back in my muddled brain, came a recognition signal. I got up on one elbow and said, "I'm in the Alexian Brothers Sanitarium. How did I get here?"

"Well, Father," he said, "I wouldn't be too concerned about it. The doctor is trying to help you. If I were you, I'd co-operate with him. He is putting you through a course of therapy he thinks will make you well. Just do as he says."

I know what happened. I had a shock treatment. The nurse told me.

"Do you want anything?" the Superior asked.

I shook my head, and he walked out.

Now, as I lay back on the cot, more of the fog lifted.

I was removed from my parish. That was it. The Bishop removed me from St. Anne's because I was drinking, and then he wouldn't see me. Now, I remember. I went back and drank all evening at the parish house, and the next morning I started for the West Coast.

Gradually, in the next few days, practically everything came back into focus except the shock treatment itself, and the events immediately leading up to it. I didn't recall those details for months.

Much later, I learned that it was very rare for a person to have deep shock treatments, such as I had, and be aware of them at all. In those days, shock therapy was used only for extreme cases. Long before they even began the therapy, the people who took them were usually too far gone to remember anything.

Deep shock carries an AC current of about 1,000 milli-amperes at 110 volts. Today, under the same circumstances, I would probably have been given sub-shock, which, with the same voltage, calls for only 20 milli-amperes, using unidirectional current.

Eventually, I got the rest of the details of my shock treatments at the State Hospital. The strong-armed men were there to keep me from leaping off the table and, possibly, seriously injuring myself. The big, wide, white object which the nurse poked down at me and which frightened me almost to death was a small tongue depresser, wrapped tightly in gauze. She had stuffed it into my mouth to keep me from biting my tongue off.

I felt much better when I awoke the morning after my first treatment. I had had plenty of sleep, and, for the first time in weeks, I felt really hungry. After breakfast, I went to see the Brother in charge, and asked if I was permitted to associate with any of the other patients.

"As long as you stay on this floor, you may talk to anyone," he said. "But don't go upstairs. That's where our incurable cases are."

There was another priest in the room across the hall, and I stopped in to pass the time of day with him. Neither of us knew what the other was there for. The last thing you ever find out in any of these institutions is why the other person's there.

After we'd talked a few minutes, I commented, "They won't let me say Mass."

"Me, neither," he said.

"Do you think we'll ever be able to?" I asked.

"Oh, yes. The Brothers here know how you're doing. As soon as they think you're all right, they tell their Bishop and yours, and you get permission."

That satisfied me. I didn't think any more about it.

I felt more and more like myself as the days went by. I was driven to the State Hospital every second or third day for shock treatments. While I never got used to them, I reached a point where I wasn't scared to death every time I walked into that chamber of horrors. I knew the treatments were helping me, and I was perfectly willing to submit to them.

A few days after I arrived at the sanitarium, I asked for drawing paper and charcoal. The Brothers found some for me, and I began sketching. Later, Jack O'Neal sent me an easel and brushes from Indianapolis, and I got oils myself on one of my trips into downtown Oshkosh with a Brother. Incidentally, Jack sent for my car, and sold it in Indianapolis. He put the money in the bank for me.

When the shock treatments were over, I was given permission to say Mass again. I had been at the sanitarium for about three weeks, and was now in a routine which centered largely around painting. It was a good hobby and I enjoyed myself. I went outside every day, set my easel up and went to work. I confined myself to still-life paintings. I started painting after breakfast, and often worked all day, only taking time out for meals.

It was weeks before my nerves quieted down to a point where I could again look back on life objectively. I realized now that I had had a narrow escape from what amounted to complete oblivion. This was my fourth nervous breakdown. There was no guarantee that I wouldn't suffer another some time in the future, but the doctor thought the shock treatments might have a lasting effect.

For the rest of the summer and early fall of 1943, I lived a quiet, relaxed life at the sanitarium. Dr. Hughes came to see me every two or three weeks, but only to ask how I was feeling. We had a few long talks such as those I had had regularly with Dr. Blanchard at Sacred Heart in Milwaukee.

My closest friend was the priest across the hall. We spent most of our spare time together. He was an avid reader, and he often sat in the sun beside me, reading while I worked with my oils. From time to time, we both stopped what we were doing, and talked.

We went downtown once a month to buy what we needed and get away from the sanitarium, always in the company of a Brother. I had no trouble getting permission to go to town more often, but I never had reason to ask for it.

One day late in October, the Superior, who had been appointed during the summer, came into my room.

"I have a letter from your Bishop," he said. "You are to report at once to Indianapolis."

"You mean I can go home?"

He nodded.

"Well, that's fine," I said. "How do I make arrangements? What do I do?"

"We'll take care of everything for you."

I took a sleeper out of Oshkosh the following evening. And, as soon as I arrived in Indianapolis, I went directly from the railroad station to the Chancery office to see the Bishop. I walked in there at about ten o'clock in the morning.

"How are you, Ralph?" he asked quietly.

"Fine."

He looked at me for a moment.

"You look all right," he said.

He sighed.

Then, "I wonder how long you'll stay that way. Well, I'm going to give you one more chance. I haven't talked to the pastor yet, but you can go to St. Joan of Arc parish and live there awhile.

"Frankly," he added, "I don't think there's a chance for you. No matter what happens, you always seem to slip back. I'm afraid you're hopeless."

It was not until years later that I was fully to realize that the Bishop was trying to shock me into positive action. But at the time . . .

Hopeless.

I've worked and prayed and worried and tried and lived in

a sanitarium for months and taken shock treatments and now he says I'm hopeless.

Where do I go from here?

No matter what I do, the odds are against me. I've got two strikes on me right now.

What's the use of trying? I can't win.

give up.

I picked up my bag, walked out and took a taxi to St. Joan of Arc. The pastor, Monsignor Clement Bosler, was well known in Indianapolis. I had met him several times, and always admired him.

He had known my uncle George, the priest, and Uncle Al, the Bishop, and was also a friend of my brother Jerry. And, in common with all the other priests in the diocese, I'm sure he was familiar with my story. Everyone was now aware of the fact that I was a problem priest, and somewhat difficult to handle.

dont like the Bishop

But Monsignor Bosler, a thorough gentleman, greeted me with a friendly welcome.

"Come in, Father Pfau," he said. "I'm glad to see you."

"Thank you, Father."

I followed him into the living room, and sat down.

"The Bishop said I was to live here," I said.

"Well, that's fine. I haven't talked to the Bishop recently, but I'm delighted to have you."

He talked as though he really were.

Later, he took me to a nice room on the second floor of the rectory.

"Make yourself at home," he said. "If you want anything, let me know. We eat at twelve and six."

After I got settled, Monsignor Bosler came back and took me around to meet the other priests. St. Joan of Arc was a big parish, and he had several assistants, all of whom I knew.

Each time he introduced me to someone, Monsignor Bosler said heartily, "Father Pfau is going to be with us now," and each time he said it, I felt a little better. He talked with such sincere enthusiasm that he nearly offset the letdown the Bishop had caused in my own outlook.

The other priests all helped to make things easier for me that first day. One came in late in the afternoon, just to tell me he was glad I was there. At supper, he and the others drew me into the general conversation. Later, I went back to my room and listened to the radio. I went to bed feeling pretty well.

I slept about seven hours, and started working on routine duties the next morning. I had no special assignment. I was simply to help with confessions, distribute Communion, say Mass and teach catechism in St. Joan of Arc parochial school, which was connected with the parish.

But I wasn't happy. Those last words of the Bishop kept coming back to haunt me, and I knew he was right. Each day, I thought of some other good reason why he should have called me hopeless. By the end of the week, I was beginning to review my life in the same old unhappy light again.

I am hopeless.

What's the use?

I dropped lower and lower on a scale of depression. The deeper I dropped, the more resentful I felt toward the Bishop. I blamed him for everything, including my present state of recurrent nerves. I refused to leave the rectory except when it was absolutely necessary. I imagined that everywhere I went, people were looking at me and saying, "There goes Father Pfau. He was pastor of St. Anne's last year, but had to be removed. He just got back from the asylum."

An old friend called me a week or so after I arrived at St. Joan of Arc.

"I just heard you were in town, Father," he said. "Glad you're back. Would you like to come out for a ride in my car?"

"I'd be delighted," I said. "Now that I don't have a car of my own, I seldom get the opportunity to go out in a car."

We rode around for a while, then my friend said, "How about a drink?"

I didn't hesitate a second. I had no defense.

"Sure," I said.

He stopped the car, reached into the glove compartment and pulled out a pint. We both took a couple of swallows. We stopped a few more times, and when the bottle was empty, we bought another.

That's the last thing I remember. I woke up the next morning back at the rectory.

Oh, God, this is the end.

I'm back one week, and I've blacked out from drinking already. The Bishop knew what he was talking about. I'm about as hopeless as you can get.

What happened? Where did I go? What did I do? Who saw me? How much trouble am I in this time?

I worried all morning. Finally, I reached my friend on the telephone and asked him to tell me what happened.

"Nothing happened, Father. You were perfectly all right. I dropped you off downtown at around eleven o'clock, and you said you were going right home. As far as I know, you did."

"Did I make myself conspicuous in any way?" I asked. "Was I obviously drunk or anything?"

"No, not a bit. You were very rational and you walked all right. Nobody would ever know you'd been drinking."

I hung up, and put my head in my hands.

I blacked out from drinking. Home a week and I blacked out from drinking. I'm lost. The shock treatments didn't do one bit of good. I might as well have saved myself the trouble of taking them.

What am I going to do now?

For the first time in my conscious thinking, it slowly began to dawn on me that *maybe alcohol was my primary problem.* I knew I had other problems, too, and I felt they were more important. However, I now began to think that perhaps I should try to get the alcohol problem straightened out first.

I went down to see a doctor—a new one this time. I got his name from one of the other priests. I told him I was jittery and depressed, and that I couldn't sleep. He gave me a prescription, and after I had it filled, I went home and took a dose. Then I lay down.

In two minutes, my head was spinning so fast I couldn't lie still. When I tried to sit, I was so dizzy I fell back on the bed. The dizziness became worse and worse. As I lay there I wanted to scream. Round and round and round I went, my whole world topsy-turvy.

I must have been there a couple of hours before the spinning stopped, and I could stand on my feet without toppling over. I made my way to a telephone and called the doctor.

"What did you give me, a stimulant or a sedative?" I asked.

"A stimulant. You told me you were depressed."

"What kind of a stimulant?"

"Benzedrine."

Without another word, I hung up. Then I called a doctor I knew, and went right down to see him. He gave me another prescription.

"This should take care of you," he said. "Take a dose before you go to bed. It'll relax you and make you sleep."

I didn't know what the stuff was, and I didn't ask. I slept well that night, but woke up jittery. I wanted a drink, but I was afraid to take one, for fear someone would see me. So, when my nerves kept kicking up in the afternoon, I took another dose of the sedative the doctor had given me, and went to my room to rest.

I closed my eyes, but couldn't sleep. Instead, I began to see pictures. They were not vague, but clear cut and sharp and beautifully colored. First, I saw a forest of trees, with the leaves changing in an autumn riot. Then I saw a downtown street scene, with yellow trolley cars dominating a picture that included wide, brilliantly lighted streets, neatly decorated store windows, long, sleek, black limousines and people dressed in multi-colored costumes. Then I saw a lake, like Winnebago, only it wasn't Winnebago, then a ball park, with the outfield a smooth, shiny expanse of green grass and the players' uniforms sharply defined, then the inside of a church.

The pictures, clear as they were, changed so fast I could hardly keep track of them. I put my hands over my eyes, but the images kept coming, all so clean and sharp that I enjoyed them. After a while, I simply relaxed and let them come. I hoped they'd go away, but I really didn't care.

Then, as suddenly as they came, the pictures disappeared. I was only aware of a pleasant sort of lassitude, which dissipated in sudden panic.

I opened my eyes, and sat up.

Now what?

Can this be the D.T.'s? It couldn't be. I haven't been drinking.
I've got to go back and see that doctor.

"You're all right, Father," he said. "You've got what we call a kaleidoscopic mind. You took a little too much of that barbital. I'm going to give you something that will neutralize it, and I'm sure you'll feel better."

I began taking the stuff the next day, for, as usual, I woke up scared and jittery. In the afternoon, I had another picture session, but it didn't last long. And, after I continued to take the medicine for another day, the pictures went away.

I carried out my parish duties in a sort of trance. I went through one day after another with that familiar vague feeling of uneasiness that comes only when you want a drink and don't dare take one. If I couldn't have a drink, I couldn't keep going. But I was terribly afraid.

If I take a drink now, I might black out again.
But I've got to have a drink.
How long can I keep this up?

I couldn't sleep at all one night. I took some of the medicine before I went to bed, but it did no good. As I lay there, nerves taut, legs stretched out, fists clenched, it was impossible to relax. Finally, I got up, went over to the window and stared out at the sleeping city.

The rectory phone rang. I was the only one up, so I rushed to answer it before it woke any of the others. On the way to the phone, I looked at my watch. It was two o'clock.

"My husband is dying, Father. Can you come right over? My son will pick you up in a few minutes."

"I'll meet him in front of the rectory," I said.

I went back to my room, put on my clothes, got the Holy Oils and went out the front door. As I closed it behind me, a car pulled up. A young man reached over from the driver's seat, and pushed the door open. I got in, and we drove off.

"What happened?" I asked.

"My dad—I'm afraid he dropped dead. The doctor's on his way."

"I'm sorry—"

As we got out of the car in front of his house, another automobile pulled up behind us. The boy led me to the front door.

"Right upstairs, Father. First room on the left. I'll hold the door open for the doctor."

I rushed upstairs, taking them two at a time. When I walked into the room, a woman was weeping. Her husband, fully dressed, was stretched out flat on the floor. He didn't move. I thought he was dead.

I nodded to the woman. They knelt down while I started to take out the Holy Oils.

"Excuse me, Father."

The doctor already had his bag open, and was filling a needle from a bottle. I moved aside to give him room. He felt the man's pulse, rolled up one sleeve, splashed on some alcohol and shoved the needle into an arm.

For a minute, nothing happened. Then, to my amazement, the man sat up and looked around.

The doctor looked at me, then smiled slyly.

"Just as I thought, Father," he said. "He's had too much liquor and barbitals. He'll be all right."

"I—thought he was dead."

"He will be if he doesn't change his habits."

We were both on our feet now. The doctor was snapping his bag shut. We turned back to the man, and helped him to his feet. Without a word, he walked to the bed under his own power, and began to get undressed. Meanwhile, his wife, badly shaken, thanked us both, and asked me to stay a few more minutes.

The doctor left, and I began talking to the woman, trying to calm her. But it was a classic case of the blind leading the blind. I wasn't the least bit calm myself. My head was spinning, and I wanted a drink.

In spite of what I had just witnessed, I wanted a drink.

My mind was far away.

Just one drink.

"—called you at this hour, Father. We appreciate your kindness in coming."

I followed the woman downstairs, and sat with her son in the living room while she heated some water. I talked mechanically to the boy. I was so jittery that it was an effort for me to say anything.

His mother came in and they had coffee. I didn't take any, since I was to say early Mass. The boy took a few sips of coffee, then stood up and walked to the door. He was going to drive me home.

As I walked out of the room a book on the mantel caught my eye. I walked over to look at it, then picked it up and riffled the pages.

"May I borrow this?" I asked.

"Certainly."

"Thank you."

The name of the book was *Alcoholics Anonymous.*

realized he had a problem

PART III

CHAPTER 15

I T WAS AFTER THREE O'CLOCK when I got back to the rectory. My heart was pounding, partly from the excitement of the previous hour, but mostly because I wanted a drink. But in three hours I would have to say Mass, so I could neither eat nor drink.

It was useless for me to try to sleep. I didn't even bother to get completely undressed. I took off my coat, my collar and my shoes, settled down in a chair and began reading the book, *Alcoholics Anonymous.* advice/help

I had never heard of Alcoholics Anonymous; I didn't know there was such an organization. The book, which explained its principles, its aims and the significance of its twelve steps to sobriety, intrigued me. I read it through in one sitting, and finished it before dawn.

And I remember thinking, as I put it down, "What a wonderful book—for those who need it."

Then I lay down and slept for an hour or so.

The next afternoon, I went to see how the man on whom I had made the sick call the night before was doing. He answered the doorbell himself.

"I'm Father Pfau," I said. "I was here last night when you were—indisposed. How are you today?"

"Oh, come in, Father," he said, shaking hands. "I'm fine. I'm sorry they sent for you at such a crazy hour. It was so good of you to come—and so unnecessary."

"Well, I must admit it *seemed* necessary at the time."

He laughed, and commented, "Appearances are deceiving, aren't they?"

We chatted for a few minutes. Then I said, "About that book I borrowed last night—"

"What book, Father?"

"*Alcoholics Anonymous.*"

"Oh—that!"

He laughed again.

"You want to know something, Father?" he said, in a confidential tone of voice. "My wife brought that home a couple of weeks ago. She thinks it would help me. But I'm a social drinker. I don't need it." *denial*

That obvious absurdity didn't register with me.

"I was just wondering if I can keep it a while longer," I said. "I'd like to read it over a few times. I think it would be helpful to me—as a priest, of course."

That obvious absurdity didn't register with me, either.

"Sure. Keep it as long as you like."

I got up to leave, a few minutes later. As Bill saw me to the door, he said, "Thanks for dropping by, Father. My wife will be sorry she missed you when I tell her you were here. And don't worry about me. That attack last night probably had something to do with my heart. I had rheumatic fever as a kid and I've got a murmur now. Every so often, it floors me."

Back at the rectory, I went to my room after supper and read the book through again. I read it much more slowly this time and, almost unconsciously, I practically memorized the Twelve Steps. When I had finished the book, it was time for bed.

As usual, I slept poorly, and I got up to look out the window several times. Then I picked up the book and went over the Twelve Steps again:

1. We admitted we were powerless over alcohol, that our life had become unmanageable.

2. Came to believe that a Power greater than ourselves could restore us to sanity.

3. Made a decision to turn our will and our life over to the care of God as we understood Him.

4. Made a searching and fearless moral inventory of ourselves.

recovery

5. Admitted to God, to ourself and to another human being the exact nature of our wrong.

6. Were entirely ready to have God remove these defects of character.

7. Humbly asked Him to remove our shortcomings.

8. Made a list of all the people we had harmed, and became willing to make amends to them all.

9. Made direct amends to such people wherever possible, except when to do so would injure them or others.

10. Continued to take personal inventory, and when we were wrong promptly admitted it.

11. Sought through prayer and meditation to improve our conscious contact with God as we understood Him, praying only for knowledge of His will for us and the power to carry that out.

12. Having had a spiritual awakening as the result of these steps, we tried to carry this message to alcoholics and to practice these principles in all of our affairs.

Interesting—interesting stuff. I wonder who devised it.

It's the kind of thing that can be applied to anyone, no matter what his religion. I'll bet it helps a lot of people—particularly those who may have lost their awareness of God. It's a good program for alcoholics.

But I'm not an alcoholic.

And I'm a priest.

I haven't lost my awareness of God.

This program is not for me.

But I couldn't keep my hands off that book. Day after day, I picked it up and read it again, sometimes once, sometimes twice, sometimes even more often. Whenever I had a spare hour or two, I was in my room reading, studying, thinking. After three or four weeks, during which I didn't miss a day reading the book through at least once, it was seared in my brain, word for word, comma for comma, question mark for question mark. I knew it from cover to cover, the stories, the philosophy, the questions, the answers—everything.

And during that entire period, I didn't take a drink.

One evening, several weeks after I began reading the book, I noticed some pamphlets on a side table in the vestibule of the rectory. First I glanced, then I stopped and looked again. On the top pamphlet was printed the words, "Alcoholics Anonymous."

I picked up some of the literature and leafed through it. It described the A.A. program in general, and the A.A. group in Indianapolis in particular.

At supper that night, I asked Monsignor Bosler, "Who brought in those pamphlets on the side table?"

"Oh—that Alcoholics Anonymous material," he said. "Doherty Sheerin asked me if it was all right to leave it there. He's a fine man—one of our most devoted parishioners. Comes from an outstanding family. I think he's the president or something of A.A. here in Indianapolis."

"How did he happen to leave that stuff here?" I asked, trying to sound casual.

"Why, he thought it would be a good idea to acquaint the priests of the parish with the movement."

"Oh."

I sighed with some relief. Except for the fact that I had never heard of Doherty Sheerin, I would have thought the pamphlets had been left there specifically for me.

After supper, I drew the pastor aside and asked if I might take them up to my room to read. He told me, by all means, to go ahead.

I read all of the pamphlets in one sitting, and, during the next few days, I read them all through several more times before returning them to the side table in the vestibule. They told stark, simple stories of despair and hopelessness and terror and defeat, and, somehow, I felt a little better each time I read them.

Of course, none of these things apply to me. I'm not an alcoholic. But these poor people have had a terrible time on account of liquor. I wish I could do something to help them. I ought to be able to, since I'm a priest.

I wasn't drinking, but I was shaky, and still plagued by sleeplessness and lack of appetite. Outside of the A.A. material, I had no particular interest in anything. I dragged myself around, listless and lifeless and continually more confused.

I replaced the void left by the absence of alcohol by stepping up the medication the doctor had prescribed after I had had that attack of kaleidoscopic pictures. This was a combination of barbitals and Dexedrine which I was supposed to take during the day, and at specific times. But they seemed to relax me, and I took them whenever I was jittery.

I didn't know what to do. I wanted a drink, but the A.A. book and the pamphlets had already begun to take hold. I was vaguely thinking that, if I really did have an alcoholic problem, A.A. might provide me with a solution to it. And, until I made up my mind what to do about it, I wanted to keep away from liquor.

I was scared, and I needed help. This I knew.

What am I going to do? I can't let myself go again. This is positively my last chance. The Bishop won't stand for any more monkey business from me. I've got to straighten myself out once and for all.

One evening, while I was reading the A.A. book, I suddenly came to a decision.

I'll call this Doherty Sheerin. What have I got to lose? I'm not an alcoholic—not really—but maybe he can help me. At least, he might give me some kind of an answer to my problem, whatever it is. I don't need A.A., but I certainly need something. It won't do any harm to talk to this Sheerin, anyhow.

So I got his phone number and put in a call for him.

"Mr. Sheerin?"

"Yes."

"This is Father Pfau—one of the priests at St. Joan of Arc."

"Oh, hello, Father. What can I do for you?"

"Well," I said, "I was just wondering—could I possibly see you some time? I'd like to talk to you about—something. There's no hurry—"

"I'll be right over, Father."

He hung up before I could say any more. And he was at the rectory fifteen minutes later. The housekeeper called me downstairs and I met him in the living room. When I went up to him, he held out his hand and said, "I'm Doherty Sheerin. Just call me Dohr."

I liked him on sight. He was a bald-headed, heavy-set man, with a tan, healthy complexion, deep, dark brown eyes and the most attractive smile I have ever seen. There was strength and character and leadership in his rather square face, and I felt almost a compulsion to put myself in his hands and let him steer me any way he wanted to.

This man will help me.

"Sit down—Dohr," I said.

"What's on your mind, Father?"

"Well, I understand you're president of Alcoholics Anonymous here in town."

"Of course, I'm not president. We don't have any such thing as president. After all, Alcoholics Anonymous is only a group of individuals all faced with the same problem, you know. We only recently began the Indianapolis group and I happen to be the first member of it, but that's neither here nor there."

"I see," I said. "I wonder if you can help me. I have some personal problems, and I thought maybe you could give me a little advice. Of course, mine isn't really an alcoholic problem. I never drank very much."

His smile never left his face.

"Yes, Father, go on."

"As I say," I continued, "I haven't ever drunk a whole lot. On occasion, I'll take a drink, and maybe once in a while I'll have a little too much. But, of course, I'm not an alcoholic."

"I know what you mean, Father," he said gently. "I don't know whether we can help you or not. All I can do is pass along a few ideas, then perhaps you can help yourself. This A.A. movement is unique. We don't teach anything. We don't lecture anybody, or tell anybody whether he is or isn't an alcoholic. All we do is suggest, 'Take another look at yourself, and form your own conclusions.'

"Why don't you go to a meeting with me? You'll learn more from one meeting than if you sat here for hours listening to me."

"Now, wait a minute," I said. "Do you mean I should go to a meeting of Alcoholics Anonymous? Remember, I'm a priest. If I should go to one of those meetings, what would people think? Why, they'd say, 'Look at that Catholic priest sitting down at a meeting with a bunch of drunks.' "

"Well, Father," Dohr said slowly, "I don't think you have to worry about that. Nobody will say anything. As a matter of fact, they're all so busy with their own problems that they won't give you a second thought."

"Maybe—maybe I'll go—"

I'll just look in as a spectator. These people won't know I've got any problems. They'll just think I'm there in my capacity as a priest to help them out. Anyhow, this Dohr Sheerin is a pretty persuasive fellow. I'll go to one meeting, and if I don't like it, I won't go to any more.

"Our next meeting is Thursday night, Father," Dohr was saying. "It starts at eight o'clock. I'll pick you up at seven-fifteen."

"Well," I said, doubtfully, "I guess that'll be O.K."

We talked a few minutes more, then Dohr got up to leave. I saw him to the door, then turned and walked slowly up to my room.

The date was November 10, 1943. It was my thirty-ninth birthday.

By Thursday, I had decided at least thirty-nine times not to go to the meeting.

There'll be nothing but drunks there. How can I be seen with those people? I'm a priest. It would be in bad taste for me to go. That's no place for a priest.

But then I would read a passage from the A.A. book, or go over the Twelve Steps, or recall Dohr's friendly smile and his penetrating eyes and simple, yet forceful words.

"We don't teach anything. We don't lecture anybody, or tell anybody whether he is or isn't an alcoholic. All we do is suggest, 'Take another look at yourself—'"

Are these the words of a drunk? Is Dohr a drunk?

Once, at the dinner table in the rectory, I brought up the subject of A.A. I asked if anyone knew about it.

"I don't know anything about A.A.," one priest said, "but I do know Doherty Sheerin, and he's a wonderful man."

"What does he do?" I asked.

"He's a retired manufacturer. He was in business for many years, and was very successful. I guess he gives all his time to Alcoholics Anonymous now."

Later, I pulled one of the other priests aside and asked him, "What do you think of this Alcoholics Anonymous?"

"I don't know much about it," he said. "But if Dohr Sheerin's got anything to do with it, it must be good."

"Do you think it's the sort of thing a priest should get involved in?"

He shook his head vigorously.

"No, no, not a priest," he said. "A.A. isn't for a priest. A priest doesn't need that. He has everything he needs for sobriety in his Church."

Promptly at seven-fifteen Thursday night, the housekeeper called me downstairs. Dohr and two others were waiting for me in his car. He introduced me to them with the words, "Father Pfau is a new priest in this parish. He's interested in alcoholism."

And I said, "I hope you gentlemen don't mind my looking in on your meeting."

We drove to a small branch library, the Rauh Library, and I stared curiously at my companions as they climbed out of the car and into the glare of a street lamp. Both of the two others were, like Dohr, not only neatly, but rather expensively dressed, and, like Dohr, they talked and acted like men of some distinction. I later found out that one was a manufacturer's representative and the other a retired banker.

It was a small meeting—only seven people altogether. One of the men was an attorney, another a hardware salesman. Neither appeared to be in financial difficulties and neither looked like a drunk, or even an ex-drunk. From all appearances, this could have been a meeting of the board of directors of the library.

Dohr gave me a jolt before I sat down. After greeting everyone, he said, "Before we get started, I want to introduce a friend of mine, a new member, Father Pfau."

A new member.

Somewhat dazed, I took a seat. We were all grouped around a long table, and everything was very informal. Dohr opened the meeting, and said, "Tonight, let's talk about honesty in maintaining sobriety."

For the next hour—the library closed at nine and we had to be out of there by then—the discussion moved back and forth between Dohr and a couple of the members. I recall one exchange vividly, because it impressed me so much at the time.

"I do a lot of traveling," a hardware salesman said, "and I'm offered a drink everywhere I go. I decline by saying, 'I've got a bad stomach, and I don't drink.' But sometimes people keep insisting, and the more they insist, the shakier I get. I'm afraid someday I might accept a drink and then I'll be off again. I don't know what to do about it."

"Well," said Dohr, "I consider A.A. a program of honesty. I feel that under circumstances like this, if we want to be freed of the shakes and all the other things that come with tension, we have to be completely honest—as honest with other people as we are with ourselves. It isn't honest to refuse a drink with the excuse that we have a bad stomach unless we really *have* a bad stomach. I think, when we refuse a drink, we should come right out and say, 'No, thanks. I can't drink. I can't handle liquor. I'm an alcoholic.' That's what I always say, and people seem to understand. Nobody ever offers me a drink a second time."

I noticed that before anyone spoke during the meeting, he always said, "I am an alcoholic," and I wondered if I would ever be able to do that—if, that is, I really *were* an alcoholic. I still was far from ready to admit that.

But I felt better than I had felt in several weeks as we rode back toward the rectory in Dohr's car. One of the others asked me how I liked the meeting.

"Fine," I said, with real enthusiasm. "Very interesting."

"That's good," Dohr said, as he pulled the car up in front of the rectory. "Now, keep coming back. Someday, everything will fall into focus."

I walked thoughtfully into the rectory and up the stairs to my room on the second floor. And, as I began to get ready for bed, I could feel the seeds of discouragement begin to crop up again.

This A.A. is great for laymen. It gives them a new awareness of God, and that helps to keep them from drinking. But I have always had a strong awareness of and faith in God, and that didn't keep me from drinking. They talked about honesty tonight— honesty with themselves and honesty with other people. I know all about honesty. Honesty is one of the virtues that any priest adheres to as a matter of course. So there are two things—aware-

*ness of God and honesty—which are keystones of success in A.A.,
and I have both, but neither stopped me from drinking.*

So what can A.A. do for me?

I went to bed, still thinking, and, when I couldn't sleep, I got up and paced the room, thinking, thinking, thinking, and the more I thought the more convinced I was that A.A. wasn't for me. I finally went back to bed, and fell into an intermittent sleep, then woke up exhausted and more discouraged than ever.

Dohr Sheerin phoned just after breakfast.

"How are you feeling, Father?"

"All right—I guess."

"Well," he said cheerfully, "I just wanted to say hello."

"Thanks," I said laconically.

Day after day, I went through the motions of carrying out my duties at the parish, but my nerves kicked up and I continued to take barbital pills. I didn't drink, but I was never free of a vague urge to do so.

Dohr called me every day, usually in the morning. About all he ever said, "How do you feel, Father?" and about all I ever replied was, "All right—I guess." But, after a few days, I began to look forward to his calls. Even though we talked briefly and only about inconsequentials, they seemed to help me, if only for a few minutes.

When he phoned the following Thursday, I was prepared to tell him that I was not going to the meeting, but he didn't give me a chance. Before I could open my mouth, he said, "This is meeting night. I'll come by for you at seven-fifteen," and I uttered an automatic, almost compulsive, "O.K."

Dohr was alone when he picked me up. He explained that the others would meet us at the library. It was a bigger meeting than the first one. There were half a dozen more people, including an elderly man from out of town. Somebody other than Dohr acted as chairman this time. It was later explained to me that most A.A. groups try to rotate the chairmanship from time to time.

The chairman asked the visitor to give us a talk. The man, a gray-haired, red-faced fellow with a raspy voice, arose and began,

"I am an alcoholic, and, let me tell you, I'm a *real* alcoholic. I drank a fifth of whiskey every day for forty years."

I shuddered, involuntarily.

A fifth a day for forty years! I'm not even forty years old yet. Why, I'm not an alcoholic. What in the world ever made me think I was? I don't have anything to be afraid of.

And, as these thoughts continued to go through my mind, the visiting member told a long, gruesome tale of heavy, stumble-bum drinking, the kind of drinking that landed him in the gutter and kept him there for years. He spoke for a long time, and every adventure he recounted was more horrible than its predecessor. He took all kinds of cures, but always went back to liquor as soon as he got out of whatever establishment he happened to be in. He woke up after long benders in places like mental institutions and Salvation Army missions and hospitals and elevated train platforms and slum flats and gutters and human pigsties of every description. Once, he opened his eyes on the sidewalk of the Brooklyn Bridge, with his feet propped up on the railing. He tried suicide three or four times and, as he put it himself, "the only reason I didn't succeed in killing myself was that I was too drunk to do it right."

I wanted to ask questions, but was too shy to say anything in front of all those people. After all those years of hopeless living, this man obviously was now dedicated to a life of sobriety. But, instead of encouraging me, his story horrified me. And it nearly drove me out of A.A.

On the way home, I said, "I don't know, Dohr. After hearing that man, I'm convinced I don't have an alcoholic problem. I really don't drink more than once in a while, and then only for old times' sake. This program is for somebody like him, and it really helped him. But I don't see how it can help me. I've got a good many more years of heavy drinking to do before I'm an alcoholic, judging by his experience."

"Well, Father," Dohr said, "I suggest you just keep coming to the meetings. Just keep coming and don't drink. Let's see what happens. Let's take one day at a time. You know, we have what we call our twenty-four-hour program. That means we're not worried about yesterday or tomorrow. We only think of today.

What are we doing today? That's the big thing. And we know that if we don't drink today we're not going to have any trouble today."

"That's fine," I said, "only I never did drink every day. I'm really not an alcoholic, Dohr."

"Well, Father, I hope you're really being honest with yourself, if not with me. And tell me, if you don't think you're an alcoholic, why—really, be honest now—why did you call me in the first place?"

"Oh, I don't know. I had just read your literature. And everyone—Monsignor Bosler and all the priests at the rectory—said you were such a nice, decent fellow."

"But why call *me?* Why bother with Alcoholics Anonymous? You must have many priest friends to consult on other problems. You could have gone to any of them. And you must know plenty of doctors who could treat you if you felt you were sick. You wouldn't be here with me, riding in my car on your way home from an A.A. meeting—you surely wouldn't have contacted A.A. or anyone in it—unless you thought you had an alcoholic problem."

That made sense. It made sense to me all the way back to the rectory. It made sense when I shook hands with Dohr and thanked him for picking me up. It made sense when we said goodnight to each other and it made sense when he promised to call me and see how I was doing.

But ten minutes after I walked into my room, it didn't make so much sense any more.

I couldn't see how the comparatively little amount of drinking I did could put me in the same class with a man who had drunk a fifth of whiskey a day for forty years.

CHAPTER 16

DOHR CONTINUED to phone me every day, and our conversations lengthened. My jitters always died down a little after I had talked to him, but it was never long before they returned. So one day, over the telephone, I asked him what I should do about them.

"You know, Father," he said, "ours is a program of many angles. Among other things, it's a program of action. When something goes wrong, we don't just sit back and wait for it to go away. We make a positive move. That's what I think you should do. As you've told me, you've been to doctors here and elsewhere, and they've helped you from time to time. A friend of mine had the same trouble you did after he stopped drinking, and he went to the Mayo Clinic, in Rochester, Minnesota. They put him through a whole course of tests, and found out what was wrong with him, and then got him straightened out. Why don't you go up there?"

I asked the pastor what he thought, and he told me to make whatever arrangements I wanted to. In order to go to the Mayo Clinic, you had to be sent by your own doctor. I talked things over with my doctor—the one who had prescribed the medication I was still taking—and he agreed that the clinic might help me. He wrote the people there a letter. In a week or so, I was on my way. It was the first time I had ever made a long trip to an institution on my own initiative. Up to then, someone else had always sent me.

After eight days at the clinic, I was told I had a nervous stomach and a touch of colitis. The doctors there prescribed phenobarbital before meals and seconal before retiring. On the day I left to return to Indianapolis, I was given two boxes, each containing a hundred pills, and I brought them home with me.

I took the pills for a week, and got some relief from them. But I noticed that it was always temporary. As soon as the effect of the latest pill wore off, I was jittery again. It worried me, because I was afraid that by the time I went through all the pills, I'd be so accustomed to them that I'd always have to take them.

That year, we had opened our "jitter-joint," officially known as the Indiana Home. This was a place where alcoholics could come and spend four or five days drying out and getting back to a point where they could eat again. It was sponsored by a member of A.A. and was—as it still is—strictly non-profit. It is operated under the supervision of a board of directors. Anyone who used it paid the regular fee. There were always twenty or thirty members dropping in, and they came at all hours of the day and night. Thus, the patients were well indoctrinated in the A.A. program. A meeting was held every Saturday night.

I stopped by often, partly to see if I could do anything and partly for my own benefit, for I had long since learned that I must never lose contact with other alcoholics if I hoped to stay sober myself. I would just sort of hang around, talking to people, perhaps having a cup of coffee or two and trying to make myself useful.

There, I had once met a hearing-aid specialist with an office in downtown Indianapolis. One day, I happened to be walking past his building, so I decided to stop in to say hello. Several people were standing outside his office when I arrived there, but they moved aside to let me in. The man was sitting in a chair, his tongue out, his lips swollen and blue and his eyes staring. The building nurse was trying to revive him.

"What's wrong?" I asked.

"He took an overdose of pills."

"What kind?"

"Seconal," the nurse said, without looking up.

"Will he be all right?"

"I think so," she said. "The doctor's on his way."

I waited for the doctor. When he told me the man would recover, I left and went right to see the doctor in charge of the Indiana Home. I told him what had happened.

"I'm scared, Doctor," I said. "I just got back from Mayo, where they gave me a couple hundred pills to take for my nervousness. But now I don't know what to do with them."

"Well," he said, "those people know what they're doing up there. Did you tell them you are an alcoholic?"

"Oh, no."

"You should have, Father. The doctors at Mayo would never have given you all those pills if they'd known that. Phenobarbital and seconal can both be dangerous drugs, especially to the alcoholic and the addictive personality. You might take too much of either without realizing it. I'm sure that's what happened to your friend, the hearing-aid man. It often happens with people who have been taking barbitals for a long time. They don't get enough relief from one, so they take two—or three—or even more—and pretty soon they've taken so many they pass out, or even die. You often read of people dying from an overdose of these drugs. It sounds like suicide, but in most cases it isn't. These people were just trying to get relief. What happens is, they have a couple of pills, then unconsciously reach for the bottle and finish it. It could happen to you."

"What shall I do with the pills, Doctor?"

"Well," he said, "it'll be tough on you for a while, but there's only one thing to do. Take those two boxes of pills and get rid of them before they get rid of you. I'll give you a shot of vitamin B-1. That will help. For a while, you ought to have one every few days."

So I went home and threw the pills out.

The doctor was right; it *was* tough on me. The next week was very tough indeed. Now, for the first time since my return from Oshkosh, I was trying to get along without pills of any kind. I was terribly jittery. I couldn't concentrate on anything. My mind wandered even when I read the A.A. book. I often had to put it down and pace the room. It was hard for me simply to sit down at the supper table, much less eat. I picked at whatever was placed in front of me, but pushed it away after taking a few nibbles. I slept an hour here, a half hour there. Most of the nights found me up and down, in and out of bed, staring out the window one minute and trying to read the next. Often, I put on my clothes and walked up and down in the back yard for hours while the rest of the city slept.

I had always been a heavy smoker, and now I was again averaging nearly three packs of cigarettes a day. I rarely let one go out without using it to light another. The first two fingers of my right hand were a deep brown, my mouth tasted like a furnace and my throat was so dry that I always felt thirsty.

The only thing that relieved my nervousness was talk, and I babbled endlessly. Now, when Dohr called, I held him in long conversations. I told him all about the trip to Rochester, and the diagnosis of the doctors, and the pills they gave me, and what happened to the hearing-aid man (who recovered), and what the doctor at the Indiana Home had told me. I told him how I had thrown all the pills away, and now wasn't taking anything, and how I hoped that was the way I'd always be.

When he picked me up in his car on meeting night, I was glad he had come alone.

"I'm terribly worried, Dohr," I said. "I've had a bad reaction from not taking pills. I'm so nervous I can't sit still."

"Well, now, Father, you've got something there that I'm not familiar with. We don't profess to know anything about barbitals. The only thing I can tell you—and it's only a personal opinion—is that if anything is worse than alcohol it's probably drugs. I imagine that monkeying around with barbitals would be the first step toward drug addiction for the alcoholic and would eventually lead to drinking again. You've lasted almost a week without those pills. If you can just go a little while longer, I should think eventually your nerves would quiet down."

It was good advice, and I followed it. I noticed that, while my nerves were jumpy and my mind wandered from time to time, my general condition was nowhere nearly as bad as in previous attacks. The vitamin B-1 helped tremendously. One factor that nearly drove me out of my mind during other shaky spells was now missing. I no longer was assailed by the deep depression and despair and the fear of the future. Those old fears had robbed me of my ability to think clearly. I couldn't take account of my own stock intelligently.

But this time I could almost stand in the wings and watch my troubles run their course on the stage. For the first time in my life, I could look at myself objectively while in the throes of a nervous reaction. Now I knew that this was only a temporary condition which would go away in due time. In the meantime, I must accept this physical restlessness as a means to an end.

As the weeks and months passed, the drugs I had taken left my system, and my nerves gradually fell back into place. I continued to go to A.A. meetings, largely because of Dohr. He never asked me if I wanted to go. He simply took it as a matter of course that I *was* going, and he always called for me. I still had no car of my own.

But, since many of the priests I knew didn't think I should be involved in the program, I still wasn't completely sold on A.A. I never spoke at a meeting, partly because I was too shy and partly because I was not ready to commit myself completely. But I listened carefully to what everyone said, and marveled at the way they all could open their talks with a baldly expressed, "I am an alcoholic." I was sure that, no matter what happened, I could never admit that, either to myself or anyone else.

In general, the other priests in the rectory, including the one who had been startled at the idea of a priest getting mixed up in A.A., approved of my interest in it. But they knew me and knew my problem. I'm sure they felt that anything was better for me than the conditions under which I had previously been living. And their great admiration for Dohr Sheerin was undoubtedly an important factor in their approval.

But whenever I mentioned A.A. to priests outside the parish, I almost invariably ran into opposition.

"This A.A. is all right for laymen, I suppose," one seminary classmate of mine remarked at a retreat one day, "but it's nothing for you, Ralph. No priest should join that sort of an organization. You don't need it."

"That's just the point," I said. "I *do* need it—or something like it."

listen to self

"You're a *priest*, Ralph. You should be able to get what you need from your Church."

He expressed the thoughts of the majority. I wondered if he was right. I *could* derive the strength to stop drinking from my Church. I asked Dohr about it later.

"You *can*, but you *won't*," he said.

"*You can, but you won't.*" *Where have I heard that before? I know—in Milwaukee. Dr. Blanchard once said something like that to me. What was it?*

I thought a moment. Then I remembered.

"*You can, but you won't.*"

I told Dohr.

"Same difference," he said. "It would be wonderful if you *could*—find the strength to stop drinking from the Church, that is. But the average alcoholic personality just won't. I didn't— and I've always been devoted to my Church. You're a priest. You've not only been devoted to your Church; you've given your life to it. But, with all of that, you still didn't get from it alone a solution for your drinking problem."

"But I must have the Church."

"Of course, you must have the Church. I must have the Church. Any good Catholic must have the Church. A.A. without the Church would be less effective for us than the Church without A.A. But, in order to stop drinking, people like you and me must have *both*. We need something to help us remove the *natural* obstacles to grace, something to *keep* us convinced we *can't* drink—that we're still alcoholics."

"How do I make other priests understand that?" I asked.

"I don't know," Dohr said. "I suppose you can only show them the results. You were drinking before you had A.A. Now that you have A.A., you've stopped drinking."

"That's not enough to convince people who don't understand," I said.

"I'm afraid you're right, Father. But the big thing for now is that you understand, yourself. After that, you can think about making other people understand."

"But how can I tell another priest why I must have A.A.? If—" I added, lamely, "it is a fact that I must have it."

"That's the whole point," said Dohr. "There can't be any 'ifs' in your own mind. First, be convinced that you must have it. Then the explanations to convince others will come easier."

Gradually, I became convinced. It took almost a year for the program to take shape. I began to see how a key principle of A.A. applied to me, reluctant as I was to admit it.

To the alcoholic, the first thing in his life is that he cannot drink.

This is basic. It may not be his most important problem. Certainly, the threat of drug addiction, which may have hung over me, was potentially more important. My neurotic tendencies, which first manifested themselves at St. Meinrad, before I had ever taken a drink in my life, were more important. If an alcoholic has a deadly disease, the disease is more important.

But, regardless of his other problems, the *first* thing an alcoholic must do is stop drinking. Once he has done that, he can tackle the other problems. But if he doesn't do it, the other problems not only will remain unsolved, but become intensified.

I learned at last what an alcoholic really is. I had always confused alcoholism with drunkenness. To me, the alcoholic was the person who daily drank himself into a disgusting mess, a stumble-bum, a guttersnipe, a weakling, hopelessly befogged day after day, week after week, month after month who, eventually, ended up a liquor-soaked corpse in the river or under the wheels of a truck. That's what I had always read, for any literature I had ever seen on the subject pinpointed alcoholics as being that way.

But now I saw how wrong I had been. During that first year in A.A., I discovered that an alcoholic is merely a person who, when he takes his first drink has no idea where he will stop. When he takes that first drink, something happens. He is no longer the same person he was before. Once he has had the first drink, he is compelled to continue drinking indefinitely.

But he can avoid the first drink. And, once he's learned to do that, he will stay sober, for it is impossible for a man to have a second drink until he has had his first.

Now, I had to apply all this to myself. I had to learn that this program was even good enough for a priest.

I sat in at one A.A. meeting after another for a full year without saying a word, but watching and listening. I saw a man come in, red-faced, bleary-eyed, sweating, jittery, disheveled, and I saw him come in a week later tired, but neat, and a week after that looking a little better until finally he appeared to regain his status as a human being. He later became one of the city's outstanding attorneys.

His case was not unusual. As I watched, others came in, not all bleary-eyed and disheveled, but all shaky and nervous and upset, and I saw them improve until they regained their niches in life.

And I learned that you don't have to be a stumble-bum to be an alcoholic. You can be a doctor, a lawyer, a college professor, a businessman, a writer, a society leader, a nurse, a stenographer, a salesman, a buyer, a mechanic, an engineer, a psychologist, a policeman, a fireman, a politician.

Or a priest.

At a meeting one night in the fall of 1944, almost a year after Dohr Sheerin first introduced me as a new member, someone asked, "How much should a person tell about himself when he speaks at a meeting?"

"I think he should go into all the moral details of his life," another member commented. "I think he should tell everything, regardless of whether or not it has anything to do with his drinking."

"I don't."

I was startled at the sound of my own voice.

Dohr, who was conducting the meeting, turned to me and said, "You don't, Father?"

I rose to my feet.

"No," I said. "I don't. I think that anyone speaking at a meeting should confine his remarks to his problem of alcoholism. The moral details of his life have no bearing on this problem, and recounting them won't help him stop drinking. Ours is not a public confession.

"I feel after listening to all the discussion for nearly a year," I went on, "that there are three basic reasons for speaking at a meeting, and none has anything to do with moral details. The first reason is to identify yourself as an alcoholic. The second is to talk about our past, and familiarize ourself so thoroughly with it that we'll drive out all the fears that made us drink in the first place. The third is to help yourself and others stay sober."

Then, a little dazed by my own boldness, I sat down.

It wasn't until later that I realized I had neglected one of my own stated reasons for speaking at a meeting. I hadn't identified myself as an alcoholic.

On the way home that night, Dohr said, "Now you're getting somewhere, Father. Do you realize that's the first time you've ever spoken in a meeting?"

"I know it," I said.

"And you brought up a good point."

"You know, Dohr, I was wondering about this business of identifying yourself as an alcoholic. Assuming that you are ready to admit it, to whom do you admit it?"

"That's up to you, Father. In A.A., we don't tell anybody else's names, or who attended meetings, but we can talk about ourselves all we like. I can tell my boss, my friends, my neighbors, my relatives, anyone at all. I can get up on the rooftops and shout about it for all the world to hear, if I want to. And I would, if I thought it would help others, or even myself. Anonymity respects the other members' names. We may do what we wish with our own."

He looked at me, and smiled.

"Are you ready to admit now that you're an alcoholic, Father?"

I smiled back.

"Well, Dohr," I said, "let's put it this way. I'm ready to admit I'm a member of Alcoholics Anonymous."

"That's something, anyhow," he said, just before bidding me goodnight.

I talked more and more about A.A. around the parish house. I found that it helped me to talk about it. I no longer made subtle references to the fact that I attended meetings. Now, I came right out at the dinner table and said, "In A.A., we think this—" or "In A.A., we think that—" The term "we" was not lost on any of my priestly colleagues. And, to my relief, all of them

now seemed to approve of my membership. Once I asked Dohr
if there were any other priests in A.A. He had never heard of
any.

Life went on smoothly for me, and I was happy both in my
parish work and in my A.A. associations. Monsignor Bosler was
very understanding, and let me do as I pleased. I didn't neglect
my duties, but I spent increasingly larger amounts of time with
A.A. My pastor didn't seem to object.

Then, in August of 1945, I got a letter from the Bishop, telling
me that Father Sullivan, who had been appointed pastor of Holy
Cross parish in Indianapolis after he got out of the army, had
asked for me to be his assistant.

"We would like you to take up residence at Holy Cross at
your earliest convenience," the letter said.

This was my first direct contact with the Bishop since I had
returned from Oshkosh a year and a half earlier. I had studiously
avoided the Chancery, for I didn't know how the Bishop would
feel about my being in A.A. The letter encouraged me. Obviously, the Bishop must have heard about it, and, just as obviously,
he didn't object or he would have said something about it.

I was delighted to rejoin Father Sullivan. Before moving in
with him, I dropped by to see him.

"Did you know I've become a member of Alcoholics Anonymous?" I asked.

"Oh, yes," Father Sullivan said. "And I know how it's helped
you, too. Now, you come out to my parish and you can give
A.A. all the time you want."

"I may end up giving it more time than the parish."

"That'll be all right, too."

I thanked him, and moved in a few days later.

At just about that time, I had begun to make Twelfth Step
calls. These are to people who, faced with the alcoholic problem, call Alcoholics Anonymous for help. Dohr had started me
off soon after I began speaking out during meetings. As far as
I knew, the only purpose in making Twelfth Step calls was to
help somebody else try to stay sober. I made half a dozen calls
in about three months, but I might as well have stayed home.

Only one of the people got straightened out, and I think he would have even without me.

The first time I made a Twelfth Step call, I went to see a Negro about forty-five years old, who was about in as bad shape from liquor as anyone I ever laid eyes on. I went to visit him in a squalid flat in the west end of town. When I got there, he was in bed, shaking the frame almost to pieces, while his wife, a thin, hard-working soul who looked as if she were at the end of her rope herself, stood by wringing her hands and sobbing.

"I'm a member of Alcoholics Anonymous," I said.

"I take a little drink and I get a little scared," he mumbled. "Then I take another drink and I get more scared. Pretty soon I just shake all over like I'm doing now."

"Sure, sure," I said, "I know how it is."

"Nobody knows," he moaned. "I take a little drink and I get a little scared—"

He went on mumbling. I tried to soothe him and tell him everything would be all right, but all he did was shake and repeat the same thing over and over. Finally, I said, "I'll be back tomorrow night at seven-thirty to take you to an A.A. meeting."

I turned to his wife.

"Can you have him ready?"

She shrugged, then managed to get out a weepy "I'll try."

The next night Dohr and I went over to pick the man up, but neither he nor his wife were there. I never did find out what happened to him, although I made two or three trips back. All I know is he didn't join A.A.

My second Twelfth Step call was no more successful. This time, I went to see a young fellow in the northeast part of town. He was married, but when I saw him, he was slobbering over a fifth of rye in the kitchen of his mother's home. She was the one who had called us. I tried to talk to him, but he was too drunk to understand what I was saying.

"Poor Charlie," his mother said, wringing her hands, "he's never done a wrong thing in his life."

I looked at her a minute, then said, "Do you want to know the reason why Charlie is in there drunk tonight? Just because of things like that last statement of yours. You've probably been telling him for years that he's never done a wrong thing in his life."

"Well, he hasn't, Father."

"Leaving his family to come back here to drink in his mother's house is hardly a right thing," I said.

"Can you help him, Father?"

"I don't know. Maybe I can help him help himself—if he wants help. Our next meeting is the day after tomorrow. We'll pick him up and take him along with us."

But two nights later, when Dohr and I went over there, the man had gone back to his own home. We followed him there, but neither he nor his wife saw any need for his joining A.A. I told them where they could reach me if he changed his mind, but I never heard from him.

I had no better luck on any of my other calls. Finally, on the way to a meeting, I said to Dohr, "Look, I've been making these Twelfth Step calls and I haven't got anyone sober."

"Well," he said, "you've stayed sober yourself, haven't you?" I nodded.

"Insurance against a slip—that's really the primary reason for Twelfth Step calls," Dohr said. "When I make one, I lay my cards on the table. I say, 'Now, look, fella, I don't care if you die drunk. I'm not interested in that. But I do care if *I* die drunk, and that's the reason I'm here. Now if you want what I've got, I'll take all the time in the world to give it to you. If you don't want it, just give me a call when you're ready.'"

But the things that worked so well with Dohr didn't work at all with me. Dohr must personally have sponsored hundreds of alcoholics during the years I knew him, and most of them made the grade. My record in those first few months was almost zero. The only person who came into the group through me was an eighty-three-year-old man. While in the throes of the shakes, he stopped in to see me at the rectory. He had taken the pledge to stop drinking, and he begged me to relieve him of it.

"Just let me be allowed to have one drink, Father," he pleaded.

"If I did that," I said, "where would you get the drink? You'd either have to buy a bottle or stop in at a tavern. If you got a bottle, you wouldn't stop with one drink. And you wouldn't stop with one if you went into a tavern, either."

Then I suggested, "How about giving you a drink?"

His eyes danced, and his face broke into a tearfully happy grin. "Father," he said, "you're the kindest person I've ever met."

I went into the kitchen, poured out a shot and brought it to him. He downed it quickly, then handed me the empty glass.

"If you must have another, come on back, and I'll give you one," I said.

He came back twice that day. But after that, he stopped. From then on, he never had another drink. He died after several years of beaming sobriety.

ended positively

× own life is improving

CHAPTER 17

Although I was staying sober myself, I wasn't satisfied. I felt that, as a Catholic priest and a member of Alcoholics Anonymous, too, I had something more to offer other alcoholics, if I could find a way to reach them. I talked it over with Dohr several times.

"Look," I said, "I'm on the give side of this thing in a different way from anybody else. As a priest, I'm in a unique position. I've got something to offer that the others haven't. But when I go out on calls, people won't accept me as anything but a priest, no matter what I tell them. As far as they're concerned, I'm moralizing."

"That's right, Father," he said. "You can do a lot more good in other ways than any of us. The only question is how to go about it."

The answer was so obvious that I felt foolish because I hadn't thought of it sooner. It had been right in front of my nose all the time. In the seminary and as a priest, we annually make a retreat. A retreat is a period of discussion and meditation which normally lasts from a day to a weekend, although it can last longer. In a Catholic retreat, there is a retreat master or retreat director who gives talks on the dogma and practice of Catholicism. There is also a regular period for questions and open discussion, as well as periods for rest and meditation. People in all walks of life attend retreats, and gain great peace and solace from them.

"How about having a retreat for alcoholics?" I suggested to Dohr one day. "After all, the whole idea of a retreat is just to pause and think things over in company with other people having the same idea in mind. We could have an A.A. retreat, with talks and questions and open discussion. And we could make it exclusively on A.A. We wouldn't go into the question of religion at all."

"You mean a retreat that wouldn't be confined only to Catholics?"

"That's right, Dohr. We'd just have members of A.A. and we'd discuss nothing that's not discussed at any A.A. meeting."

"Father," he said enthusiastically, "I think it's a splendid idea. Only where could we hold such a retreat?"

"I'll find a place," I said.

It was easier said than done. To begin with, I'd need the Bishop's permission, and I was a little apprehensive of his reaction. Except for his letter transferring me from St. Joan of Arc to Holy Cross parish, I had had no direct contact with him since the unfortunate interview after my return from the Alexian Brothers Sanitarium in Oshkosh. At that point, he apparently was sick and tired of me. I wondered how he felt about me now, a year and a half or so later.

Before writing him, I decided to try to find a location. I wanted to start with a one-day retreat in or near Indianapolis. It could start after Mass Sunday morning and last until dinnertime in the evening. That would give us time enough for a few talks, and the people could also have discussion among themselves. If it worked out, we could try something more ambitious later.

Since I had once served as chaplain for the Little Sisters of the Poor, I went to them and asked for the use of their facilities. They told me they'd be delighted. I went back to the parish house and, with some misgivings, wrote the Bishop a letter which read, in substance, as follows:

"I presume that you have at least a passing acquaintance with the Alcoholics Anonymous program. Perhaps you do not know it, but I have been associated with A.A. now for over a year. I would like to conduct a one-day retreat for the members at the

Little Sisters of the Poor, if you would be kind enough to give me permission to do so."

He wrote back by return mail, telling me that he was well aware of the A.A. program, and was thoroughly delighted that I had become a member of the movement. He added that he was happy to hear that I was planning a one-day retreat at the Little Sisters of the Poor.

The retreat was a success in all respects. We had sixty-seven men there, only about twenty of whom were Catholics. The talks were all strictly A.A., and were well received by Protestants and Catholics alike.

We had our lunch in the men's dining room. The Sisters knew what I liked, and always prepared the same type of meal for me. They also knew, of course, what A.A. was, but none of them had any idea that I was a member myself. So, when the Sister who had always brought me my lunch took it to me this time, she set a tray in front of me with sandwiches, coffee and, squarely in the middle, a nice, big, cold bottle of beer.

The place exploded, and I laughed harder than anyone. I'm afraid the poor Little Sister doesn't know to this day what struck us all so funny.

Sometime before the retreat, when I walked into a five-bed men's dormitory on the second floor of our Indiana Home, I noticed one of the patients stare wildly at me, then bury himself under the blankets, pulling them over his face. But he didn't duck fast enough. I recognized him at once. It was Bill upon whom I had made the hurry-up sick call and from whom I had borrowed the A.A. book.

I walked over to his bed, pulled the covers down and said, "Well, good morning. Fancy seeing you here!"

"Oh, no, Father, not you!" he mumbled.

"Yes, me," I said. "I read the book before you did. But it was your book. I'm glad you finally got around to reading it yourself."

"It's killing me," he groaned.

"I know," I said. "It's bad now, but you'll feel better after you're all dried out."

Bill never took another drink. He came to meetings and attended our first retreat at the Little Sisters of the Poor about a year later. He dropped dead in town from a heart attack the next day. But he died sober, and his wife and son were eternally grateful to A.A.

The one-day retreat was so successful that the members asked if I could arrange a longer one. I went to see the Bishop about having a weekend retreat, and he said, "Go ahead. If you can get a place anywhere in the diocese, you have my permission to use it."

I went to several institutions but I didn't get beyond the front door. When it was opened, I said, "I'd like to talk to someone about holding a retreat for Alcoholics Anonymous."

"Oh, no, Father, not here" was the inevitable reply.

The only other place I could think of was St. Joseph's College at Rensselaer, Indiana. I wrote there in early April, but nothing happened. When several weeks had gone by without an answer, I became pretty discouraged. Nobody seemed to want us.

I was still trying to figure out an answer when I received a letter from Father Lux, the president of St. Joseph's.

"My apologies for not having answered your letter sooner," he wrote, "but I have been away from my desk for nearly a month. We'd be most delighted to welcome you and your Alcoholics Anonymous people here for a retreat. I would suggest some time around the middle of June, after our students have returned home for summer vacation. If you'd like to talk things over with me ahead of time, why don't you come and see me at your convenience?"

The St. Joseph's retreat was the first weekend affair of its kind ever held. Previously there had only been Catholic retreats for members of A.A., which included talks on Catholic dogma and practice. The retreat at the Little Sisters had merely lasted one day and was strictly experimental. There were about ninety people there, about eighty per cent of whom were non-Catholics. We followed the pattern, but not the content of a regular Catholic retreat, giving talks, with a question period and discussion, and allowing time for meditation, all on the A.A. program.

To this day, we have a men's retreat at St. Joseph's every year.

We also have retreats, for women as well as for men, although they are held separately, in various places around the country. Our average attendance, which varies in different parts of the country, still runs about sixty-five to seventy per cent non-Catholic.

At about the time I was planning the first St. Joseph retreat, I got a letter from a priest in a large midwestern city, inquiring about Alcoholics Anonymous. He had heard I was familiar with it and wanted more information.

"I might be interested myself," he wrote, "because I think that, through it, I can help others. I know several people who need this kind of help."

By this time, the Bishop had given me permission to drive, and I had a car of my own again. I suspected that the "several people" whom the priest said needed help were non-existent, and that he was asking help for himself, so I drove over to see him. One look at him confirmed my suspicions. He was shaky and upset, and it didn't take him long to admit that he had an alcoholic problem. But, because he was a priest, he was doubtful about joining A.A. In talking about it to other priests, he had run into the same adverse reactions I had. I pointed this out to him, then told him that I now had the approval of my Bishop and that many of my colleagues who had originally frowned on the idea had changed their minds. I finally convinced him that he had nothing to worry about, and he agreed to give it a try. As far as I know, he was the second priest to join A.A. He's still very active in the program. There are now clergymen of many different faiths who have joined A.A. and found sobriety in it.

I was beginning to get pretty confident about my own ability to stay away from alcohol. By late 1945, I had not had a drink in two years, and I was getting proud of myself. When I arose every morning, I asked divine help in remaining sober for the next twenty-four hours (as I do today), and every day I remained sober. My nerves were behaving, and my jitters were gone. I was in good physical condition, eating and sleeping well and enjoying more peace of mind and satisfaction in my work than I had ever known.

I had full confidence in the A.A. program, but there was one fact which I still couldn't accept completely. That was the theory that alcoholism is a disease. From time immemorial, alcoholism had seldom been distinguished from drunkenness, and I had grown up committed to this idea. I was ashamed of my own moral weakness, and, even after two years in A.A., I still suspected that it was moral weakness which had caused me to drink.

Of course, I had learned that there are sharply defined differences between an alcoholic and a drunk. I knew that alcoholism had the element of compulsion and drunkenness did not. The quantity of liquor consumed and the resulting intoxication might be exactly the same, but the motive is altogether different. The alcoholic drinks because he has to. The drunkard drinks because he wants to. Once the alcoholic starts drinking, he can't stop. The drunkard can stop whenever he feels like it. When the alcoholic drinks, all he can think about is where he will get his next drink. When the drunkard drinks, he wants only to get high and enjoy himself. The alcoholic can't get liquor out of his mind. The drunkard can forget about it at will, if, indeed, he ever gives it much thought to begin with.

When the alcoholic wakes up in the morning, he's got the jitters and an uncontrollable craving for a drink to relieve them. When the drunkard wakes up in the morning, he feels terrible, but the only craving he has is for something to get his mind off his hangover. The last thing he wants is a drink. If the alcoholic doesn't have his drink, he can't work or do anything else. The drunkard might take something to settle his stomach, but he can always manage to drag himself off to work. He won't have a happy day, but he won't have a craving for liquor, either.

Of course, a drunkard can develop into an alcoholic. Most alcoholics started out as social drinkers. But who knows where the responsibilty for his becoming an alcoholic lies? I had been taught that it's his own responsibility. It is the normal reaction of any clergyman to accept this theory.

This was why I, as a priest, found it so hard to accept any other theory. As far as I could see, I became an alcoholic because I drank too much, not that I drank too much because I was an alcoholic. It was as simple as that. And, no matter how much Dohr tried to tell me otherwise, I refused to believe him.

Hadn't everyone told me I was no good? Hadn't they all said I was hopeless? Wasn't it always my fault that I drank? Hadn't I been told I'd never be any good if I didn't moderate my drinking?

That didn't sound as if I had a disease, did it?

I told alcoholics every day that they were sick, but I had my fingers crossed when I said it. I didn't—I couldn't—believe that it was true.

Not until the day I nearly slipped myself.

When saying Mass, a priest uses wine in the chalice. This, in our belief, becomes the Blood of Christ at the moment of Consecration. Although, according to our faith, transubstantiation actually does take place, the accidents of wine remain. This means that although the substance is changed the action of alcohol can have the same effect on the human system after the Consecration as before.

I learned early after I joined A.A. that, as a priest alcoholic, I must take a minimum of wine at Mass. The minimum for validity is about two teaspoonsful. Medically, an alcoholic would be disturbed if he took enough alcohol to penetrate his bloodstream or brain cells. Two teaspoonsful of ordinary Mass wine would not bother the worst alcoholic. While, contrary to popular opinion, it *is* a fermented drink, it has a very low alcoholic content, because the Church does not permit it to be fortified.

Commercial wine, on the other hand, is well fortified with grape alcohol. It is usually much sweeter and heavier than Mass wine, and can cause a definite reaction if taken by an alcoholic. Two teaspoonsful of some commercial wines, the minimum for saying Mass, *can* give an alcoholic trouble. A few of the heavier type Mass wines approach this commercial content.

I had always been careful about the amount of wine at Mass, and I had never had a reaction from it after I joined A.A. But one morning, at Holy Cross, I knew, the moment I consumed the Sacred Species, that this was not average Mass wine. I felt a sudden urge to keep on drinking, a compulsive craving that blocked out all reason.

The moment Mass was over, I hurried to the kitchen.

"Was there anything different about the Mass wine we used this morning?" I asked the housekeeper.

"Yes, Father," she said. "A salesman left a sample bottle, and I used it in the cruets."

"May I see the bottle, please?"

She got it out for me. I looked at the label. The wine, although Mass wine, had an alcoholic content of twenty-two per cent.

I want a drink.

I shuddered as I left the kitchen.

I want a drink.

I was scared—as scared as I had ever been in my life. This was not just a casual desire. This was a terrible, compulsive craving that overwhelmed me.

If I don't have a drink, I'll go crazy. dependence
I've got to have a drink.

I forced myself to the telephone. With shaking hands, I picked it up and called Dohr Sheerin.

I want a drink—I want a drink—I want a drink—

"Hello?"

"Dohr?"

"Hello, Father—"

"Dohr, I want a drink."

"Well, Father," he drawled, "I'm glad you called. What happened?"

I told him. I talked so fast the words tumbled out, one on top of the other. I guess I wasn't very coherent, but he didn't interrupt me. Then I said, "Dohr, I'm frightened. I've got to have a drink."

"Keep talking."

"I can't understand how this happened. It's never happened before. I've been dry two years, and now I feel as if I'd never been dry. A little wine at the Mass—that's all I took. But it was enough to set me off. Dohr, I'm afraid I'll go mad if I don't have a drink."

"A little wine has set off a lot of benders, Father," Dohr said. He was still drawling, talking in a slow, casual manner. "You

know," he went on, "you were very wise in calling me. Any
time you feel like a drink, just go to the phone and call. I'm
never very far away."

"I want a drink," I said.

"Sure, Father. I know just how you feel. You've had a reaction because the wine was too heavy. But you know you're really
all right, and you know you'll get over this craving. You've
been in A.A. a couple of years now. You know the questions,
and you know the answers. And you know you can't take another drink, because if you do there'll be no stopping. You'll
get the jitters and you'll fall apart and you'll have to get dried
out all over again. And you know what that means."

"Dohr, I've got to hang up now. I'm going to get a drink."

"Wait a minute, Father—" softly, gently persuasive—"before
you hang up, I want to tell you something. I've got a couple of
tickets to the Notre Dame game at South Bend Saturday. I want
you to come and see it with me. They've got a great team this
year, Father—"

"I want a drink."

"Do you remember Oshkosh, Father? Do you remember Milwaukee? Do you remember Vincennes? Do you remember
Snake Run? Do you remember what you were like two years
ago before you came into A.A.? Do you realize how far you've
come in those two years? Do you realize how far you're going?
You don't really want a drink, Father—"

"Yes, I do—I do, Dohr. I must have a drink—now."

"How would you like to run a high school basketball tournament, Father, just like the one you told me about in Jeffersonville? We could arrange to have all the schools, not just the
parochial schools, and it would be a big thing. We'd get help
from the newspapers, and the city and the diocese—it would
really mean something. You'd do a good job, Father—"

"I want a drink."

"No, you don't, not really, Father. You're too experienced in
A.A. to want a drink. You've seen too many people in the jitter-
joint sweating out a living death while they wait for the alcohol
to leave their systems. You've been through that yourself a dozen

times. You know what it's like. You don't ever intend to go through it again. You're too intelligent for that, Father."

"I want a drink."

"Father, how many times have you told me that you never really believed that alcoholism was a disease? Do you remember how you used to insist to me that, even though you told others it was a disease, you really thought it was a moral fault that could be controlled? Now, what do you think, Father?"

"Keep talking," I said. My throat was dry and my voice cracked and little rivulets of sweat were gushing out of every pore in my body.

Dohr kept talking. He talked for five minutes, jumping from one subject to another, filibustering like a politician, stalling me off from leaving the phone.

And I listened.

Then he said, "Father, it's been ten minutes since you've said you wanted a drink."

"Has it been that long?"

"Yes."

"Do you still want a drink, Father?"

"Keep talking, Dohr."

So he talked for another ten minutes.

"Now it's twenty minutes, Father— Do you want to talk?"

"Twenty minutes—yes—yes, Dohr, I want to talk."

I could feel the saliva in my mouth and throat, and I wasn't perspiring so much.

"What about the next retreat, Father? Is everything all arranged?"

Now *I* talked for ten or fifteen minutes. And, as I talked about the next retreat, I warmed up to the subject. Dohr reacted as though it were just an ordinary conversation. He asked me all sorts of questions, and I answered them.

Then I said, "I'm all right now, Dohr."

"Are you sure, Father?"

"Positive."

"You don't want a drink any more?"

"No, Dohr, I don't want a drink."

"All right, Father. Call me if you need me."

We both hung up.

I looked at my watch.

We had been talking nearly two solid hours.

And now I knew that alcoholism was not exclusively a moral problem. Now I knew it was a disease.

If only I could stick to this conviction without ever rationalizing the "need" for the first drink, I knew my alcoholic troubles would be over.

- never over
- constant battle

CHAPTER 18

Not long after my near-slip from the Mass wine, Dohr and I went to an A.A. anniversary meeting in Columbus, Indiana. Just as the meeting was about to close, someone turned to me and said, "Father Pfau, have you anything to say?"

I had spoken at retreats, but had never given a real talk at a meeting. The only times I opened my mouth then were in conversations, involving mostly questions and answers, or opinions about what someone else had said.

Now, I got up and said, slowly, "I am a member of the Indianapolis group of Alcoholics Anonymous. I enjoyed the meeting here. I think it was an excellent one, and I was glad to be here. Thank you."

Then I sat down.

On the way back to Indianapolis, Dohr said, "Why didn't you say you were an alcoholic, Father?"

"I tried to, Dohr. But the words stuck in my throat."

During the first weekend retreat, my theme had been on the subject, "The Spiritual Side of Alcoholics Anonymous." It went over so well that I repeated it at all the retreats I conducted the next year and, in fact, it is now on a recording. There is nothing personal in this talk. It is a general subject, designed to give the members something to think about.

In 1946, I was asked to give the talk at an A.A. meeting in Cincinnati, by a man who had attended one of our retreats. There were more than a hundred people present, filling the little meeting hall to the doors. The chairman introduced me, and I gave the talk in the same way I always had. When it was over, the chairman opened the floor for questions.

A little fellow in the back of the room got up and said, "Father, that was a fine talk. I liked it and maybe I got something out of it. But, Father, what the heck do you know about this problem? You're a priest. Or are you an alcoholic, too?"

I swallowed.

Then in a voice I hoped was steady, I said, "Yes, I'm an alcoholic."

"Well," the man said, "that's fine. Tell us about it." *Admit*

So, for the first time, I told the story of my alcoholic life in an open meeting. I told of my first nervous breakdown, my first drink, my subsequent breakdowns, the fluctuations of my alcoholic appetite, my experiences in various hospitals and sanitariums, my frequent troubles with the Bishop, everything, in fact, that I could think of. I talked for half an hour, and the place exploded with applause when I was through.

And after I sat down, I felt a deep relief, a relief from all the doubts which had assailed me ever since I first joined A.A., as though, with that first full admission before other alcoholics, I had removed the last of the blocks that seemed to separate me from them. There was nothing more for me to hide, either from them or from myself. Now, at last, I was one of them.

The next time I was asked to speak, I stood squarely on my feet, looked around at the expectant faces in front of me and said, firmly, "My name is Father Pfau. I am not going to spell it for you. You can use your imagination. Most people do. I am a member of the Indianapolis group of Alcoholics Anonymous and *I am an alcoholic.*"

I have been telling my story to alcoholics all over America ever since, starting my talk in exactly that manner, and putting into it all the basic essentials of that first talk in Cincinnati. I will venture to say I have delivered it fifteen hundred times.

In 1946, Indianapolis, which had become an archdiocese got a new archbishop. My former Bishop, himself an archbishop now, was transferred to a larger archdiocese.

At first, the change did not affect me at all. I continued with all my A.A. work, which was now beginning to entail a good deal of short-distance traveling. The more time I devoted to A.A., the less I could spare for my parish duties. Father Sullivan, my pastor, said nothing about it, but I wasn't giving him or his other assistant much help.

In October of 1947, I was asked to give a one-day retreat at the disciplinary barracks of Fort Benjamin Harrison, near Indianapolis. There was an A.A. group in the barracks, and some of the members had requested permission to invite me to address them. After a great deal of red tape had been unraveled, it was finally arranged. The retreat was to consist of three talks, following the general pattern of all our one-day retreats.

I asked Father Sullivan well in advance if it was all right for me to go, and he gave me permission. But on the day before the retreat, he changed his mind.

"I'm sorry, Ralph," he said, "but something has come up in the parish, and I simply can't spare you tomorrow."

"But, Father," I said, "I can't back out now. This thing had to be set up far ahead of time. You know what army red tape is. The members will be disappointed and the army authorities will be very much upset. They went to a great deal of trouble to arrange this retreat. If I disappoint them, they'll never invite me again, and all those fellows will be left up in the air."

"I understand that," said Father Sullivan, "but you are, after all, the assistant pastor of Holy Cross parish, and I need you here. You must realize that nothing can take precedence over your parish duties. They are more important than A.A. or anything else."

"I'm not so sure about that," I said, with some irritation. "Besides, I've given these people my word, and I'm obligated to keep it."

After a few more somewhat sharp exchanges, I finally walked away and went into my office. Fifteen or twenty minutes later, Father Sullivan came in and said, "All right, Ralph. You gave your promise. Go ahead and keep it. But don't let this sort of thing happen again."

I was deeply resentful. Up to that moment, I had been on the best of terms with Father Sullivan, but now I felt that he was interfering with something that was beyond his province. The more I thought about it, the more resentful I became, and I worked myself into quite a lather.

The next day, after the retreat at Fort Benjamin Harrison, I decided to see Dohr Sheerin.

"What's the trouble this time, Father?" he said softly, with that wonderful smile playing about his lips.

"Well," I said, "there's friction in the rectory. Father Sullivan seems to think I'm neglecting my duties. So—I'm going to quit A.A."

Dohr didn't say anything for a minute. He just stared off into space, the smile still on his face. Then he turned to me and said, "Well, now, Father, that's a new excuse—and a pretty good one."

I winced.

"But, you know," he went on, "Father Sullivan has been very good to you. He has taken you into Holy Cross, and, if you look back, you weren't any rose-geranium at the time he took you. You were just an obscure priest in a great big parish, and, because you had a reputation of being a troublemaker, you were there on sufferance. Nobody really wanted you. Father Sullivan gave you some standing with the Bishop by asking for you. And, after you joined him, he let you do pretty much as you pleased.

"He has been quite wonderful in permitting you to give so much time to A.A. He never had to do that. After all, Father, A.A. must be first with you, but not A.A. activities. Your priesthood has to be first there. But that doesn't mean you have to leave A.A. altogether."

"But what about the talks, the retreats, the traveling—all that?" I asked.

"You forget a very important point, Father," said Dohr. "Your first obligation is to stay sober. You don't have to give talks and retreats and travel around to do that. All you have to do is go to meetings as often as you can, and maintain regular contact with other alcoholics. This other stuff you're doing is fine, as long as it doesn't cause resentment or friction. But when that happens, you have to stop, because resentments can start you drinking again.

"You just do what Father Sullivan tells you, and attend meetings when they don't interfere with your parish work. I don't think your pastor will have any objection to that. He knows what A.A. has done for you, and I'm sure he doesn't want you to give it up. The only thing that concerns him is the possibility that you will let A.A. supersede your work at Holy Cross."

As usual, Dohr was right. I went to Father Sullivan and apologized. He assured me that, by all means, I was to continue my work in A.A. I, in turn, assured him that I would be available for more duties around the parish.

The next day the new Archbishop sent for me.

"I have heard about your work," he said. "How would you like to be relieved of your parish duties so that you can devote full time to Alcoholics Anonymous?"

I didn't know what to say.

I wanted to say yes, but I wasn't sure the Archbishop understood everything it would entail. Besides, I hadn't come quite far enough yet to make a decision of that importance without thinking about it.

I thanked the Archbishop, then asked, "May I have a little time to think it over?"

"Certainly," he said. "Of course, the big factor is the financing of your own living."

"That might be a problem, because Alcoholics Anonymous is not really an organization," I said. "As we say in A.A., it's nothing more than a fellowship of men and women who share their experience, strength, hope and prayers that they may all solve their common problem and help others facing the same problem. It has no dues or fees. It is not allied with any sect, faith or denomination. It has no interest in politics, and it neither opposes nor endorses any causes. The only requirement for membership is an honest desire to stop drinking. Our primary purpose is to stay sober and to help other alcoholics achieve and maintain sobriety. If I were to give full time to A.A., I would have to do so as an alcoholic, as just another member of A.A."

"But as a priest, you would have the respect of others," the

Archbishop said. "And I feel that your retreat work is important enough to people of all faiths to warrant your giving full time to it. When you have thought it over, let me know."

Dohr was delighted when I told him about it.

"Go back to the Archbishop," he said, "and tell him you accept. Actually, you are only committing yourself to one day at a time, since, in A.A., we think only in terms of the next twenty-four hours."

"But I don't have any money," I said. "I'm still in debt."

"Don't worry, Father. We'll find a way to finance you."

"Well, Dohr, let's figure out how before I go back to the Archbishop."

The next day, Dohr and I went to see A. Kiefer Mayer, a close friend of Dohr's. He was then vice-president (and now is president) of the Kiefer-Stewart Drug Company, a large wholesale house in Indianapolis. Mr. Mayer is neither a Catholic nor an alcoholic. But his offices are right across the street from the Chancery. He was a friend of both the Archbishop and his predecessor and had always had great admiration for what A.A. had done for Doherty Sherrin.

Dohr explained the situation.

"Under this kind of an arrangement, Father Pfau could help alcoholics not only here, but anywhere in the country," he said. "The Archbishop is perfectly willing to let him go wherever he sees fit. The big difficulty will be financing, and that's why we came to you."

"You came to the right person," Mr. Mayer said. "This is the finest idea I've heard for a long time. I'm all for it."

He reached for his checkbook, and passed it to me.

"Here, Father," he said. "Write your own ticket."

My annual salary had been $600. This was the amount that Mr. Mayer filled in to cover the first year.

Then he phoned the Archbishop, and congratulated him. "It's a wonderful decision," Mr. Mayer said, "and I know you'll never regret it."

The Archbishop released me from my parish duties on Christmas Day of 1947. I thanked Father Sullivan for everything he had done, then took up residence in St. Bridget's rectory in Indianapolis, which had an extra room I could use. I paid for my room and board, so I was not obligated to the parochial duties.

I started mapping out plans for retreats, beginning in June, when I could go to St. Joseph's. In the meantime, Dohr urged me to take a vacation.

"You haven't had a real vacation in years," he said. "Why don't you go off somewhere for a couple of weeks?"

"Where can I go?" I said.

"Anywhere. You'll have a million things to do from June on. Take some time off and go somewhere first. You once started for the West Coast and never got there. Why don't you go now?"

The more I thought about the idea, the better I liked it. Finally, in April, I decided to go to Los Angeles. The night before I left, Dohr came over to the rectory and helped me pack. I was about to close my suitcase when he said, "Wait a minute."

He went over to the desk and picked up my copy of the A.A. directory, a book that lists groups in various parts of the country.

"Put this right on top every day," he said. "Then, when you open your grip, it will be the first thing you see."

I left the next morning.

The itinerary I planned took me via Texarkana to Fort Worth, to El Paso, and then along the southern route to Los Angeles. I had no definite plans about what I would do on my arrival. I supposed I'd simply drive around and sight-see, then maybe go to San Francisco and, after that, head home.

It was a lovely, sunny spring day when I left Indianapolis. As I moved southwest, the loveliness faded a bit until, finally, when I pulled into Texarkana my second day on the road, it was only hot and sunny. Once there, I retired early, planning to go as far as Fort Worth the next day.

But Texas had already been in the throes of a dust storm, and, almost as soon as I got out of Texarkana, I saw signs of it. The countryside showed little patches of dust, which increased in size as I moved west. Even the road became dusty after a while. It was hot, and I wanted to keep my windows open, but that was impossible. All I could do was leave one open just enough to allow a little air in, but it was hardly comfortable driving.

Then, to my chagrin, I suddenly noticed that I was on the wrong road. When I stopped the car to look at a map, I realized I had been on the wrong road from the beginning. There were two parallel highways west from Texarkana. The southern road went to Fort Worth. I was on the northern road, headed for Amarillo, considerably north of El Paso.

But I had come so far that it would have been ridiculous to turn around, or, at that point, even head south toward Fort Worth. I was only a hundred miles or so from Wichita Falls, Texas, a place I had never heard of, but it looked sizable enough on the map. It was north and a little west of Fort Worth, so I decided to spend the night there. Then, the next day, I could head for Amarillo before turning south to El Paso.

I was hot and sticky and dusty and tired when I got into Wichita Falls at about five-thirty in the afternoon. There had been a severe dust storm there earlier in the day. I pulled the car up in front of a nice-looking hotel, parked it and hauled my grip out of the back seat. A bellhop took it from me, and I followed him into the lobby. There was dust all over the place—on the rug, on the furniture, on the walls, even at the desk, where a tired-looking clerk blinked sleepily, as though it were five-thirty in the morning instead of five-thirty in the afternoon.

I checked in, and the bellhop led me to a room on the third floor. It was perfectly adequate, but flecked with dust. The window was closed, and the boy advised me to keep it closed.

"You never know when this stuff will kick up again," he said. "If you leave your window open all night, you might wake up under a blanket of it in the morning."

After he left, I sat on the bed, and tried to organize my thoughts.

What a day! What a murderous, miserable day! Here I am, a stranger in a strange town, more than a thousand miles from home, tired, dusty, uncomfortable, hungry—and thirsty. I "need" a drink. I'm going to take a shower, change my clothes and find the nicest restaurant in town. I'll have a cocktail before dinner, a nice meal, then come back here and sleep, and I'll be all ready to drive on tomorrow.

One cocktail—that won't hurt me. I haven't had a drink for

cant shake feeling

nearly four years, and I know I'm O.K. now. Maybe I can handle anything. I don't know a soul here, and not a soul knows me, so no one will know the difference. What harm can one little cocktail do? And then, I do "need" it.

I took off my shoes and shirt and pants, and lay flat on the bed, looking up at the ceiling.

One little drink—a manhattan—a bourbon manhattan. That's what I'll have. Nice and cold, with a cherry in it. It'll go down smoothly. A bourbon manhattan always does. Of course, I'll have only one. I won't tell a soul about it, not even Dohr. I'm sure he'd understand if he knew. And I'm dead tired.

I lay there for fifteen or twenty minutes, then took off the rest of my clothes and stood under a cool shower for a long time. And all the time I stood there, with the water cascading over my tired body, I thought about that one bourbon manhattan I was going to have before dinner.

One drink!

I climbed out of the shower, and dried myself off. The big, rough towel felt good as I snapped it back and forth across my body, in even, rhythmic strokes.

One drink—one drink—one drink—

I walked out of the bathroom, and went over to my suitcase to get clean linen. And each step I took drummed out the refrain.

One drink—one drink—one drink—

I stood over the suitcase a minute. Then I bent down, undid the straps and opened the clasps on either side, then snapped up the lock.

One drink—one drink—one drink—

The first thing that caught my eye when I opened the grip was the A.A. directory.

I stood and looked at it a long minute.

Wichita Falls, Texas—I wonder if they have a group here.

I picked the book up. It was divided by states. I opened it to "Texas," and ran my eye down the list.

Wichita Falls.

A telephone number was listed. Without stopping to put any

clothes on, I went right to the phone and asked for the number. After a couple of rings, a man answered.

I didn't identify myself. I simply said, "I'm a stranger in town. I was wondering if you have A.A. meetings here."

"Yes, indeed," he said. "We're having one tonight. You're very welcome to come, if you like."

I thanked him, and hung up.

I'll go over there and meet a new group of people—people I've never known before. I'll see how A.A. works here, and, if they want to know anything about the Indianapolis group, I'll tell them how it works there.

I forgot all about the drink.

It was my last near-slip. From that day to this, I have never again had any desire for a drink. This was the last time the obsession of every alcoholic—that he must drink and that some day he will be able to control it—raised its ugly head in my case.

stayed busy, moved on

CHAPTER 19

tells his story

THE WICHITA FALLS A.A. group met on the second floor of a small building in a downtown business block near the center of town, within walking distance of the hotel. As I stood in front of the door, a man turned toward it, and I asked, "Are you going to the meeting?"

He looked at me.

"I'm a member of Alcoholics Anonymous," I said.

His face relaxed into a smile. He put his arm around me, and we went up the stairs together. He was hospitality personified. On the way, he said, "Where are you from?"

"Indianapolis, Indiana," I said. "My name is Father Pfau."

"And you're an alcoholic?"

"Yes. I'm an alcoholic."

"How about giving us a talk, Father?"

"I'd be delighted," I said.

By this time, we were in the back of the hall. It was small, and pretty crowded. There were seventy-five or eighty people there.

"Sit here a minute, Father."

The man made his way to the front of the hall. The chairman was just about to open the meeting. He and my new friend talked a moment, and I saw him nod his head and smile. Then, my friend came back and sat beside me.

After a while, the chairman said, "We have an unexpected treat tonight—a visitor from Indianapolis. I'd like to introduce Father Pfau."

As I walked toward the front of the hall, there were scattered handclaps, but nothing that could be mistaken for bursts of tumultuous applause. There was a slight chill in the air and, after a pause, a buzz of conversation was apparent in various parts of the room. I stepped up onto the platform, and shook the outstretched hand of the chairman. Then, I turned toward the crowd.

"My name is Father Pfau. I am not going to spell it for you. You can use your imagination. Most people do. I am a member of the Indianapolis group of Alcoholics Anonymous and I am an alcoholic."

The buzzing stopped. I looked around the room, and everything was quiet.

Then I told my story—a combination of the details of my life and my original talk on the spiritual side of Alcoholics Anonymous. And when I had finished, my heart glowed from the applause. It was real and spontaneous and, apparently, universal.

Later, several men came over to talk to me. One said, "Father, that was a fine talk. We'd like to have you repeat it at the Southwestern convention of A.A. It will be held in Austin in a couple of months. Can you make it?"

"If you want me, I'm sure I can arrange it," I said.

I stayed around the little hall in the middle of Wichita Falls, Texas, for a couple of hours, talking and swapping experiences with other A.A. members, and one of them drove me back to my hotel. When I got to my room, I felt a lift such as I had never known before.

Wichita Falls, Texas—over a thousand miles from home—a strange town—but now I'm not a stranger in it any more.

I have friends here.

And I can have friends anywhere—anywhere in the whole United States.

I have spoken in Wichita Falls every year since that memorable day.

A few days after the talk, I was in Los Angeles. Two or three days after I got there, I happened to be in North Hollywood, so I called the A.A. number listed in the directory. They had a clubhouse, and the caretaker, who answered the phone—I didn't identify myself as a priest—invited me over.

When I arrived, he was ice cold. I found out why the moment he opened his mouth.

"I'm an Orangeman," he said shortly.

The Orangemen, who come from the north of Ireland, are violently opposed to Catholics.

"That's all right," I said, "but you're a member of A.A., too, aren't you?"

"Yes."

"Well, so am I."

"You mean you're an alcoholic?"

"I'm an alcoholic."

"Well, now, Father—" he was eager and friendly—"we're having a meeting tonight. How about coming and giving us a talk?"

"All right," I said.

That night, he was chairman of the meeting. He stood up and said, "If my folks in Ireland knew what I am about to do, they'd turn over in their graves. And if my Orangeman friends here knew, they'd blacklist me forever. But that doesn't bother me. I think maybe it's one of the wonderful things about A.A. Denominations mean nothing as far as the program is concerned. We aren't Catholics or Protestants or Jews—we're all just alcoholics. So, it is with real pleasure that this Orangeman introduces a Catholic priest, a member of the Indianapolis group, to give us a talk."

I changed my mind about going to San Francisco. Instead, I stayed around southern California for my entire vacation.

When I heard that Bill, one of the co-founders of Alcoholics Anonymous, was in San Diego, I went there to see him before starting for home. I heard him speak, and later he invited me to accompany him to Ensenada, in Mexico, where we spent the night.

Bill, a fine gentleman, taught me something I've never forgotten.

"Father," he said, "you will do a great deal of good in a great many places. As a Catholic priest and an alcoholic, you can be instrumental in helping alcoholics wherever you go. But remember this—no matter how well you do, no matter how much you help others or how many you help, no matter what you say or how you say it, no matter what happens—you can't and won't please everyone. Wherever you go and whatever you do, someone will find a way to criticize you.

"You must take the criticism, no matter how unjustified, with tolerance and forebearance. Remember that resentments can lead to trouble, so you must work doubly hard not to harbor them. Don't ever let anything bother you. I have taken criticism from unexpected sources many times since we began this program, and so will you. Just let it roll off your back like water off a duck's, and you'll be all right."

He was quite correct. I took a good deal of criticism in the years that followed, and from many unexpected sources. But I never let it get under my skin. I don't know where I would be today if I had.

The next time I saw Bill was at the Austin convention in June. There, before twelve hundred people, the largest audience I had ever faced, I told my story. Bill was on the platform with me. There were only a handful of Catholics in the crowd which, while not hostile, was certainly skeptical when I first got up to speak. But, just as at Wichita Falls, the people relaxed when they realized that, even though I was a priest, I was one of them.

When I had finished, Bill stood up and said, "Anything I would say after that talk would be purely anticlimactic. It is my sincere desire that it will be heard by every member throughout the world some day."

Then he sat down.

Directly or indirectly as a result of that convention, I received many new invitations to speak, mostly in Texas and the Southwest. But, through a rather providential chain of circumstances, I was also asked to speak the following September at the Southeastern A.A. convention in Jacksonville, Florida.

It seems that one of the members who heard me at Austin, Texas, later "slipped." He finally ended up in Mobile, Alabama, where, at an A.A. meeting he attended in July, he met the chairman of the coming Southeastern convention.

When the Mobile meeting was over, the man who was trying

he is inspirational

to recover from his "slip," asked the chairman if the convention program had been completed.

"I'm still working on it," the chairman replied.

"Well," the man said, "I heard a Catholic priest give a talk at the Southwestern convention, and he's a member of Alcoholics Anonymous."

The chairman, himself a Catholic, was incredulous.

"A priest?" he said. "And an alcoholic, too? Where does he come from."

"Indianapolis."

A few days later, the secretary of the Indianapolis A.A. group received a letter, asking about me. When he answered that I was, indeed, both a Catholic priest in good standing and a member of A.A. as well, the convention chairman sent me an invitation to speak in Jacksonville.

Fifteen or twenty more invitations for me to address A.A. groups in the South and East came out of the Southeastern convention. Between these, the requests from Austin and the ones from Los Angeles, I set up a nation-wide itinerary, to last from November 1948 to April 1949. I included a retreat at Austin, which, incidentally, was set up for New Year's Eve.

We had held our second annual retreat at St. Joseph's in Rensselaer in June of 1947. At the request of some of the people who had attended the 1946 retreat, my talks at that time were printed in a fifty-six-page booklet with a gold cover, and distributed as a souvenir, through the generosity of Francis Madden, then owner of the *Indiana Catholic and Record*, the archdiocesan newspaper in Indianapolis. He printed six hundred booklets on credit.

After we ran out of booklets, we began getting requests for "the golden book of your retreat." I had no more copies. However, I approached Mr. Madden on the subject of printing three thousand more copies on credit, and he agreed to accept payment for them as they were sold. Mr. Louis Krieg, of Krieg Brothers Catholic Supply House, acted as distributor and took care of the shipping and merchandising the first few years.

Thus began our so-called "Golden Books." Since that time, at the rate of a new one each year, ten of these books have been printed. We pay for them as the money comes in. Up to 1957, we had sold about fifty thousand copies of the first Golden Book and some two hundred thousand of all the Golden Books combined. We have incorporated the books into two full-sized volumes, *Sobriety and Beyond,* and *Sobriety Without End,* and we're still operating on credit. At this writing, we owe the patient Mr. Madden a goodly sum.

In 1949 even professional people had little understanding of alcoholism. Although the Yale School of Alcoholic Studies, and John Hopkins University had contributed valuable information in educating the public, we still felt that it was necessary to institute similar studies within the framework of our Church. We founded the National Clergy Conference on Alcoholism to fill this need. An annual meeting of bishops, priests and laymen is sponsored by the N.C.C.A. for the purpose of studying the alcoholic problem in relation to Catholic theology. The conference has been held in many dioceses throughout the country, and the speakers have included bishops, priests, theologians, psychiatrists, doctors, superiors and members of Alcoholics Anonymous. The findings each year are bound and sent to all bishops, superiors and associate members.

I accepted support from Mr. Kiefer Mayer for two years. After that I always managed to save enough from my expense money to pay the small board and room charge to the Sisters of the Good Shepherd Convent where I live when I am in Indianapolis.

The 1948-1949 trip took me to California, Arizona, New Mexico, Texas, Louisiana, North and South Carolina, Florida, Alabama, Georgia, Mississippi and Tennessee. I dovetailed the talks so that no one group would have to bear a heavy burden of expense. There are no fees in A.A., and I have never accepted any. Each group has always been free to give whatever it could afford toward my over-all expenses. No minimum is ever set. I usually managed to balance out, although I have returned to Indianapolis in the red several times.

My first trip was especially trying, since I didn't have much money starting out, and I never knew how much to expect. But I got help from unexpected sources in unexpected ways.

When I reached Amarillo, for example. Al and Bob, two A.A.

members whom I had met at Austin, noticed that my suitcase was battered and old.

"You ought to get a new one, Father," Al said.

"Maybe I will someday," I replied.

"Someday" turned out to be the next evening. The two came to my room lugging a brand-new suitcase.

"We thought you'd be able to use it," Bob said.

I gave twelve talks in fourteen days in southern California. The schedule began almost the day I arrived, and kept right on going with practically no relief. It never occurred to me that this might be taking something out of me.

From California, I went to Texas, speaking several times on the way. In Texas, I gave seventeen talks, many on consecutive nights in widely scattered communities. I was getting tired, but I still wasn't aware that my schedule was too heavy. Then, during the retreat at Austin, I came down with a fierce cold. My voice went hoarse, and I coughed and sniffled, but I didn't have time to stop and rest.

I kept on going, and so did the cold. I didn't do anything about it for a couple of weeks after the retreat. Then, when the cold persisted, I went to a hospital in New Orleans for a physical checkup. The doctor couldn't find anything organically wrong, but he did insist that I rest for a couple of days, so I stayed right in the hospital. I finally shook off the cold, and resumed my trip. This was the only break of more than a day on my whole trip.

On the invitation of a minister, I spoke before six hundred people in the courthouse in Rome, Georgia. There were exactly five Catholics in the audience. The minister was the first Protestant clergyman member of A.A. He and I remained close friends until the day of his death a few years ago.

I was in Miami, Florida, for an A.A. anniversary dinner on St. Patrick's Day. It was held in a large dining room, with an adjoining bar. Right in the middle of my talk, a drunk suddenly began raising the roof. The crowd got restless, and I had to do something to relieve a growing tension.

"Well," I said, "let's not worry about him. It won't be long before he'll be over here with us."

I kept on going—back to Georgia, Alabama, Tennessee, the

Carolinas. I wound up the trip in April in North Carolina, then headed for home.

In the meantime, by mail and phone, I had set up ten retreats for the summer, two in Indiana, but most of them in the South and Southwest. I also took time to go to Montreal for an anniversary talk. Finally, I went to Richmond, Virginia, for the 1949 Southeastern convention, which ended on September 3. Then, utterly exhausted, I dragged myself back to Indianapolis.

Dohr came over to see me the day I got home. He took one look, then said, "Father, how long since you've had a rest?"

I smiled, a little wanly, I guess.

"Rest?" I said. "What's that?"

"What you're going to take—right now."

"I can't, Dohr. I've got too much to do."

"Cancel everything. If you don't, I'll do it for you."

I was too tired to argue. I felt washed-up, beaten, empty of all feeling, thoroughly and completely done in. In the back of my mind were vague fears, and I was overwhelmed by a deep, indefinable depression. I couldn't think of any reason for it. I was active, busy and I certainly should have been happy. Instead, the depression became so acute and persistent that I feared another neurosis was beginning.

"I'm worried, Dohr," I said, one day. "I can't shake off this depression. No matter what I do, it stays with me."

"Father, let's face it," Dohr said. "You're still a neurotic. You've had four nervous breakdowns and you may be facing another. You've controlled the alcoholic problem, but you still have this other one. At least, now, you can cope with it sober."

"I know, Dohr. I think I'd better see a doctor. I haven't felt like this since I was in the Alexian Brothers Hospital in Oshkosh. My depression was relieved there by shock treatments. I wonder if they would help me now."

"Let's find out," Dohr said.

He arranged for me to see Dr. Earl Mericle, an Indianapolis psychiatrist. I told Dr. Mericle about my depression and my inability to shake it. In the course of our conversation I mentioned that shock treatments had helped me on a previous occasion.

"How about my taking them again?" I suggested. "Do you think they might help me now?"

"I believe they would," he said. "At least we can try. They won't do any harm. You took deep shock treatments. Today, we use sub-shock. It's much milder."

After leaving Dr. Mericle, I went to the Chancery office and asked the Archbishop's permission to take the treatments. He gave me the permission and his blessing without hesitation.

I phoned the doctor and he arranged for me to enter St. Vincent's Hospital in Indianapolis. I took my first treatment the next morning. There was only one point of similarity between these treatments and the ones I had taken at Oshkosh. Just before the nurse gave me the shot in the arm to put me to sleep, she handed me a stick wrapped in gauze. She grinned as I stuck it in my mouth.

"I was just going to tell you to do that, Father," she said. "You must have been through this before."

"M-m-m-m-m-m-m—" I mumbled.

I was out of the hospital a week later. Dr. Mericle told me to take a vacation, and to accept no speaking engagements for several months.

"And when you do start giving talks again," he said, "don't bite off more than you can chew. You're only human, and if you let yourself get all tired out, you'll have another breakdown."

"How can I refuse to speak if people ask me?" I said.

"Simply by saying no. Tell them you're under doctor's orders. They'll understand. Set up a sensible schedule before you start, and don't deviate from it. Allow enough time between talks to get your proper amount of rest. And be sure you allow plenty of time for traveling. Trying to keep an engagement can be pretty nerveracking when you've shaved your travel time too thin."

"But I can't stay away from A.A. meetings," I said. "I have to keep on attending them if for no other reason than to stay sober myself."

"That's perfectly all right, Father. But you're not to speak at these meetings unless a talk is on your original schedule."

The shock treatments relieved me of my anxieties and helped lift my depression, but they brought to the surface an old, old unsolved problem. For years, I had had deep-seated doubts about the validity of my ordination into the priesthood. I had never consulted anyone, and always pushed the question aside. Actually, in all those years, I was afraid to seek an expert opinion, for fear that my priesthood might really be invalid.

One day, I mentioned the matter to Dohr.

"What makes you doubt the validity of your ordination at this late stage?" he asked.

"I've always doubted it," I said. "I'm not sure I wanted to become a priest in the first place. And I was under tremendous pressure when I received the diaconate. I don't think anyone can validly receive major orders when he is under pressure. This is the first time I've discussed it with anybody."

"Well, let's not just sit and stew about it," Dohr said. "Let's go after expert opinion. Who can give us one?"

"Father Donovan—in St. Louis," I said. "He's one of the Church's outstanding canonists in this country."

"Let's go and see him," said Dohr.

A canonist is a priest well versed in canon law—a sort of ecclesiastical lawyer. When Dohr and I went to see Father Donovan, I told him the whole story of my doubts and fears and worries at the time of my diaconate.

"I think this must have bothered me throughout my priesthood," I said. "I have always had a vague feeling that, because of the pressures, I did not receive my diaconate as a fully voluntary procedure. I'm really concerned about two things—whether these pressures caused invalidity of my diaconate, and—if this is so—whether my priesthood is invalid, too."

"Did you have pressure and anxiety before your ordination to the priesthood, or only before the diaconate?" Father Donovan asked.

"Only before the diaconate."

He smiled.

"You have nothing to worry about, Father," he said. "Even if the diaconate was not valid, the ordination to the priesthood was. This is the law of the Church. You are perfectly all right."

I may never be sure whether I wanted to be a priest, but now I can be sure God wanted me to be a priest.

I felt much better going back to Indianapolis than I had on leaving. On the way home, Dohr said, "I think half your nervous troubles were due to this indecision. Way down deep, you were always afraid that your priesthood was invalid. Now that you know it wasn't, you shouldn't have any more trouble."

My first trip after returning from St. Louis took me to the South and West. I went to Jacksonville, Tampa, St. Petersburg and Miami, then stopped for a week or so in North Carolina on my way home. And, wherever I went, I was asked the same question.

"How about giving us a talk, Father?"

"Sorry, I can't. Doctor's orders."

Once, when I stopped in a small town in the Carolinas, I decided to go to an A.A. meeting incognito. It was raining hard, and I was in shirt sleeves and a raincoat. I sat down and listened to the talks. Then the chairman said, "I see Father Pfau sitting back there. Would you like to give us a talk, Father?"

When I had recovered from my astonishment, I explained the situation, and everyone accepted it. Later, I found out that the chairman had heard me speak the year before.

At another meeting in the South I again sat in the back of the room and was led to believe that no one had paid any attention to me. But half an hour after the meeting was over, I got a call at my hotel.

"Hello, Father," a man said. "I saw you at the meeting. Will you be in town long enough to give us a talk?"

He'd not only recognized me but, in typical alcoholic fashion, had also ferreted out where I was staying.

When I got home, I made several important decisions. With a few isolated exceptions, I manage to live up to them to this day. When I arrange my itinerary, I rarely give talks on successive nights. Sometimes, this can't be avoided, but it doesn't happen often. I have always kept at least one day out of every four absolutely free of appointments or obligations, so I can just rest. I allow no less than two days a week to attend to my mail, so that it won't all be piled up in a hopeless mess when I get home. I give myself plenty of time to go from place to place. I always drive, and always alone.

Before I resumed my regular speaking schedule in 1950, Father James D. Moriarty, the Chaplain of the Good Shepherd Convent in Indianapolis and Retreat Director of Our Lady of Fatima Retreat House, suggested that we take a short vacation trip together.

En route, I remarked about the difficulty of living in a rectory when not actually attached to the parish.

"There always seems to be unavoidable friction," I mused. "Almost every time I agree to help out, something comes up in my work with alcoholics and there's conflict of obligation again."

"Why don't you come and live at the convent?" he asked. "I'm sure the Mother Superior would be glad to have you."

"That sounds great," I said. "Then I can set my schedule without worrying about possible conflicts."

"I'll ask Mother Austin when we return and let you know. However, I feel sure she will find a room for you."

Two days after we returned to Indianapolis, Father Moriarty phoned. "It's all fixed for you," he told me. "The Mother says you can take up residence here whenever you wish."

I went over to see her. She showed me my room and we agreed on a modest sum to be paid for board and room. Then with that simple universal faith of nuns everywhere, she remarked as I left to get my belongings, "It will be wonderful for us to have an extra Mass offered in our chapel every morning you are here."

Little did she dream what the next few years would bring.

Today the Good Shepherd Convent is a beehive of activity. Typing, printing, filing, and answering telephones is now part of the daily routine for three of the Magdalen nuns who are secretary, file clerk, shipping clerk, and printer. They do their work in a large office and a printing room.

I still keep my little one-room living quarters. It serves as my private office by day, and my bedroom by night. My seminary training in making my own bed has served me well.

Two private telephone lines lead into this room, and both can also be switched to the Sister's office. Calls come from all parts of the world—and at any hour of the day or night—from alcoholics, people interested in alcoholics, and friends. Some of the callers are sober, some are sobering up, some are not sober. A few years back a lady not quite sober called me from Paris. She just wanted to talk—at twelve dollars for three minutes. It took her three-quarters of an hour to tell me what was on her mind.

When I am away from Indianapolis, Sister answers the phone. She is acquiring a post-graduate education and is adding many words to her vocabulary, some good, some not so good. At night she turns the phone on automatic answering. One morning she heard a rather inebriated voice on the recording exclaim in no uncertain terms to the long distance operator, "Aw—he'sh got that darned canned stuff on again."

Each day brings an average of fifty pieces of mail. Since the nuns are cloistered, arrangements have been made with a lay person to go to the post office each day. Whatever Sister is unable to answer herself is forwarded to me every three days when I am on the road.

Each year the demands on my time at my office have grown to such an extent that I have been forced gradually to cut down on the number of speaking engagements. There are hundreds of invitations on file from groups whom I simply do not have the time to visit. I plan to continue my retreats as long as I am physically able to do so. However, I also want to give more and more time to my office, to my writings, and to my own people in and around Indianapolis.

In 1953, Doherty Sheerin died. I was on the West Coast at the time, with a full schedule of talks, retreats and meetings facing me. I had known he was sick, and I was concerned about him, but one of the last things he ever said to me was not to worry. As usual, he was putting the problems of others ahead of his own.

The first thing I thought, after I heard that Dohr was gone, was, "If ever a man went straight to heaven, he did."

He was a wonderful person—in his way, the most remarkable man I have ever known. His wisdom, his interest, his understanding and his strength were sources of deep inspiration to me from the day I first laid eyes on him when he came to see me at St. Joan of Arc rectory in Indianapolis.

In the last years of his life, he received Holy Communion every day and attended Mass every morning. He was a very humble man. There is no question in my mind, if I may say so, that Dohr died a saint. I think about him often, and have said Mass for him many times. I seldom give a talk that I do not mention him.

I decided not to return to Indianapolis for his funeral. I somehow knew that Dohr would prefer that I continue my work rather than interrupt it on his account.

My brother Jerry was another source of great inspiration to me. He and I first became close when I entered St. Meinrad Seminary, and he was always ready when I needed help in later years.

He died of a stroke in June of 1957, after suffering through eight years of terrible pain. A combination of illnesses—tuberculosis, diabetes, cancer and cirrhosis—all plagued him in his last years. There is no doubt in my mind that his sufferings, Dohr's guidance and the grace of God have everything to do with whatever success I may achieve.

I have traveled nearly 750,000 miles in ten years of working with alcoholics. I have spoken before nearly two hundred thousand members of A.A. at retreats, meetings and conventions, and personally discussed their problems with more than ten thousand alcoholics. Many ask me if A.A. is the only avenue of recovery open to alcoholics.

This is what my experience has taught me. The approach of the Twelve Steps, used in an appropriate group, constitutes the best means available today to give sobriety to the alcoholic. However, I feel that the present structural setup of A.A. is very imperfect. It tends far too much to organization and this, in dealing with spiritual entities, could prove disastrous. To me, the greatest security for A.A. is in the preservation of its autonomy down to each and every individual member. Authority in A.A. would be fatal.

There has been and continues to be much criticism of my activities both from within and from without Alcoholics Anonymous. Most of it is caused by misunderstanding, although some is the result of ever-present jealousy and bigotry. I simply ignore it all, on the theory that whoever does anything involving large numbers of people lays himself open to criticism and misunderstanding. I prefer to concern myself with doing the best I can, and working at the maintenance of my own sobriety and serenity.

Once, not long ago, a friend of mine phoned me in Indianapolis from San Antonio, Texas. When I answered the phone, he said, "Well, Father, it's certainly good to hear your voice."

"I'm glad you like the sound of it," I said. "But you must have a better reason than that for calling me up. Why all this sudden concern?"

"There's a rumor here that you're drunk in El Paso."

"I am," I said, "get right down there and sober me up."

Many people have asked me how they can tell if they will develop into alcoholics. That's not an easy question to answer because so many factors are involved. In one group of a hundred persons, there may not be a single alcoholic; in another, they may all be alcoholics; in a third, some might be and others might not. The person who drinks for pleasure today may be drinking tomorrow because he must. The person who wakes up with a hangover and wants no part of alcohol this year may wake up with a craving for liquor a year or two from now.

But, by the same token, the person who drinks for pleasure now may be drinking for pleasure for the rest of his life. He may wake up with a hangover every morning, but never become an alcoholic, because he can stop drinking whenever he feels like it and can also moderate his drinking when he chooses to.

There are high-bottom drinkers and low-bottom drinkers. A high-bottom drinker drinks when things are going well. I was a high-bottom drinker; I couldn't stand prosperity. A low-bottom drinker drinks when things are going wrong. Yet, even here, there are no hard and fast rules. Some people in these brackets become alcoholics; some never do. Most alcoholics, incidentally, are both high-bottom and low-bottom drinkers.

My experience, dealing with alcoholics both in passing and under intimate circumstances, is that the only static factor is the *element of increase*. If a person who has been drinking at least three years (a shorter period cannot give a conclusive result), finds that he is drinking increasingly more alcohol increasingly more often, he is *probably* on the road to alcoholism. If, on the other hand, a person who even got drunk three times a week ten, or five, or three years ago, still gets drunk three times a week, the chances are he's not, and never will be an alcoholic.

If you are an alcoholic, you cannot discipline yourself into moderate drinking. This is why we in A.A. avoid the first drink. When we succeed in doing that, we stay dry.

Why did I ever drink?

I don't really know. I don't believe any alcoholic knows.

Will I ever take another drink?

Again, all I can say is, I don't really know. Only God knows the future. I don't think I will ever drink again, and at present, I don't have the slightest desire for a drink.

There is a saying among some A.A. groups that "A.A. brings about an expulsion of a compulsion by a Higher Power—by Almighty God."

I am only sure of one thing—all that I am, and all that I have is from God. I had nothing to do with it. God did it all. So, too, my future is entirely in His hands, mine is only the footwork.

-nothing is definite

need more

on A. A. exp.

- people he met, etc.